The Rooster

To Gillian,

Thank you for writing
Every Secret Thing: My Family, My
Country. Your memoir has served
as an inspiration for me when
I was writing The Rooster.

With love,

Sibel.

The Rooster

Discovering My Father's Memories from the Jasenovac Concentration Camp

Sibel Roller

ROWMAN & LITTLEFIELD
Lanham • Boulder • New York • London

Published by Rowman & Littlefield
An imprint of The Rowman & Littlefield Publishing Group, Inc.
4501 Forbes Boulevard, Suite 200, Lanham, Maryland 20706
www.rowman.com

86-90 Paul Street, London EC2A 4NE

British Library Cataloguing in Publication Information Available

Library of Congress Cataloging-in-Publication Data

Names: Roller, Sibel, author.
Title: The rooster : discovering my father's memories from the Jasenovac Concentration
 Camp / Sibel Roller.
Other titles: Discovering my father's memories from the Jasenovac Concentration Camp
Description: Lanham, Maryland : Rowman & Littlefield, [2024] | Includes
 bibliographical references and index.
Identifiers: LCCN 2023047655 (print) | LCCN 2023047656 (ebook) |
 ISBN 9781538186916 (cloth) | ISBN 9781538186930 (epub)
Subjects: LCSH: Roller, Dragan. | Jasenovac (Concentration camp)--Biography.
 | World War, 1939-1945--Prisoners and prisons, Croatian. | World War,
 1939-1945--Concentration camps--Croatia. | Diplomats--Yugoslavia--Biography. |
 Zagreb (Croatia)--Biography. | Roller, Sibel.
Classification: LCC D805.5.J37 R65 2024 (print) | LCC D805.5.J37 (ebook) | DDC
 940.53/1854972--dc23/eng/20231208
LC record available at https://lccn.loc.gov/2023047655
LC ebook record available at https://lccn.loc.gov/2023047656

When the rooster sings in Jasenovac, you can hear it in three empires.

—Dragan Roller, 1922–2003

Contents

Maps

Map 1. Dragan was born in 1922 in the Kingdom of Serbs, Croats, and Slovenes, renamed in 1929 as the Kingdom of Yugoslavia.

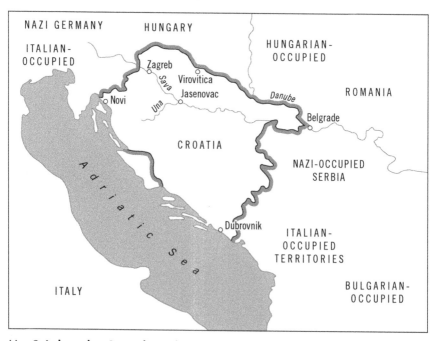

Map 2. Independent State of Croatia, 1941–1945.

Map 3. Socialist Federal Republic of Yugoslavia, 1945–1991.

Map 4. Republic of Croatia, 1991–present.

The Story

Ode to My Father, Dragan

This story is about you
And the way I never knew you
Until you passed away.
You left a string of words behind you,
Locked in a dusty room.

Our home inside the forest
All gingerbread and spice,
I thought it'd last forever,
In my heart at least.

You hid your Baba Yaga
Deep inside your soul,
But a trail of white pebbles
Led her to our home.

She came back to get you,
Wreaked her vengeance on you.
Now I know your secret,
I'd like to walk beside you.

—Sibel Roller

A Brief Note on Croatian Pronunciation and Language

Š, š	sh (as in fish)	Miloš (Milosh), Ustaša (Ustasha)
C, c	tz (as in *pizza*)	Virovitica (*Veeroveeteetza*)
Ć, ć and Č, č	ch (as in *church*)	Klaić (*Klaaeech*), Vuković (*Voocoveech*)
J, j	y (as in *yellow*)	Jasenovac (*Yasenovatz*)
Đ, đ	dj (as in *juice*)	Tuđman (*Toojman*)
Ž, ž	zh (as in *pleasure*)	Hanža (*Hanzha*)

In Croatian, Ustaša is singular; Ustaše is plural. For simplicity, I have used Ustaša throughout this book.

Chapter 1

Dear Dad

On a sultry day in August 2006, I uncovered your secret. It was the day the British police disrupted a terrorist plot to blow up ten transatlantic planes using explosives smuggled in fizzy drinks. Your secret involved terror, too, but of a different kind. That day, my memories of you were thrown into chaos, like the air traffic over Europe and America.

I was in Zagreb at the time, clearing the family home of its contents. The spacious fourth-floor apartment in a sleek, geometric 1930s block in the city center had once been a place of reconnection for family and friends. Without its occupants and stripped of most of its furnishings, it had become a ghost of its former self, waiting for a new owner to revive it. The buyer had signed the contract, and the handover date was imminent. Everything had to go.

In the previous year, I'd traveled from London to Zagreb five times to sift through a lifetime of possessions. Your possessions, but also Mama's and Grandma's and Grandpa's. Two generations, four lifetimes. Every visit was a mix of grimy physical work, difficult decisions, and energy-sapping nostalgia. After every trip, I returned to London with a sense of relief but also with the knowledge there was more to be done. This time, I'd had enough. I did not want to make a sixth visit.

Earlier in the day, as I walked around the apartment with my to-do list, ticking off all the jobs done, I remembered there was a storeroom on the ground floor that belonged with the apartment. Do you recall that storeroom? Now don't try to deny it. It was next to the elevator. In the gloom of the corridor, we rarely acknowledged its existence, except when something needed storing or disposing of at a future date. Then, the old iron key emerged, and someone trudged downstairs to enter its murky depths. It was a place where unwanted detritus languished for months or years until someone summoned up the energy to have the contents removed to the dump. You're not smiling, but I can see in your eyes you have remembered. Was it a case of "out of sight, out of mind"?

I hadn't ventured into the storeroom for a decade, and I dreaded what I might find there. I suspected it would be full of junk. I grabbed the key from its rusty hook in the kitchen and headed downstairs.

I turned the key once, twice. The door creaked inward to darkness. A hint of dust made my nose twitch. I made a mental note to take an antihistamine tablet as soon as I got back upstairs. I tapped my hand along the wall, searching for a light switch. Eventually, my fingers landed on a smooth Bakelite dial. I turned it clockwise. The bare bulb flickered on and bathed the windowless room in a yellow haze. I stepped inside, blinking. The contents gradually came into focus. There wasn't as much dross there as I'd feared. How nice to be proven wrong! This lot wouldn't take long to clear.

In one corner, a couple of stacked armchairs leaned skew-whiff against the wall. I lifted one of the chairs to check its condition. The upholstered seat released a cloud of dust. When you bought the chairs in the 1960s, they made a stylish addition to our sitting room. Now they seemed to have lost much of their appeal. However, retro furniture was back in fashion in London. Maybe someone would buy them? I'd seen upcycled midcentury furniture selling for hundreds of pounds on King's Road. As I lowered the chair to the floor, an armrest snapped, leaving me clutching a splintered strip of cherrywood. The rest of the chair hit the floor with a thud. Decision made. These chairs were going to the dump.

Next to the armchairs, I recognized the ghostly silhouette of the plastic commode Mama bought for you when you became bedbound. You used it reluctantly for less than a month before the end came. Mama must have put it in the storeroom so it wouldn't remind her of your last days. After you passed away, she seemed to give up on life. Gradually, she allowed her ailments to overwhelm her. We buried her eighteen months after your funeral. She'd always been such a confident woman, energetic, opinionated, strong. Why didn't she use her strength to live a little longer? The commode was nearly new, but it didn't seem appropriate to donate it to a charity. Another item for the dump.

There was something else. A dark object lurked under the commode. I reached down and pulled out a cardboard box of indeterminate age. I considered dumping it in the wheelie bin outside without checking the contents, but I hesitated. The apartment upstairs had been a cache of precious family heirlooms and photographs, jumbled together with plastic shopping bags, decades-old receipts for household appliances that no longer functioned, and Christmas cards from long-forgotten acquaintances. After checking my watch, I decided to take a quick look.

The box was only half full. On top, a collection of early-twentieth-century black-and-white postcards of European cities looked intriguing, but I resisted the temptation to browse through them. They could go in the trunk destined for long-term storage. I pressed on.

Underneath the cards, a buff folder bulged with papers. I noticed your handwriting on the cover. It read, "Literary attempts." I stared at it, baffled. You'd often said you wanted to write once you retired from your job at the United Nations in New York, but I thought you never got around to it. Perhaps I was about to be proven wrong again.

My curiosity pricked, I ignored the voice in my head that told me I didn't have time for this and sat down gingerly on the rickety armchair. I wondered what you, Dragan Roller, had written about? Was it about the itinerant life we led as a family? Athens in the 1950s, then Baghdad and Belgrade in the 1960s? Or was it about our sojourn to Africa, the lush green shores of Lake Victoria following on from the sand dunes of the Sahara Desert? How we seemed to escape catastrophic regime changes by moving on to another country just in time? Perhaps it was about New York, where you lived longer than anywhere else. Or was it about something else? Anyhow, what were these "literary attempts" doing in a dusty storeroom?

I opened the folder. Gossamer-like pages, some handwritten, some typed, glided silently to the floor. I picked one up. It was a poem:

> When the wings of history brush past me
> And remind me of our days of misery and woe
> I ask myself: What happened to us?
> Why does the pain refuse to go?
> [Prošlosti tamne kad me takne krilo
> I sjetim se dana nesreće i jada
> Uvjek se pitam što se s nama zbilo
> Zašto uspomena bol ne prolazi ni sada?]

More poems cascaded from the folder to the floor, scores of drafts covered with inked and penciled comments. A loose booklet with a makeshift cover made of hand-cut sepia card bound some poems together.

I gaped at the verses in front of me, my mouth so dry I could barely swallow. How was it possible that you, my big, strong dad, the hard-nosed economist, wrote poetry? I remembered watching you number-crunch your way through stacks of macroeconomic tables and household bills, the corners of your graphite moustache turning up gently after every completed sheet. Your hands, big enough to wrap around a five-hundred-page paperback with ease, sorted the papers neatly on the table in front of you, like soldiers in a Mayday parade. Even after calculators became commonplace, you still sometimes added up the numbers by hand to check the machine was working properly.

You got annoyed with Mama and me when we started sentences with "I suppose that . . . " or "I'm assuming that . . . " to express an opinion.

"Don't suppose or assume, girls," you fumed. "Support your views with evidence. Facts and figures, please!"

You stood for objectivity and impartiality, the antithesis of emotion that was at the heart of poetry. What of the sadness and pain expressed in your poem? This was not the father I knew, the man about town, laughing and dancing and enjoying life to the fullest. This was a stranger.

I flicked through the papers again, searching for dates. The typeface looked vaguely familiar but not recent. Was it the product of that battered cast-iron typewriter you used to hammer out long letters to family and friends? We still had it in our Manhattan apartment before I left home for good. You insisted on keeping it even after Mama bought a shiny new IBM Selectric in the 1970s. Did you write those poems then? I rifled through the papers repeatedly. Finally, I located two poems with dates: November 1952 and December 1952. You were still firmly rooted in Yugoslavia in the early 1950s. You had met Mama, but you weren't married yet.

There was more. Underneath the poems, a chunky stack of pages densely typed with the thinnest of margins around the edges. A manuscript. There was no title, no indication of what was inside. I read a few lines selected at random:

> *Still smarting from the slaps and blows received at reception, we ate our dinner, three boiled potatoes each, stone cold. As newcomers, we stood huddled together, slightly apart from the other prisoners. We slid the skins off our potatoes with our hands. No cutlery apart from spoons was allowed in the camp. An older inmate approached us, picked up the peelings off the frozen snow beneath our feet and stuffed them greedily into his mouth.*

I sat back, dazed. I knew you'd survived three years in the Jasenovac concentration camp during World War II. You'd told me this yourself when I was still a schoolgirl. Situated on the River Sava 110 kilometers east of Zagreb, the camp was notorious for its brutality. Some called it the Auschwitz of the Balkans. But I knew nothing about your personal experiences there. Whenever I asked you questions about it, your face went blank, and you lapsed into stony silence. After a while, I stopped asking. Years later, after you testified at the war crimes trial of the camp commandant Dinko Šakić, you gave me newspaper cuttings about your testimony to read. Again, no word came out of your mouth.

My head whirred with questions. Why wasn't this folder stored upstairs in the apartment? Did you bring it to this storeroom to be disposed of, in the hope of erasing the memories it held? Did Mama know about the folder?

Had Mama ever read your writing? Did she know about your secret? I nearly threw the whole thing away!

I jumped as the elevator next door juddered into action. Catapulted back into the twenty-first century, I snapped the folder shut and tucked it under my arm. It was coming with me to London in my handbag. I sensed that I'd discovered something precious, a document with the weight of history behind it. I was not to know it was the beginning of a journey that would reveal a whole new side of you, another dad who remained in hiding for a lifetime.

The new security measures banning all liquids from hand luggage added several hours to my flight back to London that summer. There would be plenty of time to read.

Chapter 2

The Manuscript

I was curious about your manuscript. I wanted to know what was in it, but I suspected it might not be an easy read.

On my return to London, I opened your "Literary attempts" once again, taking care not to tear the delicate pages as I leafed through them. The words *roll call* caught my eye. I was aware they'd been a feature of daily life in Nazi concentration camps, an effective means of instilling fear into prisoners. Was it the same in Jasenovac?

I woke up with a start, my head crashing into the bunk bed above. My temples throbbed with the din of the siren blasting outside our barracks. I looked down at my trousers. There were patches of white frost on the fabric where the blanket had slipped off overnight.

"Come on, hurry up! Stop staring at yourself," shouted Milan as he leapt from the berth above down to the floor. "Quickly!"

The guards were waiting outside, metallic muzzles pointing at us.

"U nastup! Roll call!" they yelled as we fell into ranks. We stood shivering in a row. "Faster!"

"What are we doing today?" the guards sniggered. "Every fifth or tenth? They need to be punished!"

"Every tenth!" the officer in front screamed.

"One, two, three . . . " the guards counted.

"Your mates have tried to escape!"

"Four, five, six . . . "

"This is to teach you a lesson, you filthy animals!"

"Seven, eight, nine . . . "

"It is impossible to escape from Jasenovac. Not even a bird can escape! Remember that!"

"Tenth! Kneel!"

A crack and a thud. I flinched. A dark shape rolled sideways to the ground. The smell of cordite filled the compound.

And then it started all over again. They were getting closer.

"One, two, three . . . "

My heart pounded like a drum inside my ears.
"Four, five, six . . . " the counting continued.
A shadow dashed past me and ran toward the barbed-wire fence. Another
ear-splitting pop of the gun. They shot number 7 in the back.
"Shuffle up, the rest of you!"
Stomach heaving, I counted with them. Was I ninth or tenth?
"Where were we? Seven, eight, nine, ten! Kneel!"
Another crack.
The man next to me slumped to the ground.
Did the comrade on the barbed wire save my life?
I didn't even know his name.

With a lump in my throat, I slammed the folder shut.

Maybe I could read this later, spread over several weeks. Perhaps a slow drip-feed would soften the blows in your stories. I placed your file in the top drawer of my night table, underneath a contemporary Fay Weldon novel and the latest issue of the *New Scientist*. I would read the manuscript in bed, interspersed with bouts of lighthearted fiction and the weekly news from my world of work.

Several novels and dozens of magazines later, the manuscript languished in my drawer untouched. I told myself there was time enough. The folder was safe, not gathering dust in a storeroom in Zagreb. It would not be forgotten. It could not be forgotten.

What stopped me from reading your papers straight through? Yes, the demands of family and dual careers kept us crazy busy. Was that the real reason for my procrastination? Perhaps I was afraid of the truths I might uncover. The horrors of war were hardly a suitable subject for some light bedtime reading. My drawer had become my own version of a dusty storeroom.

Reluctant to delve too deeply into the content, I sometimes leafed through the sepia pages, searching for clues about the nature of your manuscript. Was it a book? There was no title anywhere. No chapter numbers or indications of a sequence. At more than sixty closely typed pages and another thirty or so handwritten, it was more than an essay but maybe not long enough for a book. At the top of the first page, a note in your handwriting read, "Rewrite these twelve pages and change position." Clearly not a final draft. Perhaps it was a first draft.

What kind of a book were you writing anyway? A memoir, a political autobiography, or maybe a kind of hybrid bionovel? I seemed to remember that you didn't think much of memoirs. You considered them too subjective, too emotional. You'd started reading Leon Trotsky's autobiography, translated from Russian into French, but never finished it because you found it too frivolous. You peppered the margins of the weighty, three-volume tome with caustic handwritten comments. The early chapters about Trotsky's childhood and family bore the brunt of your scorn. You found them "boring," "insubstantial," and "meaningless." At the end of chapter 5, you wrote, "Everything up to here could be deleted. The book could start with chapter 6." Toward the end of the first volume, as Trotsky delved more deeply into his role in the Russian Revolution, your comments softened to "getting more interesting" and "this could be interpreted differently." About halfway through the second volume, your annotations dried up, leaving behind a scrap of gift-wrap paper as a bookmark. The rest of the oeuvre remained in pristine condition.

I closed the folder and was about to return it to months of neglect in my drawer when I noticed, once again, your handwritten comment on top of the first page: "Rewrite these twelve pages and change position." What came after the first twelve pages? I reopened the folder and leafed through the brittle sheets again. You numbered the first twelve pages consecutively, but on page 13, you restarted the numbering from scratch. Was this a new chapter in your book? I scanned the first few lines for key words. *Virovitica*, your hometown, and *1940* caught my eye. Was this a flashback to your early activism? Perhaps it would reveal the reasons for your arrest. What was it that earned you a sentence of hard labor in a concentration camp? Why were you there in the first place? I could read that first and return to the first twelve pages another time.

Chapter 3

The Awakening

Virovitica, 150 kilometers east of Zagreb

On a cold February morning in 1940, Zvonko and I paced the platform at Virovitica Station, waiting for the train to take us to the national table tennis championship. We were in our last year in school, and neither of us had turned eighteen yet. We had a vague interest in table tennis, but that wasn't the real reason for our journey. My hands thrust deep into my coat pockets, I fidgeted with my third-class ticket. Slender wisps of fog curled around our hunched shoulders.

"We're a little early. Do you think there'll be crowds at the first game?" I said loudly.

"Oh yes. We need to arrive early to get the best seats. We wouldn't want to miss a single game," replied Zvonko, perhaps a little too loudly. We scanned the platform for passengers traveling alone.

We looked up in unison as a hoot announced the imminent arrival of the train. The gray hulk of the engine emerged from around a bend in the tracks and came to a halt, grinding and screeching, at the platform. A pair of ruffled, sleepy passengers staggered out. We waited with a group of peasants taking their produce to market. A woman in a floral country scarf and gray overcoat shoved her way through the crowd using her wicker basket containing a couple of screeching geese as a battering ram. We ducked out of her way as the birds flapped and pecked at everything around them. The woman swore at the geese; the panicky birds swore back. Once she'd located a seat and tucked the basket under the bench, woman and geese settled down and promptly fell asleep in the warmth of the carriage.

Zvonko and I sat next to the window, facing each other. As the train jolted into action, we watched the fog gradually lift to reveal a landscape of neatly ploughed fields, waiting for the green shoots of spring. The other three passengers in our compartment, all burly men of the land, took their cue from the moving train to unpack their bags. One of them sliced a loaf of crusty bread into thick slices, another disjointed a roast chicken with his bare hands and the third removed the cork from a bottle of homemade plum brandy. He waved the bottle in our direction.

"Come on, boys, take a swig!"

It would have been rude to refuse, so we both sampled the brandy. The clear liquid slid down our throats, leaving a warm glow in its path. The men offered us food, but we declined politely. They worked their way through their provisions slowly and methodically, their lips smacking after every mouthful. The woman with the geese snored gently in the corner.

I closed my eyes and allowed my thoughts to wander. I'd met comrade Vuković two years earlier in the public library. I visited the library every week to borrow books to read, or rather devour, looking for answers to questions I could not articulate. My grades in school were excellent, but my teachers complained I was stubborn. When I questioned the church council's pronouncements about the infallibility of the pope, the school catechist told me off for being arrogant. I read Miroslav Krleža, Émile Zola, and Ivan Turgenev.[1] Vuković could see I was searching for something. He recommended a few titles. Lenin's Imperialism, for example. One day, he gave me a copy of the Hammer and Sickle magazine to take home. He suggested I share it with friends. I gathered several of my school friends together, and we started a book club to discuss our readings and talk politics. My best friend, Zvonko, joined the group, too.

After some months, Vuković introduced us to Hanža, a law student. Tall and blond, Hanža took us to a patisserie, treated us to all the cakes we could eat, and explained we were now members of the Communist Youth League of Yugoslavia. Hanža was one of the leaders of the organization, and he promised to keep us informed of developments.

At first, we carried on reading books and discussing them between ourselves, but in our final year in school, we took action. We designed and printed an antifascist leaflet and distributed it around town. Vuković and Hanža were pleased with us and invited us to talk about it to senior party members at a plenary meeting.

On the train that day, I rehearsed the speech we prepared over and over again in my head. Hanža met us at the station and took us to the first game of the tournament. The ball pinged back and forth. Points were won and lost, but my mind was elsewhere. I can't remember what the final score was.

After a hearty lunch of country stew with dumplings, Hanža took us to a property on the outskirts of town. We walked past the house through a large garden with a vegetable patch and entered a barn tucked away at the back. Inside, instead of animals, several half-finished sculptures stood on plinths surrounded by stone blocks and bags of clay. We walked through the studio into an adjoining room. It was packed with young people sitting around a couple of chess players hunched over a table in the center of the room. After we sat down, one of the players stood up and asked for everyone's attention. He did not introduce himself. We had to listen carefully, as his voice was barely louder than a whisper. He welcomed us and all the other new delegates from the neighboring towns. He talked at length about the work of the party, the war in Europe, and the dangers of fascism.

"The Nazis and the Soviets have carved up Poland between them already, but they won't stay friends for long," he said. "Mark my words. The Molotov Ribbentrop Pact is a marriage of convenience."[2]

His words were all new to me. Invigorating, inspirational. When he finished speaking, there was no clapping, just nodding and appreciative looks.

Then it was our turn. Zvonko and I told the group of our leafleting campaign and how it provoked an investigation by the school authorities. The headmaster was livid when he discovered we'd used the school hectograph to print hundreds of inflammatory pamphlets. Without a moment's hesitation, he expelled us from school. But we'd both been good pupils, so he arranged for us to sit our final exams at another school in Belgrade.

At the end of the meeting, the chess-playing speaker came over to shake our hands but warned us to be more careful in future.

"There is trouble ahead. Get ready for war with the Far Right. The fascists will attack soon," he said. His words rang in my ears on the train back home.

I was relieved. Our presentation had gone well. I could sit back and come up with a conspiratorial nickname. That's what the little black book said you should do. The chapter entitled "Conspiracy" urged all comrades to adopt a pseudonym.

I considered Slovene. *My mother was from Slovenia, but then I remembered my school reading of a Slovenian poem that went disastrously wrong. When I was about twelve, our teacher had asked us to read our favorite poem out loud in class. I'd always been a bit of a show-off, so I was the first to raise my hand. The sonnet "The Willow" by the Slovenian poet Prešeren had impressed me deeply.*[3] *The teacher was delighted. Knowing my parentage, she expected an immaculately enunciated reading. But I wasn't fluent in Slovenian, and I didn't know how to express my feelings about the poem. I stumbled and mumbled. My voice oscillated wildly between deep notes and girlish screeches. The class burst out laughing. The teacher thanked me politely, but after that episode I was taunted mercilessly by my schoolmates. No,* Slovene *would not do.*

Maybe an old Slav name would suit. No. Too old-fashioned. Or a name reflecting my personality. Perhaps Braveheart. *No. Too pompous. My friends sometimes called me* Dragan Crni *or* Blackie *for my dark looks. Maybe I could stick with that. Yes, my nom de guerre is Blackie.*

I'd swot up for my exams. It was important to do well in exams. My place in medical school in Zagreb depended on good grades.

On reading your manuscript, I sensed you were a committed antifascist, but the promise of adventure drew you to the cause just as much. The adrenaline rush of forbidden action propelled you to do more.

The Communist Party was illegal when you were young. Meetings had to be clandestine. Far from putting you off, the need for secrecy made activism all the more appealing. No shouting or slamming of fists on tables—someone might overhear and report you to the authorities. You listened respectfully to your leaders, the student demigods of the revolution. Head buzzing with ideas, you thrived on the fervor of political debate. The thrill of it was palpable: impassioned whispering in smoke-filled rooms, elbow to elbow with your fellow conspirators, you plotted your next move. The world was about to change, and you were determined to be part of the transformation.

Chapter 4

Dragan and Biserka

By the fall of 1940, you'd moved from Virovitica to Zagreb to start your university course in medicine. Full-scale war was already raging in the rest of Europe. Allied troops had been swept aside and forced to evacuate at Dunkirk, clearing the way for the German invasion of France. That summer, Hitler took a triumphant tour of Paris, posing in front of the Eiffel Tower with his closest associates. But he didn't stay long. He had more work to do, more countries to conquer. It was only a matter of time before the German behemoth would reach the Balkans.

You were an idealist. You carried on fighting for change and social justice. But you also wanted to be a doctor. You had to buckle down to your studies. And then you met a girl . . .

If I hadn't got into medicine, I would never have met Biserka.

It happened at a Youth League meeting in Zagreb, shortly after I started my studies in the fall of 1940. Our leader, Baba, addressed a crowd of us in the students' union. We didn't know his real name. He looked like a real revolutionary. One of his front teeth was chipped as if he'd been in a fight. His long, slightly greasy hair curled its way down the back of his neck. I was captivated by his bohemian appearance, his words, his performance. He spoke about the tasks ahead of us.

About ten minutes into Baba's speech, a shadow slipped discreetly into the seat next to him. She wore a suit in ordinary gray, but the fine tailoring caught my eye. This was no hand-me-down from an older sibling. Trimmed at the neck and cuffs with fur, the outfit emphasized her shapely figure. She sat down without a word of apology, flicked her blond hair off her face, and scanned the room with a cool gaze. Baba ignored the late arrival and carried on talking.

In my hometown, I led our local youth group. Supported by several full party members, I called the meetings, set the program for discussion, and started the debates. I was a seasoned activist at those meetings. But here in Zagreb, I was a novice in a crowd of old revolutionaries. They had an aura of mystery around them. Some of them had already been imprisoned for a few days. They wore the halos of martyrs. This made me feel green. I still had a lot to learn.

As Baba spoke, my eyes kept returning to the lady in gray. Big conspirator. Revolutionary maiden, possibly wealthy, she would have joined the movement because of her idealism. She was a triumph of ideas over everyday comfort. She'd be invisible in the eyes of the police. Why would anybody think this bour-geois was a communist? She had the perfect cover. Her stockings—they were made of silk. And the shoes—expensive, beautifully coordinated with her suit. I simply had to meet her.

We were all assigned specific roles at the meeting. I was to be the librarian for the group. My duty was to monitor legal and illegal publications and ensure that members read and passed on the literature in a timely manner. I asked everyone to let me know what books and brochures they were willing to share. I would keep track of the materials in a conspiratorial way. No written lists. Everything was to be stored in the head.

I couldn't believe my luck when the lady in gray approached me after the meeting. She introduced herself as Biserka. She was studying medicine, too. She had loads of books she wanted to share. She rattled them off in a single breath: Ernst Toller's pacifist autobiography A Youth in Germany, *Zygmunt Nowakowski's* Cape of Good Hope *and Ilf and Petrov's satire* One-Storied America.[1] *I was thrilled but also too embarrassed to admit I hadn't yet read these books myself. She was clearly ideologically ahead of me. I asked her to bring along some of the books to our lectures on the following day. I told her I knew a lot of comrades who'd want to read them.*

We left the meeting together, chatting about literature and the forthcoming exam on the bones of the skull. My embarrassment gradually dissipated. I didn't dare ask her if she had a boyfriend. After all, she was a fellow revolutionary, a fighter. A comrade in arms. I had to stick strictly to business.

In the following weeks, I used any pretext to see Biserka as often as possible without being too obvious about it. My role as the designated librarian for our group helped. She brought piles of books for sharing every day. I picked one in each of her consignments and read it cover to cover overnight. When we'd next meet, I casually dropped the subject of the book into our conversation and then talked knowledgeably about it as if I'd known it for years.

We attended some lectures together, but we were too busy taking notes to pay each other much attention in class. Our professors were merciless. They churned out Latin names of bones and muscles at a blistering pace and expected us to absorb and regurgitate them in an endless succession of tests and exams. The material wasn't difficult, but there was a lot of it. At the same time, our party leaders demanded more of us at grassroots level. They were enraged by the war engulfing Europe. The Nazi onslaught seemed unstoppable. One after the other, the countries of central and western Europe fell, like dominoes, to the German Army. Every day we heard news of another brazen air raid on London. Experienced party members stood up minutes before our professors arrived for our lectures and made announcements, urging us to become more active.

In meetings, we debated endlessly what we would do when the war reached us. What would our government do? Would the royal family buckle under Hitler's might? They, too, would have heard Joseph Goebbels threaten anyone who dared resist with "Wir werden sie koventrieren!" *The annihilation of Coventry by the Luftwaffe earlier that year had become a verb.*

Sometimes I met with Biserka at designated points in the city to sell the Hammer and Sickle *to passersby. Our favorite spot was near the Well of Life. Bronze statues of men, women, and children writhed softly in a circular embrace, their shapes reflected in the well water at their center. Located between the main entrance to the Faculty of Law and the National Theater, the sculpture was an ideal spot for us boys, armed with bats and hammers hidden under our coats, to loiter, while the girls sold our literature. We timed our action to coincide with the end of the teaching day and watched the law students, dominated by right-wingers, head for our female comrades, their faces red with rage. Invariably, they stopped in their tracks when they noticed the crowd of mysterious-looking men parading around the well. I hoped for a confrontation at least once that fall, but I was out of luck. Even the most vicious of the lawyers didn't dare attack the girls, knowing reinforcements were nearby. They'd buy a paper, throw it on the floor, and stomp all over it in a pathetic display of bravado and contempt.*

Zagreb was Biserka's hometown. She lived with her parents, so she never ate in the student canteen. On my bursary, I couldn't afford to take her out to a restaurant, even if I could have plucked up the courage to invite her out. And I didn't know how to behave with Biserka. Her curves, her perfume, the way her hips swayed when she walked beguiled me. On one occasion, I accidentally brushed against her right breast. I imagined she trembled at my touch. Or was it me who was trembling? A flush rushed up my face to my ears. I mumbled an apology. I felt like a clumsy provincial recently arrived in the big city. Petit bourgeois. But her face didn't change. She didn't even notice my apology, or maybe she pretended not to notice. I hoped she wouldn't dismiss our accidental contact as a vulgar shove of the sort she might experience on a crowded tram. Perhaps she did notice but ignored my confusion so as not to embarrass me even more.

One evening we were assigned to paste red star stickers and write slogans on walls around the city center. The stickers were easy work. We glued them to lampposts and shop windows in well-lit squares and thoroughfares. The streets rustled with auburn leaves, the smell of roasting chestnuts everywhere.

"Chestnuts, roasted chestnuts! Young man, get some for the young lady, one dinar per pack!"

The slogans took longer to write in chalk, so we sought out the darker alleyways. We split our slogan in two. Biserka wrote SMRT FAŠIZMU, *DEATH TO FASCISM, and I chalked* SLOBODA NARODU, *FREEDOM TO THE PEOPLE. While one of us wrote, the other stood guard. I was about halfway through mine when Biserka noticed the glint of a policeman's helmet coming toward us. She threw herself at me and kissed me. I remembered reading about this subterfuge in my little black book. I embraced her back. Her curves pressed against me. I let go slightly, lest she noticed my excitement. We stayed close as the policeman walked by. He seemed to be taking forever. Eventually, he was gone. Biserka laughed. I didn't know if she was laughing at me or the policeman.*

"Comrade Blackie, it looks like leafleting in mixed company is commonplace for you, as you seem to know how to kiss," said Biserka. Was there a hint of irony in her voice?

I turned away and finished working on the slogan I'd started earlier.

"The policeman thought our embrace was real," I said.

I wanted to tell her our kiss went beyond the call of duty as prescribed in our little black book of conspiracy. She'd reciprocated not only as a comrade but as a woman. But I stopped myself. Saying anything would have made our action profane, kind of vulgar. Our cell entrusted us to do our job, not canoodle in dark corners.

"Yes, we were convincing," Biserka said calmly. "Anyway, we've finished in this district. We've been here for some time. We'd better scamper."

She grabbed my hand, and we ran down the cobbled street toward the bright lights on the main square, giggling like children who had played a trick on their teacher and got away with it.

When we parted that evening, I saw a gentle glow in her green eyes. Our formal handshake lasted a heartbeat longer than usual. We agreed to meet the following day after the anatomy practical.

My face beamed as I walked down Ilica Street, bathed in the lights from shop windows crammed with St. Nicholas Day presents.[2] The festive season was upon us. My thoughts kept wandering to Biserka, her almond-shaped eyes, her long eyelashes, her curvaceous hips. Turning the corner toward my student digs, I inhaled the nutty, autumnal scent of roasting chestnuts.

"Hot chestnuts, young man! Come get them!"

* * *

After our practical on the following day, Biserka told me she'd forgotten to bring Mikhail Sholokhov's And Quiet Flows the Don.[3] *She promised to bring it along next time.*

"Or if you have no other plans, we could pop over to mine to get it," she said. "It's a heavy tome, so you can help me carry it. I live a few minutes' walk away."

I was thrilled. I would get to see her innermost sanctum.

She opened the front door of the apartment. It led into a hexagonal hall lined with oil paintings of landscapes. A marble bust of a man stood on a pedestal in the middle of the hall on a floor of highly polished parquet. There was no one at home. A heavy oak door led to her room, a vast cavern filled with the scent of her perfume. A small writing desk like the one I'd always dreamed of having myself stood by the tall double window. In one corner, there was a wide, red couch with scatter cushions. A bookcase filled to bursting point stretched along the inner wall of the room. A few easy chairs surrounded a glass coffee

*table strewn with magazines. Biserka took my coat and disappeared through
another door.*

*When she returned, I had to suppress a gasp. She wore a pale green house-
dress made of some kind of slinky fabric that clung to her curves. The garment
was drawn together carelessly, offering a fleeting glimpse of leg or neckline
every time she moved. The dress shimmered as she drifted around the room. She
sat next to me on the couch, reclined backward onto the cushions, and pushed
off her pom-pom-topped slippers.*

"What do you think of my little corner?" she asked me with a smile.

*"Would you like a glass of liqueur?" she said, before I had a chance
to answer.*

*She jumped up and opened the door to a sideboard beneath the bookshelves.
Her robe slid down her back, revealing a lacy shoulder strap. The next thing I
knew, she was standing in front of me holding a crystal glass filled with amber
liquid, her willowy silhouette outlined in the downlight of the gilded chandelier
above her.*

*I drained the glass, coughing and spluttering as the liquid seared my throat.
It was all getting too much. I stood up briskly.*

*"I need to go now. I have to write up this afternoon's practical," I blurted
out. She stood in my way.*

*"Don't be so provincial," she whispered. The heady scent of her perfume
wrapped itself around me. I didn't know where it started or finished. My body
filled with desire.*

*We tore at each other. Our embrace was crumpled, clumsy at times, passion-
ate. We found ourselves on the couch. I sought a hasty path toward her body,
breathless as I sensed her soft smooth skin beneath my fingers. We lost ourselves
in each other, wanting time to stop.*

When I came to, I felt her slipping away from me. I pulled her back toward me.

"No, no. Not yet. I'm not letting you go."

*"My dear little boy," she whispered. "You are a wild man. You haven't taken
care. I'm going to the bathroom, I'll come back soon."*

*With a single lithe movement, she wriggled out of my embrace like a cat and
disappeared into the bathroom. I watched the shadows dancing on the ceiling
and dozed while I waited for her to return into my arms.*

*That night, I walked home humming. I dodged the puddles with a swing of the
hips, like a samba dancer, imagining I was partnering Biserka at a grand ball.*

*It was the first of our beautiful fall nights together. Sholokhov remained on
Biserka's bookshelf, but he was not forgotten. His book was our alibi, an excuse
for my visitations, if anyone should ever ask why I was there.*

*Biserka taught me little tricks. She stopped our lovemaking to remind me to
take care she doesn't get pregnant. She became my teacher.*

We were comrades during the day, lovers at night.

* * *

By March 1941, we were busy preparing for the inevitable. The hectograph at the Faculty of Medicine was put to good use, not only to print off our lecture notes, but also to reproduce political leaflets. We distributed thousands of them around town. We collected donations for our fellow freedom fighters in Spain imprisoned in concentration camps. The torrent of daily news meant we couldn't print the student newspaper fast enough, so we stood on street corners shouting out the latest developments.

"Bulgaria signs the Tripartite Pact!" we screamed until we were hoarse.[4] "Join the resistance! Down with fascism!"

Medicine and politics took up nearly all our time and energy. There was little time for love. When I embraced Biserka, she was mine and I was hers, but I sensed a coldness setting in as soon as we'd satisfied our desires. She brought me Alexandra Kollontai's Free Love to read and rejected any signs of tenderness in public, calling them provincial.

Our side won a landslide victory in the Student Union elections that year. Medicine was overwhelmingly socialist, but we made great strides in other faculties, too. The conservatives lost heart, even in the Faculty of Law. Biserka won a seat on the influential University Management Committee with wide-ranging powers across all faculties.

Our election euphoria didn't last long. Prewar psychosis was setting in. Some students were reluctant to become politically active in the atmosphere of uncertainty. Many did not want to take sides that would cost them dearly later. Bigger and more powerful countries than our own little Kingdom of Yugoslavia had fallen victim to the Blitzkrieg. Hitler was so confident of his military supremacy that he sent Rommel to conquer Africa. After the invasion of Poland and France and the bombing of Britain, we didn't stand a chance. Our closest neighbors, Hungary, Romania, and Bulgaria, buckled under the onslaught. Mussolini occupied Albania and attacked Greece. We were surrounded by the Axis powers and their allies. Either Germany or Italy or both were sure to invade.

The crunch came on March 25, 1941. Our government signed a pact to join the powerful trio of Germany, Italy, and Japan. We weren't having it. We organized a protest demonstration, to start from the main train station and wind its way through the city streets to the German Travel Agency opposite Zrinski Park. We loitered around the station in an atmosphere of expectation.

But something wasn't right. There were rumors. There'd been a fight with the police near the National Theater. The starting point of our march changed. It would now begin in Maksimir, on the other side of the city. We would not get there on time. Feeling despondent, a small group of us walked toward Zrinski Park anyway.

We stood on the lawn under the hundred-year-old plane trees and faced the German travel agency.

"Down with Hitler!" someone in the group shouted.

We had to show the citizens of Zagreb there were people who did not approve of the pact.

"Down with the pact!"

"Down with fascism!" we screamed.

"Down with war!"

Early-evening strollers hoping for some peace in the park left swiftly. We could see the employees of the bureau, a man and two women, through the glass frontage. The women gathered their papers quickly and withdrew behind the door at the back of the shop. The man tried to dial a number on the office phone, without success, judging by his nervous demeanor and repeated tapping of the cradle. He was probably calling the police.

The police never came, and we soon got tired of shouting. I retreated with Igor and Fran to the bandstand in the center of the park. We leaned on the ornate wrought-iron balustrade and discussed the following day's exam in chemistry, as if nothing had happened.

I noticed a dark silhouette of a man walking toward us. I wouldn't have given him a second thought if he hadn't almost imperceptibly changed direction when he saw me looking. I stared at him. He reached into his coat and pulled out a gun.

"Hands up! Police!" he yelled.

The gun was huge. I raised my hands up and froze. Igor and Fran turned on their heels and bolted in opposite directions from each other. Emboldened by their quick reactions, I dashed off in a third direction.

"Stop!" the man shouted.

Something whistled over my head. I don't remember hearing the crack of the gun, but there must have been one. Or did he have a silencer? Perhaps he was a professional assassin. I ran faster. Another whistle rushed past my ear, but this time it was louder. I changed direction, left, right, left, right, diving into doorways to catch my breath. Several streets later, I slowed down, still breathing hard. There was no one about. Once my heart stopped beating wildly, I congratulated myself for escaping an agent with a gun. He can't have been a professional. He couldn't even shoot straight! Perhaps he was a new recruit.

On my way home to my garret, I thought about my adventure and how easily I got away. I imagined what would have happened if I'd owned a gun of my own, if I'd fired it from the pavilion. I wouldn't have aimed to kill. I would have scared him off by shooting at his feet.

The excitement of the chase made me hungry. I dropped into my local dairy restaurant and ordered a glass of milk and a piece of cornbread for one dinar and twenty paras. I poured the milk over the yellow, stale bread to make it more palatable. As I chewed, I carried on daydreaming about my first gunfight with a plainclothes policeman. There would be many more fights. My meal tasted so much better laced with radical fervor. The revolution was well on its way.

* * *

I didn't see any of my comrades until late the following day. When I finally bumped into them at the clubhouse, they all shouted at once.

"Pustili su te! They've let you go!"

"Biserka went looking for you with a basket of cakes, but they told her at the police station you weren't there."

"We didn't believe them but now we can see it's true—they've let you go already!"

It gradually dawned on me what had happened. They thought I'd been arrested and went looking for me at the main city police station.

"What the devil did you do that for? You've compromised my cover! Thanks to you, I'm a suspect now. The police will want to know why my friends thought I'd been arrested. And what was Biserka doing with her basket of food like Little Red Riding Hood? What did she tell them?"

"She said she was your fiancée," said Igor with a mocking glint in his eye. *"What's more, they believed her."*

"Well, you should have looked behind you while you were running. I bet your heart was in your pants, and you didn't stop until you got to Old Town," I said.

"I retreated strategically," Igor said. *"I was much faster than you. I used my arms to propel me instead of holding them up like you did."* He burst out laughing.

"Here's Biserka," Igor turned toward the lithe figure approaching us. *"Can we all come to yours to help you polish off the lovely cakes you've made for Dragan in his prison cell?"*

"Yes, good idea! Bring Zdenka, and I'll let some of my other friends know, too."

"What's the matter with you?" she turned toward me. *"Why are you sulking? You should be happy you're not in prison. My parents are not in, so we can turn up the music and have a dance. Half past seven everyone!"*

"Aren't you lucky?" said Igor as we watched Biserka's frame undulating away from us. *"You'll get to stay afterward, too,"* he shoved me in the ribs, his face beaming with a lecherous grin.

I blushed. No amount of willpower seemed to control the heat rising up my neck. I turned away from Igor hoping he wouldn't notice the fire in my face. Did he know about me and Biserka, or was he probing? Did the whole group know about it? Maybe I should have told them openly? Revolutionaries mustn't keep secrets from their comrades. Maybe they've found out anyway, and now they don't trust me because I didn't tell them myself? But where would Igor know this from? Had Biserka said something? Maybe she'd confided in Zdenka, who then passed it on to Igor?

We didn't know it at the time, but the evening we gorged on my "prison provisions" would be the last of our carefree gatherings. Igor and Zdenka, Fran and Mira, Zorka and a few others—we all descended on Biserka's. I wound up the gramophone and chose the dance music. First, a few tangos from Georges Boulanger's virtuoso violin. His *"Avant de mourir"* always got everyone up on their feet. And then the Russian romance song *"Ochi Charnye," "Black Eyes,"* my favorite. I swayed with Biserka in the darkest corner of her room, hoping no one would notice how tightly we were wrapped around each other. But the others didn't seem to care. Igor and Zdenka groped each other openly on the couch.

They stood up occasionally without unraveling and weaved their way across the room, sliding effortlessly on the parquet floor.

In one corner, Fran and Mira raised their voices. We could hear them arguing while we danced. Mira's usual pallor had turned into a rosy glow.

"The Soviets haven't hacked Poland to death, as you say," Mira insisted. "On the contrary, they've protected Poland from the imperialists' perfidy. Sadly, they couldn't save the whole country. Anyway, the Polish bourgeoisie helped Hitler to partition Czechoslovakia. Now their greed has come back to bite them."

"Yes, but the Polish people have paid the price in blood," said Fran. "And it's going to get worse for them. Stalin's so-called friendship with Hitler—it's a big trick. It won't last. Everyone says the Russian is as much of an imperialist as the German."

"Nah. The Soviet Army is weak," objected Mira. "The Molotov Agreement is a delay tactic. Their soldiers carry their rifles on pieces of string. Their tanks stop every time they hit a pothole in the road."

"The Russians aren't weak," Fran countered. "They know what they're doing. They want the capitalists to think the first socialist state is feeble. Eventually, the imperialists will believe their own propaganda and lies about the Soviet Union. That'll put them to sleep. Russia is huge, rich, well endowed with material and spiritual wealth. Even Napoleon couldn't conquer it. It is no longer a country impoverished by the Romanovs and the tsar's generals."

Mira leaned forward to make another point but sat back as a coughing fit wracked her body. Fran poured a glass of water for Mira and rubbed her back gently until the fit subsided. Her battle with TB wasn't getting any easier.

Zorka, our cell leader, sat quietly, listening to the discussion. She didn't come to many parties. She spent all her energies on political work and her studies. Her straight black hair was simply cut, almost like a man's hairdo. She always wore a determined expression, accentuated by her sharp facial features and pockmarks left behind by smallpox.

Zorka's widowed mother ran a small dairy restaurant. It made barely enough money to feed the six children in the family. Zorka often helped at the tills, but even then, she used her position to further the socialist cause. She gave pamphlets to the girls who worked as servants in rich households. Some showed the leaflets to their employers. Horrified, the ma'ams forbade any further purchases from the dairy. Zorka's mother knew all her customers. She asked them why they no longer sent their maids to buy bread and milk in her shop. The ladies sympathized with her. They knew she had many mouths to feed, but none had the courage to tell her the real reason for withdrawing their custom. It wasn't the old woman's fault she had a crazy daughter.

Eventually, Zorka worked it out for herself.

"Ma'am will not permit such godless literature in the house," a maidservant said to Zorka. "She threatened to dismiss me if I bring Lucifer's post to her house again."

Zorka shrugged her shoulders. Life was difficult for the working classes. Not only did they have to put up with crumbs from their masters' tables, but they weren't even allowed to read about themselves. Maids and housecleaners were the least self-aware workers. She tried a different approach. She visited their families at home, bringing gifts of butter and cheese from the dairy.

"Everyone has the right to bread," Zorka said earnestly. "In the Soviet Union, bread will soon be distributed for free. There is no poverty in Russia. There is no unemployment. Everyone gets a pension, so there's no need to worry about getting old. Everyone has a job, men and women. The children go to beautiful state nurseries. The community looks after the upbringing of children."

The women and their hungry families listened, enraptured, to these stories of a distant, fairy-tale land. The children's imagination was ignited. Free bread and maybe free cakes, too! The kids wanted to go to this magical place.

After Zorka left, the mothers swore the children to secrecy.

"You'll be arrested if you tell anyone these stories!"

"Why? Why hasn't Zorka been arrested, then?" the kids wailed.

"Go and stand in the corner for ten minutes. That'll teach you about free bread and cakes!"

Zorka talked about nothing else but the revolution. No other topic of conversation interested her. When our attention turned to Greta Garbo's latest role or the football results, she went quiet, dark, and unapproachable. She was an excellent student and did well in her exams. Her knowledge of medicine was, for her, a weapon to fight the capitalist enemy with. She insisted weak students couldn't influence their colleagues. Her studies were motivated by her political work.

When the dancing paused, I approached Zorka. I told her our group was getting too big and diffuse. Smaller cells would be more agile. Cliques were forming within the larger group anyway.

"Yes, cliques of mutual admirers," said Zorka.

"Why not? Mutual admirers, what's wrong with that?" I said. "Smaller groups are safer. Everyone trusts each other. Isn't that better for a conspiracy? How do we know our large group doesn't harbor a few traitors? We know already there are plenty of lazybones. They don't even read the leaflets they are distributing. All they do is talk. They do little else."

"Yes. Small groups are more secure against enemy infiltration," said Zorka. I've talked to Baba about this already, and he agrees. We must strengthen our conspiracy. When the Germans attack, our feeble royal army will crumble. The air stinks of betrayal and treason."

"I'm going home to Virovitica tomorrow for the semester break," I said to Zorka. "War may well start . . . "

Shrieks and giggles interrupted our conversation. Igor had painted a small black moustache on his upper lip with Zdenka's eyeliner. He smoothed his hair down onto his forehead, raised his arm in a straight-limbed salute, and clicked the back of his heels.

"Bei uns in Deutschland, Millionen essen nur Kartoffeln, aber in Amerika, sie essen gebackene Truthahn mit Palatchinken. Darum müssen wir kämpfen.

... Here in Germany, millions subsist on potatoes, but in America, they eat roast turkey and pancakes. That's why we must fight. . . . " Igor shouted out.

We roared with laughter. The sound cascaded through the window, nudged open to keep the dancers cool, to the street below us; it twisted and turned between lampposts until it came to a shuddering halt in the depths of a shadowy, sinister alley. There would be dark days ahead.

Reading through your account of your student activism raised more than the occasional smile on my face. Here was the man I knew, the dad who often hummed the timeless tune "Ochi Charnye," the dad who loved dancing, the man who had an eye for beautiful women. Biserka's party in 1940 triggered my own memories of your weekly soirées with friends, some twenty years later.

It's a hot evening at our home in Baghdad. I'm perched on the landing on top of the staircase. I'm about five or six, in my nightie and barefoot. My ears are on full alert. I hear voices, your voice, the voices of your friends. I'm supposed to be in bed fast asleep. The scratch of stylus against vinyl on our gramophone announces the start of the musical part of the evening. Rhythmic bass guitar mingles with the honeyed baritone of Dean Martin. The languid notes weave themselves around the spindles to the top of the stairs, twisting and turning. I sway with Dean. On the wall opposite the staircase, the shadows of dancers undulate.

"It's a rumba," Mama says between peals of laughter. "Why are you doing the tango?"

"I don't care what it is. I'll dance what I like!" you retort. "Why don't we invent a new dance? A rumgo or a tanba?"

You wrap your arm around Mama's waist. She bends over backward and kicks her right leg up in the air. Upstairs, I hold onto the banister with both hands, lean backward, and kick my leg out in my own version of tanba.

This was the dad I was used to, confident, fun loving, happy. Not the stranger in the first twelve pages of your manuscript.

Your writing triggered more memories of landmarks in Zagreb I was familiar with. On my next trip to the city, I revisited some of them in the hope of seeing them with fresh eyes. Zrinski Park, where you dodged bullets from a plainclothes policeman, was an oasis of calm, revealing little of its turbulent past. The neat rows of ancient plane trees and manicured flower beds exuded a sense of order, offering passersby a respite from the hustle and bustle of the city center. Teenagers lingered around the ornate bandstand like you did so many decades earlier. Perhaps they, too, harbored hopes and dreams of a better world. Or were they more concerned with the present, like passing their chemistry exam or tweeting their friends on their mobiles?

I strolled down Tesla Street toward the Well of Life, where you taunted your right-wing opponents with the *Hammer and Sickle*. Sandwiched between the main university building and the baroque splendor of the National Theater, the fountain was set a few steps below street level to create a tranquil haven. The bronze statues still writhed in a gentle embrace, like they did all those years ago when you were here. I tried to imagine you in a group of hot-headed firebrands loitering around the well, but I was distracted by a mother and toddler sharing an ice cream. They giggled at each other and took turns licking the pink mounds of sweetness dripping from the wafer cone. The immediacy of the present elbowed the past aside.

I made one more attempt at reimagining your youth. I headed for Tomašićeva Street, a brisk fifteen-minute walk from the theater. I'd read that the dairy restaurant where your cell leader Zorka Klašnja worked was located there, but I didn't know the house number. Perhaps I could guess the exact address by peering into modern-day establishments. Zorka fought tirelessly for the cause, distributing leaflets and organizing clandestine meetings while helping her mother run the business. I scoured the short street lined with apartment buildings and a parade of shops at ground level. I searched for clues. Was it one of the two sprawling cafés, always thronging with people? Or was it Veganšpek, Vegan Bacon, the restaurant eager to please both vegetarians and meat eaters? Or was it the fishing tackle shop tucked away in a basement? Or possibly the tiny experimental theater with its hand-painted posters announcing the next performance? Or the bakery, the bank, or one of the two mini supermarkets? It was impossible to tell. Too many businesses, too little information. You didn't know it at the time, but a fourth-floor apartment in a building on Lopašićeva Street, around the corner from Zorka's dairy, would one day become your permanent home.

I returned to your manuscript. There was tension in your writing between your idealism and your pragmatism. The fighter in you also wanted to be a doctor. Your studies could not be neglected. And there was Biserka. Sweet Biserka. Comrade in arms and beautiful lover. What would be your next move?

Chapter 5

War, 1941

On the day you traveled from Zagreb to your hometown, Virovitica, for your semester break, there was more disturbing news. A group of Yugoslav Air Force officers, unhappy with the terms of the pact with the Axis powers, staged a coup and overthrew the government. Hitler was incensed. How dare a pimple of a nation like Yugoslavia stand up to the German colossus? The only way to deal with the impertinence was to squash it.

Virovitica, April 6, 1941

My father crashed into my bedroom yelling, "The Luftwaffe is bombing Belgrade!" Startled out of a deep sleep, I stumbled out of bed and joined him in front of the radio. We flicked through the stations, twirling the knob, searching for news. Radio Zagreb was talking war. Radio Vienna played military marches with occasional clips from the Führer's speeches. The war in Yugoslavia had begun.

I went out to investigate.

Virovitica was preparing for battle. A red-faced farmer, his uniform reeking of mothballs and straining at the buttons around his middle, pulled a bullock cart loaded with a small cannon along our street toward the main square. He shouted obscenities in the animal's ear and half-heartedly cracked the whip. Better used to ploughing the fields, the beast snorted and plodded on.

"There's our elite antitank force!" someone shouted. "The Krauts will quake in their boots!"

The newly formed cavalry, made up of reservists, rode past. Their pack horses brayed and kicked, trying to dislodge their riders. Judging by the mud on their uniforms, a few had already been thrown off their prized farm animals. Sabers rattled and saddle straps squeaked as they filed past. Were they intending to attack German tanks with sabers? The air smelled of leather and manure. The riders filed past in long columns in one direction, only to return in the opposite direction a few minutes later. Hasn't anyone told them which way to go? Wasn't anyone in charge?

The townspeople stared from the pavements. Women wept and embraced their sons and husbands on their doorsteps.

After the thunder of horses' hooves subsided, an eerie silence descended onto the streets. If all the army units have left, who would defend our town? Where was the infantry?

The explosions started that afternoon. A blast near the bridge across the River Drava was followed closely by another at the train station. Our little town shivered.

By the evening, more troops of newly clad peasant knights galloped through. It was impossible to tell if they were on some urgent mission or they couldn't stop because their horses were spooked. Or maybe they were rushing back to their villages for their dinner?

Overnight, bursts of machine-gun fire and sirens from the fire station kept us awake. Not that we could sleep, anyway. We listened for airplanes. None came.

The following morning, cold and gray. Curtains twitching across the street.

At midday, soldiers thundered past our house, this time on foot.

"The Germans are coming," said one of them.

Our neighbor two doors down dashed home in full uniform, looking around over his shoulder before stepping in through his front door. He emerged a half-hour later in civilian clothes and carrying a suitcase. What did he do with the uniform? And where was his rifle?

Afternoon. Still no sign of the Germans. I emerged from the house for a peek.

Walking past the army barracks, I noticed there were no guards. Instead, men and women carried blankets and bags laden with flour and tinned food out of the provisions room. A captain walked briskly in the opposite direction, toward the station.

"Where are you going?" I shouted after him. "Shouldn't you be watching the garrison?"

"Fuck off, kid!" he barked. "Mind your own business! Go back to Mommy and wash behind your ears." He waved his gun toward me.

Machine-gun fire crackled in the hills. A blanket of twiglets landed on my shoulders from the chestnut tree canopy above me. Could stray bullets reach this far into town?

Everyone running. Soldiers, officers, civilians, everyone. I ran, too, back home.

Crashing through the front door, I called out to Mom and Dad, Milena and Zlatko.

"Down here," I heard a muffled voice from somewhere below. The four of them sat huddled together on an old mattress in the basement.

"It's probably safer down here for the moment," said Dad.

Buzz of engines in the distance. Were they ours or theirs? The hum became more insistent, combative. It was too rhythmic and methodical to be our own. The German army attacked slowly and systematically, one step at a time.

We were under occupation. Long columns of armored vehicles packed with German soldiers trundled past our windows toward the barracks. Officers stationed along key crossroads directed the leaden traffic. Unlike our own makeshift army, they seemed to know where they were going.

* * *

April 10, 1941

Another announcement on the radio.

"Long live the Independent State of Croatia! Long live the great German Reich!" screamed the news reader.

We were no longer Yugoslavs. The royal family fled the country, taking the nation's gold reserves with them. The Yugoslavia of my youth disintegrated.

"Long live our supreme leader, Ante Pavelić!"[1]

They'd done it. The fascist Ustaša paramilitaries have taken over.[2]

On the following day, Dad tried to stop me from going out, but I refused to cower all day at home. As soon as I stepped out, a youth in Ustaša uniform approached me. It was Danilo. He'd been two years below me in school, and I remembered helping him with his math homework. There was barely a suggestion of hair on his chin. He pointed his gun at me. The bayonet was awfully long.

"Come with me! Now!" he barked.

"Hello Danilo! How's your math? Has it improved at all?"

"Come now!" he yelled, his voice wavering.

"And whom do you represent?" I asked him.

"We're going to an Ustaša base. You have sinned against the Independent State of Croatia."

"Alright then, let's go to this lair of yours," I said, stuffed my hands in my pockets, and whistled the "Lili Marleen."[3]

The "Ustaša base" was a makeshift shed, hastily converted into an office. Inside, more uniformed youths awaited. Some of the faces looked familiar, but I couldn't remember their names.

"You're a communist agitator." Danilo screamed. "Admit it!"

I remained silent.

"Admit it! We have photographic evidence of you printing propaganda leaflets in the school basement!" he yelled.

"Come on, boys! Show me the photograph. Why are you bothering to question me if you have the evidence?"

I thought of our trusty hectograph in the windowless basement of our school. We always worked by candlelight. It was so dark in there. No one could have taken a photograph. Their threats did not ring true. They were almost comical.

They whispered among themselves. One lad took out his bayonet and carved his name on the table in front of him. Steel blade thumped softly against cherrywood.

"You were in the Youth League!" shouted one of them.

"So were you!" I retorted.

"I was forced to join."

"So was I."

Silence. Then more whispers.

"You are under house arrest for your activities against the Croatian people and the Ustaša movement!" announced Danilo. "Now go!"

I was marched out and escorted home by a boy soldier younger than Danilo. Tanks and armored vehicles thundered by.

Over the next few days, I discovered some of my comrades from the Youth League were also under house arrest. This didn't stop us from seeing each other. We left by our back gardens, jumped over a few fences, and ran along the secret maze of footpaths we'd created when we still played at cowboys and Indians. We met in Zvonko's house, where we pretended to play cards. We'd deal out the cards, open a bottle of plum brandy, and pour the fiery liquid into glasses. Then we talked politics. If the police were to raid us, we'd have a valid excuse for being together.

The new Ustaša regime wasted no time making changes. Within days, Jews and Serbs were rounded up and taken to prison. Some of them were put to work sweeping the streets.

One morning they found the body of tailor Matija, a Serb and known sympathizer of the Reds, on the parade ground behind the army barracks. He had been stabbed. Some said he was found naked. Others said his face had been mauled by pigs. No one knew when or where he was murdered. His widow buried him quickly and quietly. No priest. The priest had already left town. But how was Matija killed? Who killed him? Was it the Germans or the Ustaša? The townspeople discussed his death in whispers. A sense of dread descended on our little town.

Then there was the message from Vuković, my old mentor from the library. "Destroy your papers. Your house could be raided. They can use whatever they find as evidence against you and your family. When you've finished reading this message, burn it."

I didn't want to waste my diary, my poems, my little collection of angry leaflets, but I couldn't leave them with my parents. Too incriminating. With a heavy heart, I made a fire in the kitchen stove and burned the lot.

Mom and Dad were worried. But I had to get back to Zagreb to continue my studies. I left Virovitica, the town of my youth, the next day. Somehow, I knew I would never return.

Not for the first time, your writing reminded me of how shaky my knowledge of World War II history was. I was broadly aware of major events but would have been hard-pressed to produce an accurate timeline of the war. Croatian history was a particular weakness. Although the names *Ustaša* and *Ante Pavelić* were familiar, I would not have been able to write more than a single sentence about them. Without a historical context, your story didn't make much sense. On my next trip to Zagreb, I purchased a heap of Croatian history books, paying dearly for excess luggage on my flight back to London. But it was a price well worth bearing.

After weeks and months of reading, I learned that your birth country, the Kingdom of Yugoslavia, had been an uneasy alliance of ethnic groups with diverging allegiances. During your childhood, a spate of tit-for-tat assassinations of prominent Croatian and Serb leaders by ultranationalist groups brought the country to the brink of civil war at least twice. The kingdom turned into a repressive dictatorship. All around you, social inequality was rife. You riled against it.

When you left Virovitica to return to your studies in Zagreb, your home country had changed beyond recognition. Almost overnight, the large multiethnic kingdom metamorphosed into a smaller fascist state ruled by the extreme nationalist group, the Ustaša. With Benito Mussolini's blessing, they'd been training for a takeover in paramilitary camps in Italy, waiting for the right moment to strike. That moment came when the German Army invaded Yugoslavia. Ante Pavelić, a hitherto little-known officer, returned from a twelve-year exile and seized power. Hitler was delighted. What better way to rule a conquered land than using its own natives to subjugate the populace? He could save his own troops for the western front.

Pavelić and his militant supporters wasted no time in terrorizing the population. But you were not afraid, at least not in your hometown, Virovitica. You were not intimidated by boy soldiers, most of whom you'd known from school. Would it be the same in Zagreb?

"I see the young gentleman is traveling somewhere," a voice boomed behind me as I boarded the train to Zagreb. It was Stipe, a friend from school.

"Going back to Zagreb for your studies, now the war is over?" Stipe said overly loudly. He took a good look around and sat down opposite me. The train wasn't full. We sat some distance away from the other passengers.

"What are we to make of this?" he whispered, leaning toward me. "The Krauts will conquer the world. I've never seen so much heavy weaponry in my life. And now they've installed the Ustaša, we're done for . . . " His words gushed out of his mouth like a waterfall.

"They come to our village to take food for their soldiers. People are hiding their wheat harvest. I've hidden some, too," said Stipe. "My old man, he's so ill, he can hardly walk anymore. He says I should hide the whole lot. That's how it was in the Great War. There was more and more money but less and less food. Who's going to win this war?"

Behind Stipe's back, I could see Ivo coming down the aisle toward us. I signaled to Stipe to pipe down. Ivo was my first failed attempt at recruiting someone new to the Youth League. His father was an unskilled laborer who couldn't afford to look after his family of five children. It was hard to imagine what it was like to be so dirt poor. We needed more children of factory workers and laborers to join the Youth League. Not peasants or traders or intellectuals but workers who had only their pure labor to sell. Not artisans or craftsmen or even semiskilled workers but raw, unskilled laborers. Ivo was the son of such a worker. Ivo was hardworking and industrious, always top of his class. He won prizes. At every school performance, he was asked to read his poetry or essays.

The Franciscan friars were so impressed, they awarded him a scholarship in their school.

I often walked home from school with Ivo. We discussed themes like virtue, humanity, and freedom. I tried to steer our conversation toward politics, but Ivo resisted.

"I'm not interested in politics," Ivo said. "I'm poor and I'll lose all my support if I engage in politics. My father was honest and worked all his life, but there was never enough to feed us all. If he'd engaged in politics, we would have been worse off. I want to be educated, go to university, and live like a gentleman. I don't want to go hungry. I'm lucky to have the help of our God-fearing monks."

When the Nazis invaded, Ivo's father was thrilled. He said it was high time for the old Yugoslavia to perish because it was governed by Jews and Freemasons.

"How are you, Ivo?" I said as he sat down next to us on the train. "Are you living better now the end is near for all the undesirables? There will be more room for us Croatian scholars," I goaded him.

"That's right. All these Jews, Freemasons, Serbs—they were poisoning our society. We've finished with all that. There will be progress now. A motorized army can't be fought with ox carts. We Croats understand this. We need to have links with advanced nations in the West, the Germans and the Italians. The East beyond the River Drina is doomed. Balkan backwardness, it's all about eating and drinking, swearing, and other lowly passions."

"Ivo, you've changed. A few weeks ago, you didn't want to engage in politics. Now you're expressing some strong opinions."

"I have changed because I've had my eyes opened," said Ivo in a shaky voice. "I know now who was responsible for all my troubles over the years. Germany has shown us the way. You should change your politics, too, if you know what's good for you. The time for chattering and linguistic sparring is over. You won't just lose your place at university. You'll lose your head."

"I can see, Ivo, the German Army has impressed you. Hitler has smashed the Yugoslav ox cart with a single blow of his steely fist. He's installed new coachmen, too. But the cart has stayed the same."

"Give it up!" snarled Ivo. He rose and leaned toward me, fist clenched.

"Hey, boys, try some asparagus from my dad's farm," interrupted Stipe and shoved a glass jar full of pale green spears between us. "My old ma made it. I've got some fresh cornbread and plum brandy, too."

We sat back and tucked in, lips smacking, fingers licking. We swigged from the bottle of country brandy, strong and tart, and slapped each other on the back like we used to in our schooldays. By the time the twin towers of Zagreb Cathedral emerged from the evening fog on the horizon, we were sprawled over the benches, basking in the warm glow of the brandy we'd shared, our earlier arguments forgotten.

In reading your account of your early days of political activism, it struck me how easily your verbal sparring with former school friends dissolved into camaraderie and sharing of food and drink in good cheer. But Pavelić and his militants had set to rule the new Croatia with an iron fist, modeled on Nazi Germany. The new country tolerated communism even less than the old kingdom did. There would be no debates with the new regime. Anyone daring to object would be stamped on, and stamped on hard.

Chapter 6

The Action

Shortly after taking control, the Ustaša government ratified new laws intended to protect the "purity" of the Croatian people, whom they considered of Aryan or Germanic origin rather than Slav. Discrimination against Serbs, Jews, Roma, and political "enemies of the state" became legal. Anyone who dared threaten the "honor of the Croatian people" or questioned the existence of the Independent State of Croatia could be arrested and imprisoned on grounds of being "objectionable and dangerous." Political activism of any kind became perilous.

May 1941

Zagreb thronged with soldiers. German soldiers marched in neat processions, singing "The Erika."[1] Some carried sacks and suitcases laden with mysterious goods. Young Ustaša in new uniforms topped with red berets strutted down the streets, proud of their allegiance to the new world order. A poster on the church bulletin board in the city center announced the times of the Wehrmachtsdienst, *a mass served entirely in German. Directly beneath it, someone pinned a hand-written note with the address and opening hours of the* Wehrmachtsbordell, *the German Army brothel, and* Wir sprechen Deutsch, *We speak German!*

At the university, new deans and vice chancellor were in post. Several professors had already left, some of their own accord; others were arrested.

Many students didn't return to their studies. There were fewer leftists around. The Ustaša attended lectures in uniform with enormous handguns strapped to their belts. If a Jew or Serb had the temerity to sit next to them, they glared at them and fingered their weapons until they moved away.

Fascist students took it upon themselves to clear the faculty of "undesirables." Early on in the semester, I witnessed their methods in the middle of a chemistry practical. Anton barged into the lab in full Ustaša uniform.

"Židovi, Srbi, komunisti! Marš van!" "Jews, Serbs, communists! Out!" he screamed.

Several students collected their satchels and made their way out. Beyond the lab door, thugs in uniform formed two rows along the corridor and down the stairwell leading to the exit. They punched, pushed, and scratched the departing students all the way down the stairs. Relieved to reach the exit alive, the students picked themselves up, straightened their torn clothes, and wiped their bloodied faces with their hands. They headed home in silence, never to be seen again.

I stayed put with my comrades and continued working on our practical assignment. Anton approached me.

"Did you hear the announcement?" he said.

"I did. I am not Jewish or Serbian," I said.

"But you are a communist."

"Look, you're making a serious allegation here. I could take offense," I said as I decanted concentrated sulfuric acid from a five-liter demijohn into a glass beaker on the bench. Anton took one look at the vapors coming out of the beaker and stepped back.

"We'll see about that," he muttered.

Behind him, our lab demonstrator fumed almost like the acid itself. He stepped up to Anton and glared into his eyes at close range.

"I haven't had any orders from the dean to stop Serbs and Jews from studying!" he squeaked.

Anton eyed him with a look of disgust, then turned away without saying a word.

"I'm telling the dean! You won't get away with this!" he screeched. He waved a desiccated fist at Anton's back.

"I won't tolerate violence in my classes," he announced to the remaining students. "This glassware is precious. I'm going to see the dean right now. Pauza! *Take your break now!"*

The atmosphere in town was tense. Public protests were few and far between. People stopped making loud comments in the street for fear of being overheard and reported to the police. Posters announcing executions of Jewish and Serbian communists shocked the populace into silence. Young people wearing the yellow star were rarely seen in the company of people without the Jewish emblem. After a while, the yellow star disappeared altogether from city streets.

My mother sent me a newspaper clip listing all the misdemeanors punishable by death. Distribution of leaflets against the state or the mere possession of such leaflets were on the list. Special tribunals were set up to determine if people accused of such crimes were guilty or innocent. Errands as innocuous as distributing books by the "wrong" authors could land you in front of a tribunal.

Some of my comrades avoided me. When they saw me approaching, they crossed the street to the other side. At first, I laughed off their spineless behavior, but then I realized I was the same. I put off seeing Biserka with the excuse of having too much studying to do. I gave up love because I was too scared. I had no right to laugh at others when I was a coward myself.

I avoided Zorka, too, but she sought me out. She approached me in the anatomy lab. We were dissecting the muscles of the leg. I'd removed my specimen from its formalin-soaked wrapping, when she sidled up to me and pointed at the long, reddish-brown strip on the inside of the thigh.

"What muscle is this?" she said.

"Musculus sartorius," I replied. *"It's been named after the tailoring profes-sion. The muscle has an important role when crossing your legs, the way tailors do when they're working,"* I said slowly and deliberately.

"Where have you been?" she hissed. *"I haven't seen you at a Youth League meeting for ages."*

"I went home to Virovitica and watched the Yugoslav Army fall to pieces. Soldiers and officers alike deserted the army. They ran from the enemy, their guns slung around their shoulders pointing downward, like recreational hunt-ers. Disgraceful," I whispered, hoping to deflect her question.

"Meeting tonight at seven, Sava River promenade. Six of us. No more meet-ings in each other's homes. And no excuses," she breathed, then raised her voice and continued. *"When you've finished with the leg, make sure you return my lecture notes. I've got a test coming up."* Zorka moved away quickly.

I looked down at the leg in front of me. It belonged to a person once. It was alive once. It took its owner to work, for a walk in the woods, maybe to a wed-ding or a dance. I wrapped the specimen up and placed it gingerly in the metal container with all the other legs and arms. The bin reeked of formalin.

What was happening to me? I'd always viewed anatomy specimens dispas-sionately. They were samples to be studied and learned from. They were no different from lecture notes. But now . . .

I had to make up my mind. What was the point of being a great conspirator if you got caught? The Ustaša had no scruples. If they found you guilty, you were shot. If not, you ended up in prison anyway. In a few years, if I carried on studying, I would become a doctor. Our country needed doctors. And what was the point of fighting? I would never become a doctor in prison. And who knows what would happen to Mom and Dad, Milena and Zlatko? They'd be persecuted, too, because of my actions.

But what about the revolution? Freedom, equality, social justice? Am I going to allow the Ustaša to tell me what to do? What about Anton, who failed his exam on the bones of the skull three times? He is one of their leaders now, shout-ing his mouth off and beating people up. He is a colleague. He'll be a doctor, too, one day. And we can't expect the Russians to save us. After all, they are friends with the Nazis. And even if they end up fighting each other eventually, we'll be left by the wayside. They don't care about us.

I made fun of the Ustaša boy soldiers in Virovitica, and I got away with it. It won't be so easy in Zagreb. The prisons are full of our people. I won't last long if I carry on agitating. But I can't stop now. You can't live without ideals. A life without ideals is like a Christmas tree without decorations. Dull, empty, cold.

There were two sides to me. One side wanted peace and quiet; the other craved a battle. One side wanted to study medicine; the other, to change the world.

Maybe I'd skip the Sava meeting? But Biserka would be there . . .

That evening, the river sparkled against the apricot haze of the setting sun. I walked down the promenade toward our meeting point and spotted Biserka already waiting there. As soon as she saw me, she waved and skipped toward *me like a little girl. My heart fluttered. She shoved her left hand into my right coat pocket and squeezed my hand already in there.*

We paired off, Igor and Zdenka, Biserka and I, Mira and Zorka. We pretended we were casual strollers, enjoying the afternoon and chatting with each other. There was nowhere to sit. The grass around us was still wet from the morning rain. The whole thing felt awkward and tense. It wasn't ideal, but it was better than congregating in the city center.

"Many comrades have been arrested; some have been shot," Zorka said. "Large-scale demonstrations are out. So are leaflets. Hide all your books and all your writing. If the police raid your digs, your writing could incriminate you. The Ustaša have infiltrated the police, so don't expect any sympathy from them," she continued breathlessly.

"But we must remain active. Try to recruit more first-year students. You'll have to approach them individually. No more pamphlets."

"And try sabotage. Puncture a few wheels or destroy a phone box," she suggested.

After the meeting, we couldn't go to Biserka's home. It was too dangerous. We went to my room instead. Biserka took her shoes off and tiptoed her way to my bedroom, so the landlady could hear one set of footsteps on the staircase. It was like the first time we'd been together. We clung to each other, bathed in the yellow light of the bedside lamp, surrounded by a sea of darkness. If only we could have stopped time.

Our Youth League meetings got ever smaller. No more sessions in the student union. Gone were the printed materials, but chalking slogans was still possible, provided we were quick about it. Loitering was not allowed.

Igor and I were returning from a slogan-writing assignment when we came across a crowd of Ustaša students straddling the road ahead of us. They stared hard at each passerby, deciding whether or not to let them through the cordon. We couldn't turn around and walk away. It would have been too obvious. We walked on and pretended we didn't notice the human net forming ahead. Would they recognize us?

"Where have you been, you two? Spit it out!"

"We had dinner in the canteen. We've been studying for a chemistry exam," I said quickly. We produced our student ID cards.

"Were you at a communist meeting?"

"We don't know anything about that. We're not interested in politics. We're interested in passing our exams," said Igor.

After a quick frisk, they let us go.

"Gubi se! Get lost!" they shouted.

"Serves me right for hanging out with you," said Igor. "If I'd been out with Zdenka, we could have had a good smooch, and they would have left us alone. Maybe next time I'll write slogans with Zdenka."

There was something ominous in the air. Our small actions were like the hoots of an owl in front of a hospice for the terminally ill. There was talk of the Nazis attacking Russia. Leftists looked forward to it. They predicted that Hitler, like Napoleon in 1812, would end up mauled. Let him attack the hornet's nest. This wasn't the Maginot or the Siegfried Line. The Russians were invincible. Fascists looked forward to it, too, for different reasons. Drang nach Osten—*The push toward the East. The Nazis wanted more* Lebensraum, *living space, for their perfect Aryan race. They would clear out the backward, mystical Slavs from their territories and cleanse the land of communism and atheism. The only people against the war were our mothers. They cared little about fighting. They wanted their sons and daughters to stay alive. To not be heroes.*

* * *

Our end-of-year exams were fast approaching. I cocooned myself in my garret and swotted, day and night.

* * *

June 22, 1941
I needed a break, so I headed off to the student canteen for a meal. The atmosphere in the streets was electric. People laughing nervously. Whispers all around. Has something happened? Or was it my exam nerves?
Goran approached my table as I tucked into my soup. Goran was a good friend, a centrist who never crossed the street to avoid me, unlike some of my Youth League comrades. His face beamed.
"So, what do you say? It's happened, finally!" he said.
"What? What's finally happened?"
"You mean you don't know? You're joking!" exclaimed Goran.
"I've had my nose in my books for days."
"Hitler has attacked the Soviet Union. He hasn't even declared war formally. His troops have crossed the border," blurted out Goran.
"Ah, that explains the tense atmosphere in the streets. I'll have to buy a paper. My landlady doesn't have a radio. I've been a bit cut off from the world."
"Don't tell me: you've lost interest in politics!" said Goran with a smirk on his face.
"No, no, not at all. I'm lying low until these exams are over. But now the Nazis and the Soviets are at war, there will be no middle ground. You'll have to jump left or right, not sit on the fence," I said.
"Aw yes, you keep telling me that. I'm not sitting on the fence. We are demo-crats against totalitarianism in all shapes and sizes," he carried on while I munched on the gristly slop passing off as stew. "I wonder how the Western democracies will view this attack on Russia? They said nothing when the Germans and the Russians decimated Poland between them, like jackals. Leave them to their own devices, they said. With a bit of luck, they'll annihilate each other. But they did the exact opposite. Living proof totalitarian regimes can coexist, provided their dictators agree with each other. Their methods are the

same. Muzzle public opinion and get the intelligentsia to invent lofty theories explaining and justifying their actions."

"The West is in hot water now," I said between mouthfuls. "How will they explain to their public the Russians are on their side? They'll have to resort to pro-Soviet propaganda. How will they explain the Siberian gulags? The Russians, too, will have to pipe down with their anticapitalist propaganda. They'll even have to tone down their rhetoric on worldwide revolution."

"Ah, that won't last long," said Goran. "Hitler's Blitzkrieg will be much faster than Napoleon's armies were. As long as Hitler wins before the winter sets in, Stalin will lose the war."

"What nonsense," I retorted. "This isn't 1812, you know. Wars are fought differently now. The Russians have the most modern army on Earth. Hitler's not the only one with a wall of tanks."

"You're such a fantasist, Dragan! Do you think Molotov would have bothered signing a peace agreement with Ribbentrop if the Russians were that powerful? Of course not! Don't kid yourself!"

"We'll see. History will prove us right or wrong."

"I hope you are right, Dragan, but I fear we'll have to put up with the Nazis for a few more years. Until America joins the war, that is. Americans need so long to get ready for war. We know that from the Great War. In America, men are called up with jazz music. If someone doesn't want to serve their country, they don't have to. They can be conscientious objectors. America can't compete with dictatorial regimes. Hitler's machine must be supported by all. People don't need to think for themselves because Hitler is doing all the thinking for them."

"Sometimes it's no good if everyone thinks differently. In war, we must be united," I said.

"We have to unite against fascism, but we don't all have to think the same thoughts. We should look for common goals, not dwell on our differences. If we agree we all hate fascism, we can fight against it together."

"We can fight better if we have a common approach," I said.

"But we won't win the fight if we become automatons, robots obeying orders. Hitler is strong with his army of robots, but therein lies a fatal weakness, too. Robots are good at conquering unarmed people. But they don't have a freethinking brain. You must not extinguish freedom of thought. Freedom to think can win against the robots. Maybe not today or tomorrow, but in the long run . . . "

"Sshhh!" I interrupted him. "Anton is coming up behind you. We'd better talk about something else . . . "

I went back to my books that evening, but I couldn't help thinking about the front in those distant lands. Young men like me fighting for their lives. Here I was, memorizing my organic chemistry, while others died fighting. As soon as these exams were over, I would get back into action.

The war raged on. By the summer of 1941, the Germans reached Kyiv, with huge losses on both sides. At home, the noose tightened.

In reading through your manuscript, I couldn't believe that people were executed simply for expressing their political views. I searched the historical newspaper archives. The evidence was not difficult to find. In *Hrvatski Narod, Croatian People*, a pro-Ustaša newspaper, the following notice appeared:

Zagreb, July 6, 1941
Communist Agitator Put to Death
The Ministry of Home Affairs has announced the following:
On June 24, 1941, Ivan Bučica from Blato, 20 years old, shouted out,
"Long live Soviet Russia," during a live radio broadcast. He was arrested
and tried by special tribunal in Zagreb on July 5, 1941. He was found
guilty and sentenced to death. He was shot the same day at 4:30 p.m.

And there was more. On July 10, 1941, ten communists were executed for injuring an Ustaša guard. The accused ranged in age from twenty-seven to fifty. They were painters and decorators, professors and journalists. Some were Jewish; others were Serb. The perpetrators were punished using a 10:1 formula for reprisals. The Ustaša regime was virulently anticommunist and determined to crush all dissent by scaring the population into submission.

As in Nazi Germany, all power lay with a single self-proclaimed leader, Ante Pavelić, on the Führer principle. Pavelić appointed all ministers, judges, and members of the academy. Always dour in photographs of the period, he was intent on "cleansing" the country of undesirables. He cultivated the cult of revenge, blaming the Serbs for all of Croatia's historical ills. Serbs, Jews, and Roma lost their citizens' rights. Property and land were confiscated, and their owners deported. Mass shootings occurred from the beginning of the regime. And yet the "Independent" State of Croatia was anything but. Decrees had to be agreed by Nazi Germany. Diplomatic relations with countries other than the Axis signatories failed. In the eyes of the West, Pavelić was shunned for coordinating the assassination of the Yugoslav King Alexander in Marseilles in the 1930s.[2]

In September 1941, Pavelić dispatched a delegation to Germany to learn about the Nazi network of concentration camps. On their return, the new camp at Jasenovac was built, modeled on the well-established Sachsenhausen camp in Oranienburg near Berlin. Both Sachsenhausen and Jasenovac started off as labor camps but evolved into death camps as the war progressed.

Fall 1941
We enrolled in our second year of medicine. Our assignments got harder. I worked part-time as a chemistry demonstrator to supplement my bursary. Yet we always found time for our Youth League work, too.

Enraged by news of Soviet casualties, our cell of three—Igor, Biserka, and I—stepped up our action. We retrieved our red star stickers from the previous year's campaign and stuck them on doors around the academy. We watched from a distance as angry Ustaša students tried to tear them off. Spending more on quality glue had paid off. The stars held onto the doors for a long time afterward. It took a stiff brush, soap, and lots of elbow grease to remove them entirely. But it wasn't enough. We wanted to do more.

Without prompting from the leadership, we planned our next move. The army cavalry stored animal feed in an open-sided shed near the main barracks west of the city center. The shed was packed with bales of hay harvested over the long summer. The plan was to set the straw on fire. But the barracks were heavily guarded. We made a sketch of the streets and worked out where the sentry points were.

There was another problem. A chicken-wire fence surrounded the shed. We couldn't get close enough to simply flick a lit match or cigarette at the hay. We needed some form of incendiary device we could sling over the fence. We searched our chemistry textbook for examples of exothermic reactions. We filled a cylindrical metal biscuit box about halfway with calcium chlorate crystals and a test tube with sulfuric acid, sealed at the top with a condom. The reagents were safe as long as they were kept apart. At the appropriate moment, we would turn the test tube upside down, bury it in the crystals, and close the metal lid. After less than a minute, the acid would dissolve the rubber and flood the crystals, generating enough heat to start a fire. With a bit of luck, the reaction might even produce a bang.

Biserka and I visited our target to work out how often the guards patrolled the premises. We stopped to kiss every few minutes, watching the men in uniform from the corner of the eye. The guards leered and moved us on, their orders accompanied by smutty remarks.

We took action the following day at dusk, shortly before the night watch closed the streets surrounding the barracks. Igor and Biserka approached from the north, while I closed in from the west. We synchronized our watches and agreed to throw our lab-made bombs at exactly 6:30 p.m. The bales of hay basked in a warm orange glow as the autumnal sun sank toward the horizon.

I held onto my box of calcium chlorate in one pocket and the test tube with acid in the other, hoping to look like a casual stroller. I walked slowly down the street toward the shed, swaying slightly, pretending to be tipsy. A guard was marching in the opposite direction. He looked at me with a bored expression as we passed each other. There was another minute to go. I counted backward, 60, 59, 58, 57 . . . the guard's boots carried on thumping rhythmically against the pavement. Would he turn around to take another look at me? I crept up to the fence.

48, 47, 46, 45 . . . Was he looking? Maybe I shouldn't have imitated a drunkard. Perhaps I've attracted too much attention.

32, 31, 30, 29 . . . I pretended I needed to take a leak.

16, 15, 14, 13 . . . I took the test tube out of my right pocket and held it ready against my side. With my other hand, I reached deeper into my left pocket to remove the box.

10, 9, 8, 7 . . . The box snagged against the pocket lining. I couldn't get it out. Blood rushed to my head. I pulled again more vigorously, but it wouldn't move. Stay calm, stay calm.

3, 2, 1 . . . I gave it another tug. I was late. If the fire has already started at the north end, I'd make a perfect target for the guard.

"Oy, you! Drunken bastard! Get lost! Find yourself another pissoir!" the guard yelled.

With my back partly turned toward the guard, I jerked the box out of my pocket, ripping the seams in the process. I quickly tipped the test tube into the box and slung it over the fence. It landed on top of a pile of loose hay, rolled down the side and stopped at the foot of a full-sized bale. Perfect place to start a fire.

My plan was to stick with the drunkard role and stumble for a few paces to the nearest street corner. Once out of sight of the guard, I would walk briskly up the narrow street to the first vestibule and courtyard, then jump over the low fence at the back into the next street, which led to the western train station. There I would board a train, due at 6:40 p.m., and travel to the main station.

But the guard was too quick. He rang the alarm bell in the sentry box with one hand and pulled the rifle off his shoulder with the other. There was no time for role play. I turned on my heels and ran.

"Get the drunk! He's started a fire!"

Boots pounded the pavement behind me. More guards appeared out of nowhere.

"Shoot the bastard," someone yelled.

"No, get the water buckets first!"

"Motherfucking commies!"

A gunshot cracked behind me. A bullet ricocheted off the pavement to my left. I ran faster.

A fire engine siren wailed in the distance.

Rat-a-tat-tat . . . Sounds of gunfire from the north end of the barracks. I hoped Biserka and Igor were alright.

With my heart in my throat, I flew around the corner and up the alleyway as planned. I crashed into the first vestibule and dove for the courtyard. I stopped for a second to rest my burning lungs and look back at the street. Passersby were ducking into doorways, too. More boots pounding. The smell of cordite filled the air. I looked up. Red tongues of fire flickered beneath thick plumes of smoke rising above the rooftops. Yes! We'd done it!

But wait! This courtyard didn't look right. Instead of a fence at the back, there was a workshop with a brick wall and sloping slate roof. I'd taken the wrong turn. I was trapped!

Footsteps outside. People running, more sirens blaring. This time they sounded like the police. I had to get out.

There was a fruit tree next to the workshop. Dense, brittle branches not made for climbing. I pulled myself up through the crown, boughs snapping beneath me. I grabbed onto the gutter and heaved myself up onto the roof. The tiles were slippery. I kept going on all fours. My hands and nails finally clamped onto the apex. Over to the other side, I let myself slide, then jumped down as I reached the edge. As I picked myself up to run toward the gate, I stopped in my tracks. A little girl with pigtails, eyes wide open, stood next to me, staring. She was as stunned as I was. Neither of us screamed.

"Ssshhh," I whispered, my forefinger raised to my mouth. "Don't be afraid, little girl!"

Before she had a chance to call for help, I leaped through the gate onto the street.

I hurried through unfamiliar streets toward the railway station, hoping I hadn't lost my sense of direction. I rubbed my hands together to remove some of the soot and blood. Dusk had turned into night, and lights were coming on inside houses. I was getting my breath back, but my heart thumped so hard I worried passersby might hear it. My left pocket hung out of my trousers in shreds. There were blood stains on my shirt. I couldn't travel by train in a state like this. I would attract too much attention. I carried on walking.

We were due to reconvene at 7 o'clock, but I couldn't turn up the way I looked. Home was too far away. I went to Fran's house instead.

"What's the matter with you?" he said with a look of horror on his face. "You're as pale as a ghost. And what's happened to your hands?"

"Don't ask. I jumped from a tram and slipped. I'm due to meet Biserka and don't have time to go home to change. Please can I exchange this coat for yours? I'll return yours tomorrow in class."

"And can I wash my hands? Have you got any iodine? No, I don't need any bandages. These are abrasions."

I got to the meeting on time. Igor and Biserka were already there. We couldn't talk in public, so we went back to Igor's digs. Igor and Biserka had managed to drop their bombs as planned. They didn't have to run. They walked away from the scene.

The next day, everyone talked about the fire at the barracks. Three months' supply of animal feed had burned down, but the firemen stopped the blaze before it spread to the main buildings. We were elated. We won! It was our most daring act ever.

* * *

Ours wasn't the only diversion that fall. There was an explosion at the post office, then a fire at the sports stadium organized by Youth League members from the technical high school in Zagreb. Rumor had it Biserka's younger brother was involved. When I asked her about it, she claimed not to know anything. Didn't she trust me?

When two Nazi officers were found dead in one of the parks in broad daylight, the Ustaša panicked. They didn't go anywhere unarmed. Some took their guns with them to bed, too. They were afraid of young saboteurs. The curfew was extended.

Emboldened by our success, we wanted to do more, make bigger missiles, cause more mayhem. But bigger bombs required more sulfuric acid. As a lab demonstrator, I could smuggle out small amounts without anyone noticing. For larger quantities, we needed an insider, perhaps a permanent member of staff.

Biserka suggested Luka, the lab technician in the Physiology Department. We didn't think much of Luka. Some dismissed him as a dull-witted peasant. But Biserka assured us he seemed genuinely interested in the cause. He offered to help and donated twenty kuna to the Red Cross, a euphemism for the collection we organized for our partisans. We all knew this was against the rules. Student organizations were not supposed to recruit academic or technical staff. The faculty had its own groups. They knew each other well and were better placed to decide who was trustworthy. A good-looking student whispering with a technician would have attracted unwanted attention in and of itself. But Luka kept paying up, twenty or thirty kuna every week.

Biserka argued Luka could have reported her as soon as they started discussing politics. His word would have been enough to put her in prison for being "objectionable and dangerous." But he didn't report her. So perhaps he was genuine, after all.

Next time Luka offered help, Biserka asked him for concentrated sulfuric acid. She stopped short of inviting him to a cell meeting. Luka was disappointed he would not be able to meet his fellow conspirators but agreed to procure the acid. Biserka assured him the cell did trust him but explained this was the safest way of operating under the circumstances. Luka agreed to fill two beer bottles with acid that evening and leave them in the lab for Biserka to collect.

After our chemistry practical on the following day, I saw Biserka leaving the university buildings carrying a canvas shopping bag.

I never laid eyes on her again.

Chapter 7

I, Slave

Biserka disappeared from your life as abruptly as your writing stopped. There was no follow-up on her story. What happened to her? Was she arrested?

Perhaps the twelve pages contained a clue. Many months had passed since I read about the roll call, yet I could not put it out of my head. What was it like to fear for your life when your comrades were being shot at point-blank range? I couldn't imagine, but I could sense your heart hammering and your ears ringing during countdown.

The time for skirting around the subject was over. In my quest to know you, to understand you, I had to dive into the twelve pages.

Spring 1942

I sat on a rock in front of the leather workshop, sunbathing my swollen ankles. The day was unseasonably warm. Tiny jets of murky groundwater bubbled through the mud beneath my feet. River Sava threatened to breach the flood barriers.

I looked down at the hands in front of me. Long fingers extended ghoulishly from the rake-thin forearms. They reminded me of the skeleton in the anatomy lab at the medical school in Zagreb. It seemed like such a long time ago. Anatomy came easily to me. All I had to do was memorize the Latin names of bones and muscles. I earned top grades in my first-year exams. These arms would have made good lecture exhibits—the radius and the ulna were clearly outlined under my skin.

It didn't take long to get to this decrepit state. At the time of my arrest, I was nineteen and strong. A few weeks in this wretched place and I've been reduced to a skeleton wrapped loosely in a leathery sack of sallow skin. A mere simulacrum of a man. Other prisoners commented on my thinness. The closely cropped stubble of indeterminate color on top of my head was all that remained of my black, glossy hair. But my eyes shone like torches out of the pits of my sockets, or so I was told by my comrades.

"Keep those eyes glowing!" they said.

The hands lifted occasionally to rub the wrinkled forehead.

"You're sunbathing like a lizard," someone shouted.

Lizards were clever. They harnessed energy from the sun. They had to be careful not to be disturbed while sunbathing. I was the same. I wallowed in the spring sunshine, keeping a watchful eye out for guards and their spies. As an old prisoner, I could feel the guards approaching even before I could see them. I'd been in the camp two months, but this made me an old prisoner. In that short period, you either learned quickly, or you died. Little tricks of the survival trade made all the difference between life and death. I learned when to respond to a guard's question with a broad smile and when it was smarter to be serious. I knew how to lie when questioned about where I was heading. I had a long list of lies and excuses. I learned when to move as little as possible to conserve energy and when to work with all my might in front of the guards. Any sign of laziness could mean death.

The learning started as soon as we arrived in the camp. February 18, 1942. A date I will never forget. There were twelve of us students, five medics and seven engineers. We were dragged out of our cells at the police station in Zagreb before dawn, shackled together in chains, and herded into cattle wagons. We sat on the filthy floor and huddled together for warmth. The winter was bitterly cold. As day broke, we took it in turns to stand on our toes and peek out through the only air vent in the freight carriage. The train trundled slowly through the snow-covered landscape, stopping and starting. Clickety-clack, clickety-clack.

It was late afternoon when the train stopped for the last time. The sliding metal doors shrieked open. Better used to the gloom of prison, we were dazzled by the blazing snowscape ahead of us. All I could make out in the distance was a gray chimney stack rising out of the mist.

We were met by shouts of abuse. Gray figures, guns at the ready, ordered us out.

"Out! Motherfucking traitors!"

We stumbled out of the train and onto the frozen platform, then marched briskly through the main street of the deserted village. Where was everybody? Didn't anyone live here? There was no time to look. It took all our energies to walk in step lest the chains tripped us up.

Out of the village and down a muddy track, the chimney was getting closer. Eventually, we reached an arched gate with a sign above it: Labor Camp III. We staggered through the entrance and into a courtyard flanked by uniformly gray buildings. The gates crashed shut behind us. Only then were the chains removed from our ankles. We were ordered to line up and wait.

We waited, feet tapping, arms waving gingerly. Mustn't provoke the guards. Around us, rolls of barbed wire stretched to the horizon, punctuated by wooden watchtowers. The guards could see far into the marshlands from these towers. To one side, parts of the wire fence had been replaced by a brick wall so high that it looked unscalable. The rumors about Jasenovac were correct. Escape did not seem possible.

We waited. And waited.

With the last glimmers of the day fading, the guards marshaled us into a cavernous reception room. It was bare, apart from a desk at one end. A gaunt man of indeterminate age sat hunched at the table, his pale, bony fingers scratching

notes on a piece of paper in front of him. The rags covering his torso resembled
a jacket. A couple of men in black flanked the desk, guns trained on us.

Ljubo Miloš stood in front of the desk, his mouth twisted into a smirk as he
watched us file in. He needed no introduction. The cutthroat of Jasenovac. The
look he gave us behind his thick-framed black spectacles did not bode well. A
beret, worn at an angle, contained his unruly mop of dark curls. A revolver and
truncheon were slung prominently on each hip. He stood with his feet apart, his
left arm behind his back, his right arm wrapped around the leash restraining his
wolfhound. The beast lunged forward, its white canines flashed in our direction.
The commandant tugged sharply on the leash. The hound sat down. I reminded
myself: Never look a wolf in the eye.

We stood rigidly in rows of five, facing the desk.

The buttons on Miloš's uniform flickered in the last of the evening light as he
moved toward us. The hound stayed sitting behind him.

I was first in line. He stopped in front of me.

"Name and occupation!" he barked. "Why are you here?"

"Dragan Roller, medical student, for donating ten kuna to the Red cause," I
spat the words out.

In a flash, he swung his arm back and slapped me across the face. My knees
buckled. I crashed backward a couple of paces but managed to stop myself
from falling.

"How dare you speak to me with your hat on! Take it off this instant!"

I whipped my hat off and pulled myself upright quickly, staring into the
middle distance. Never look a wolf in the eye. My left cheek stung like the lash
of a whip.

He moved onto the next student, Vlado, who promptly removed his hat.

"Are you a communist? Medicine is full of communists!" Miloš bellowed.

Vlado looked at the floor and said nothing. The scribe at the table shuffled
his papers. The guards stepped back a little, like onlookers clearing a space for
a shootout in a Wild West movie. This would be a shootout, too. Miloš was the
gun-slinging stranger, but what about Vlado? He was unarmed.

Miloš leaned into Vlado's face.

"I'm asking you: are you a communist?" he roared.

I could hear my blood throbbing against my temples.

Vlado raised his head and looked Miloš straight in the eye.

"I was," he squeaked.

I stared at the icicles hanging down, swordlike, from the only window in the
room, waiting for the blow. Someone in the lineup fidgeted with the contents of
his pockets.

Miloš's lips twitched as he glared at Vlado.

He spun on his heels to face our group head-on.

"This guy's better off! He admits his guilt," he hollered.

He stepped back toward his dog. The scribe dropped his shoulders and
sighed. The guards cackled obsequiously. Miloš picked up his walking stick from

the table and stretched it out in front of his hound. The animal stood up and jumped over the stick to the other side.

"Good boy," Miloš praised him. He waved us on without so much as a glance in our direction.

The guards pointed us to the opposite side of the room. There was a blanket laid on the floor with a pile of belongings on it.

"Empty your pockets," they screamed. "Everything! Money, watches, pens, cigarettes, medicines, food! If you keep any of it, you'll be shot!"

We watched as the heap grew in front of us: rucksacks, satchels, wallets, thermos bottles. Everything our families had managed to bring to us while we were in prison. Vlado was allowed to keep a small piece of cheese as a reward for his confession, but the rest of his food was confiscated.

And then they frisked us, reaching into our pockets and sliding their hands all over our bodies, kicking and punching at every opportunity.

We were allowed to keep the clothes we arrived in. We'd heard rumors that prisoners died of frostbite in Jasenovac, so we all dressed in several layers of trousers, socks, and jumpers as soon as we suspected our fate. I wore my paja- mas underneath my street clothes. I was pleased with myself for being so clever. Later, I realized we needn't have bothered. There were plenty of clothes in the camp. The guards were thrifty. No clothes or boots of any quality went to waste. Dead prisoners were buried or thrown in the river naked.

There was a commotion. One of the guards was spitting at Milan. Milan Špalj. Civil-engineering student and party activist. Brave. Fearless. I admired him from my first day at the university. We were brought to trial together in Zagreb. When the judge asked him if he was a member of the Communist Party, Milan took off his shoes and showed him his blackened toenails.

"Sir, if you had hot needles inserted under your nails, you, too, would admit to being a communist."

The guard had found a dinar coin from the previous regime in Milan's pocket. Milan kept the coin as a souvenir of his first date with his girlfriend on 10 April 1941, the day the Nazis marched into Zagreb. Coins from the old Kingdom of Yugoslavia were no longer legal tender, but keeping them in the camp was a heinous crime, reported instantly to the commander. On hearing this, Miloš charged over to our group and crashed the butt of his revolver across Milan's face.

Blood gushed out of his nose to the floor.

"It was a souvenir! Souvenir!" Milan wailed.

I stood by, rooted to the spot, staring at his writhing figure.

"Do something! You're a medic!" a voice screamed inside my head. But I couldn't move. I stood there and watched in silence.

Next to me, Radovan hiccupped wildly. Did Radovan betray us? Someone did. Or was it Biserka? Sweet Biserka. Someone must have told the interrogators about our cell. Who was the traitor? But the police had ways of extracting any confession they wanted. It could have been any one of us. Radovan's incessant hiccups were annoying and dangerous. They could provoke the guards. He could get us all into trouble. He had to stop. Stop!

Relieved of all our possessions, we were marched to the shack serving as the camp kitchen. Groups of prisoners surrounded the building, eating in silence and tapping their feet on the frozen ground. Still smarting from the slaps and blows received at reception, we ate our dinner, three boiled potatoes each, stone cold. As newcomers, we stood huddled together, slightly apart from the other prisoners. We slid the skins off our potatoes with our hands. No cutlery apart from spoons was allowed in the camp. An older inmate approached us, picked up the peelings off the frozen snow at our feet, and stuffed them greedily into his mouth.

"Comrade, if you want to eat the skins, we'll hand them to you. You don't need to pick them off the ground," I said.

Two days later, I had to apologize to the same prisoner for not giving him the skins at all. I ate them myself.

Our reception in the camp on that winter's day was just the beginning. We arrived in Jasenovac with lofty ideals about civilization and social justice. The historic town had a strategic location around the confluence of the River Una into Sava and was once a tripoint of the Austrian, Ottoman, and French Empires.

When the rooster sings in Jasenovac, you can hear it in three empires, the locals used to say.

This tripoint was now witness to events we never read about in our books.

That night in the barracks, we learned we were the first group of communists admitted to the camp without losing at least one comrade to the execution squad. We got away with it and stayed alive. Some even called us heroes. Quite undeservedly, I thought to myself a few weeks later, while basking in the spring sunshine.

All my suspicions about your camp experience were confirmed. The cold and the hunger, the loss of freedom and dignity, the thefts and the beatings—they were all bad enough. But most of all, the thought of my proud, tall dad being humiliated by a nasty man in uniform made my head steam. How dare he? I was outraged.

In your writing, you were fearful of Miloš's hound. Or had you transferred your fear of Miloš to the four-legged monster at your feet? Whatever the answer, I knew you as an animal lover. Dogs, in particular, were creatures in need of our protection, as you'd often told me. Do you remember Laika, our bouncy Gordon setter puppy we took on in Baghdad, when I was about five? We were so enthralled by rockets and stars, we named her after the dog the Russians sent into space in the Sputnik program. When Laika got a bit too boisterous for her own good, you'd cradle her in your arms and gently coo in her ear while stroking her long, silky ears. She trained her soft round eyes on you and cooed back, like a little dove. You were not a man who was afraid of dogs.

For several years after we left Iraq, I had a recurring nightmare in which you and I were in a snake pit desperately trying to save our Gordon setter puppies from being devoured. We were barefoot; the ground was slippery. We stumbled and slid as we clutched the soft, warm puppies, one under each armpit. They were mute with terror while the serpents hissed, writhed, and lunged at us. Forked tongues fanned the air. The torment ended only when I woke up. My puppy nightmare was the product of a child's imagination. Your nightmare in Jasenovac was real.

My mother gave me a new pair of boots when she visited me in prison in Zagreb. She had to sell the oak sideboard in the dining room to buy them. The camp guards didn't notice them at first, but when they did, I was promptly relieved of such unnecessary luxury. I walked around barefoot for a couple of days until I found an old pair of shoes in the garbage. The soles were riddled with holes, but they were better than nothing. I kept them in place with pieces of string scavenged from the leather workshop. The guards laughed at my newly found shoes.

"These must be the latest fashion trend from Soviet paradise," they sniggered.

"Do they wear better shoes in the Soviet Union?" they wanted to know.

The first time I was taunted in this way, I ignored their remarks and walked away. I was rewarded for my insolence with a blow to my back. They made me walk barefoot again with the shoes slung around my neck. After a while, they got bored and found someone else to pick on. I was grateful to be allowed to put my shoes back on, holes and all. Next time I was goaded about my footwear, I nodded politely.

"Shoes worn in Soviet paradise are much worse than these," I said. "These are made of good-quality leather."

Lesson learned: never ignore or contradict the guards.

Other clothing mattered, too. Mother had knitted a white woolly hat for me. On my first day in Jasenovac, I donned the hat and was thankful to my wise old mother for the warmth it provided. But when selecting prisoners for the hardest jobs that morning, the guards picked me first.

"Guy with the white hat! Over here!" they screamed.

We were ordered to push a heavy wagon, but despite the efforts of ten men, it wouldn't move.

"Hit the guy with the white hat!" the guards yelled.

That day, I got more than my fair share of beatings. Nothing else in the camp was white, not even the snow. I tore the hat off and never wore it again. Instead, I made a head cover out of an old rag I found on the dump. I learned to blend in with the gray mass of prisoners. It was safer that way. Attract as little attention as possible.

I learned some new work habits, too. A bookworm and mama's boy, I wasn't used to physical work of any kind. I knew nothing about carrying heavy loads. This did not escape the notice of my fellow prisoners. They got me to carry a railway sleeper in the middle with shorter men supporting the front and back.

As a tall man, I bore the brunt of the weight. I groaned and bent under the strain like a willow tree, straightening up only when prodded by a guard's rifle butt. The prisoners had no time for sentimentality. Another lesson quickly learned.

There was a time when I believed I was a revolutionary. But here in the camp, I had to greet the lowliest of foot soldiers with deference. I learned to read the insignia on their uniforms. If the guard was a private or a lance corporal, I addressed him as corporal. If he was a lance sergeant, I addressed him as sergeant.

At first, I ignored the twelve-year-old woodworking apprentice who sometimes strutted around the camp in full black uniform. But the older prisoners warned me to be careful. Rumor had it the boy had personally killed several people. So when the youngster stopped me to ask where I was from and why I was here, I stood to attention and responded to his questions politely and respectfully, like I used to address the faculty dean when I needed a discount voucher for the student canteen. Did this subservience make me less of a revolutionary?

I was learning to be a slave.

No, I was less than a slave.

I was a number, worth less than a head of cattle.

A zero.

I, slave.

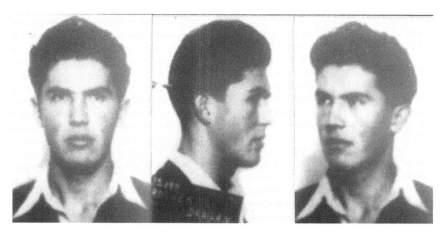

Figure 7.1. Arrest photos of Dragan Roller taken by Ustaša police in Zagreb, Independent State of Croatia. November 1941.

Chapter 8

Delirium

Twelve pages. You'd condensed the monstrosity of Jasenovac into a dozen densely typed sheets of paper. Your prose reflected on the terror, hunger, and disease in the camp. There was more.

I watched Uncle Marko scavenging through the pile of garbage behind the kitchen, poking here and there with a long stick. We called him Uncle because of his gray hair and slight limp, but he was probably not much older than forty. He collected all kinds of things: gristle, vegetable peelings, bones.

"A good base for a healthy soup," said Uncle Marko. We admired him. He had guts of steel.

What was the difference between Uncle Marko and the rest of us? We ate the skins on our ration of potatoes, but he ate them off the dump. Potato peelings were potato peelings. Marko was a tramp or perhaps a gypsy, as some people said, and we were so-called intellectuals. So what? Was there truly any difference?

Gravedigger Mordo once chewed away strips of fat from pig entrails discarded by the cook onto the dump. Mordo had two doctorates, one in pharmacy and another in philosophy, but he still ate the fat. He'd studied in Paris, but all the same, he ate the fat raw, straight off the garbage pile. Do workers, peasants, and intellectuals feel hunger differently? Some put up with it more easily than others. The less hungry were lucky. I was no better than any of the others. In the previous week, I'd gulped down the raw legs of a poor little frog, but I removed the skin first. I didn't eat all of it, just the legs. I threw away the rest.

I didn't think much about death and dying, especially not my own death. It was no use thinking too hard about other people's deaths either. We kept track of numbers. Gravedigger Mordo and ragman Iggy supplied them every day. The dead were stripped before burial, and their clothing was recycled in the workshops. We compared the numbers today with yesterday's numbers. Were they going up or down? Was the situation getting better or worse? We drew conclusions from the numbers. They were important for that reason only.

Death was a release from everyday misery, but it also closed the door on real life. Real life was worth surviving for. It was what we all dreamed of. Real life was a breakfast of sunny-yellow eggs and bacon, served on a tray in a clean, soft bed. Real life was a hot bath, a fragrant terry towel, and a crisply ironed snow-white shirt. Real life was a glass of freshly squeezed lemonade sweetened with honey. Or a glass of good country wine followed by some more food. Yes. Food. Lots of it.

The difficult winter months were over. Spring was on its way, but then the ice melted. The river rose. We were ordered to build up the flood barriers with soil from a nearby pit. Some of us had to dig; others pushed the wheelbarrows loaded with dirt and gravel. I winced as I heaved the full wheelbarrow up the slope of the bank and tipped it out on top. Our comrades with practical skills were lucky. Those with tailoring, woodworking, or cobbling experience were assigned to the workshops. At least they had a roof over their heads. The rest of us were relegated to hard physical labor outdoors.

We were ordered to move pine logs from the riverbanks to the workshops before the spring meltwaters washed them away. We had to wade into the icy water up to our knees. I heaved a heavy log at the front, comrade Milan at the back. We shuffled past the garbage dump. A gray figure crouched on top of the stinking mound, picking out scraps and stuffing them hastily into his mouth. Was it Uncle Marko? We couldn't tell. His back was turned to us. He didn't see the dark shadow approaching. It was Miloš.

"Lezi! Lie down!" he screamed.

The prisoner obeyed instantly, hitting the ground face down. Miloš pulled out his knife, lifted the man's forehead and slit his throat with one sweep of the arm. He wiped the blade on the prisoner's clothes, then straightened himself up.

I stopped in my tracks and stared open-mouthed.

Milan shoved me in the back with the log.

"Idiot!" he hissed. "Keep moving! He'll kill you, too, if he sees you staring!"

I stumbled on, my heart in my throat. It can't have been Uncle Marko. He would have been more careful. Must remain calm.

* * *

River Sava surged. The floodwaters brought us lice, millions of them. The guards ordered a disinfection day. I undressed for the dip bath, its acrid smell irritating my nostrils, and looked down at my protruding knee joints. My legs were like those of the bony figures in a Goya etching I remembered from our history schoolbook. Beneath my knees, my feet had turned into melon-like swellings.

Your reference to a Goya etching set me on a mission to identify exactly which image might have been reproduced in a history schoolbook. Profoundly affected by the wars between Napoleon's French Empire and Spain in the early 1800s, Francisco Goya produced a series of shadowy prints depicting scenes of violence against soldiers and civilians. The prints were later called by art historians *The Disasters of War*. Goya kept them private during his lifetime, but all eighty-two plates are now available to view on the Prado Museum website. Perhaps, like you with your writing, he preferred to keep some of his works out of sight. Plates 48 to 64 focus on scenes of wartime famine in Madrid, but I could not determine exactly which one might have been reproduced in a schoolbook.

"You have Myodegeneratio cordis, comrade," said Joshua, the camp doctor. "Wasting of the heart muscle. Have you covered it in med school yet?" We had but only superficially. Cardiology specialization was scheduled for the third year. Would I ever reach the third year?

Joshua sent me to the hospital wing, a barracks no different from the others except for the presence of doctors. They were prisoners, too. They tried to help, but they had no medicines other than a few bottles of aspirin. There was no operating equipment to speak of. We were allowed to make linden tea on a tiny wood-burning stove. It was a little warmer than in the other barracks.

The lower bunkbeds in the hospital were all occupied. I struggled to climb into the upper bunk allocated to me. Every day, a new semiconscious inmate staggered into the bed below mine, only for him to die in the night and be replaced by yet another patient. After a week, I had several blankets from those who had died. The dead didn't need blankets, and the gravediggers would have taken them for themselves anyway. My bed became softer and more comfortable the longer I stayed in hospital. Sometimes the comrade in the bunk below died in the evening but no one came to collect the body until the following morning.

The food in the hospital was the same as elsewhere in the camp, but the portions were smaller.

"Prisoners who don't work don't deserve a lot of food," the guards said. A ladle of sickly sour turnip soup for lunch, two potatoes for dinner. A piece of brown bread was a rare treat.

After a few days, I felt better. My feet regained their former shape. The river continued its ascent.

One day, the guards ordered the transfer of all seriously ill patients to the new hospital wing on higher ground.

"Everyone up! Stand next to your beds," they shouted.

We were inspected one by one. The guards demanded to know the nature of our illness and asked Joshua to confirm our answers. Joshua suspected the real fate of selected patients and downplayed our conditions as much as possible. He chose his words carefully. If a prisoner was not deemed seriously ill, the doctors were beaten for sabotaging the camp's productivity by keeping healthy men in the hospital.

It was my turn. It took all my energy to stand up straight.

"What's the matter with you?" said the guard, his voice muffled by the handkerchief he held over his nose and mouth. His eyes were full of loathing and contempt.

"I've made a full recovery," I explained through gritted teeth. "I'm returning to work tomorrow morning." Joshua nodded. The guard moved on.

Some patients were too weak to stand.

Those of us on our feet were ordered to bundle the bedridden patients in their blankets and carry them to the new wing. This turned out to be an empty room next to the brickmaking kilns. There were no beds in this room. We laid the patients down in a row on the floor.

Vlado and I carried a dying man to the new wing. His fingers were like the claws of a bird, blue flesh falling off the bone.

"Frostbite," Vlado said the day before when he'd asked me to help him bandage the man's hands. We'd run out of clean bandages and had to use strips torn from old blankets to stem the blood flow. By morning, the rags on his hands were dripping crimson. He'd lost so much blood overnight he could not stand up next to his bed.

When all the selected men had been moved to the new wing, we ran back to our barracks as fast as we could. The guards locked us in. We sat silently and listened out for gunshots. There was one. Had the frostbitten man tried to run?

Sometime later, figures in black marched past the barracks windows, bayonets fastened to their rifles. One of the guards waved a sledgehammer in wide arcs above his head. Clumps of hair were still attached to it.

On the following day, a gray drizzle forced the smoke from the kilns downward from the chimneys to the ground. The whole camp stank—a nauseating, pungent stench of burning fat.

"Picilli's ovens," someone whispered. Engineer Picilli had kept his promise. He'd converted the brick kilns into crematoria.

I was ashamed. Ashamed for carrying my comrades to their fate in the kiln.

The smell from the makeshift crematoria—didn't anyone in the surrounding villages notice? Didn't anyone question it? What did people know about the killings in the camp? Were they complicit? Later, I read that the entire prewar population of Serbs in the village of Jasenovac had been deported at the beginning of the war and replaced with Ustaša forces, their families, and sympathizers. The town had become an Ustaša garrison.

The flood barriers collapsed in April. Swirling with mud, the water was waist high in places. Brown eddies lapped against the walls of the brick factory.

Work ceased, and we were evacuated to Camp V in Stara Gradiška, nearly twenty miles downriver from Jasenovac. Officers traveled by jeep. We were packed into cattle wagons and shipped to the village of Okučani. We completed the rest of the journey on foot.

The old fortress in Stara Gradiška was a border outpost built by the Habsburgs to protect themselves from the Ottoman Turks. When the Austro-Hungarian Empire collapsed, the imposing structure was made into a prison. Perched above the two wings of cells was the tower, built of walls so thick they looked medieval. The dank, cavernous rooms were linked by long, gloomy corridors with arched ceilings. At the end of each corridor was a small, barred window letting in a single shaft of light. The place stank of mildew.

We were packed into the basement of the tower, twenty or thirty of us to a room. Instead of beds, there was hay on the cold floor. The straw swarmed with ravenous lice. Our weakened bodies made easy work for them. Their guts burned with the fire of tiny rickettsia bacteria multiplying and bursting to get out. They gorged on our blood, leaving their infected feces behind on our skin. We were their giant latrines. Every bite caused maddening itching. We scratched and scratched.

Typhus spread through the prison like wildfire. It was only a matter of time before I would get it, too.

The fever was relentless. Every night I was delirious.

One night, a rabid dog came charging at me. Or was it a wolf? The animal stood on my chest, howling and snapping, its saliva dripping on my face. A gunshot popped somewhere in the distance. Maybe someone tried to shoot the dog? But still, it didn't stop. It carried on snapping.

Another night, I sat on top of the brick kiln to warm up. But then I heard the half-dead people inside screaming as they burned. A clawlike hand waved at me from the mass of bodies below. I wanted to move away, but the warmth of the kiln kept me rooted to the spot. The hand waved on, blue flesh falling off the bone.

And then, one night, I met my double. His name was Dragan. He was a medical student, too. He usually stood behind me.

"It's your fault," he said. "You had to see Biserka, didn't you? She took you home. You slept with the traitor," he carped on and on.

Sometimes, Biserka joined us, her long blond tresses cascading down her shoulders. I tried to send her away.

"Biserka, why are you here? I've never loved you. I was only ever interested in your sensuous curves. They wrapped themselves so readily around me. But now, they no longer tempt me."

"When will I see you again?" she said sweetly, tilting her head slightly to the left. "I miss you."

I didn't answer. I didn't want to return to her, ever. Biserka paid no notice. She hovered around us while Dragan and I bickered.

One night, my double brought an orange with him. This time he stood in front of me. He peeled the fruit, then sucked on the segments, forcing me to watch. The fragrant juice drooled down his chin. I reached out for the orange. He faded out. Then he was back.

"I need a pee," I said to Dragan.

"I don't," he said.

"Why is it always me who must go? Can't you go for a change?"

"I don't want to go."

"Go on, you go!"

"No, you go," echoed my double.

Eventually, my distended bladder woke me, and I realized I was alone. I heaved myself up and stumbled to the slop bucket.

The fever raged on.

There was a window at one end of the room with iron bars across it. I walked over to the opening and grabbed the rails with both hands. I leaned my forehead on the frigid metal, blood thumping in my temples. Gradually, my head cooled down. Beyond the fortress ramparts, I glimpsed a snowscape glistening in the moonshine. Dragan disappeared for a few moments. When I could no longer stand on the icy floor, I returned to my straw pit and quarrelsome twin.

Getting up in the morning and going to work was a relief. Staying in bed was not an option. Anyone who couldn't work was a useless mouth and was shot. I could not allow the guards to suspect I had typhus. They were afraid of epidemics, and sometimes they caught typhus, too. Eliminating the source of infection, the prisoners, was their preferred method of halting an epidemic. Not one we were taught in medical school.

The prisoner doctors tried to protect us. They called typhus "the flu." But the guards didn't tolerate influenza, either. Every few nights, they came for the sickest of us.

I carried on working.

The fever scrambled my brain and made movement difficult. I could feel every limb and organ inside me.

We were ordered to work in the sawmill. We formed a human chain from the wood store to the workshop and passed planks to each other. The planks were heavy, as if made of stone. The distance between my hands and those of the other prisoners lengthened. The job was taking forever. Every plank was heavier than the last. My arms were leaden. Every muscle fiber rubbed against another. Textus muscularis striatus skeletalis. Femur grated against tibia as if someone had poured fine sand into the synovial fluid.

My mouth was dry. Why was my mouth so dry? Did it have to be so dry?

I looked down at the aluminum ration bowl hanging from a string around my neck. I had to have some water. There was a well within sight of the mill. They'd removed a woman's body from it a few days earlier. She'd jumped in one night. I told myself it didn't matter. The water would have changed itself several times since then. Her body was discovered on the morning after she drowned. Not enough time for decomposition to start. The water was drinkable. What was she thinking of, jumping into the well everyone drank from? Clearly, she hadn't been thinking. I had to drink. Water . . .

I left the plank-passing row. Comrade Milan looked worried as he stepped up a place in the human chain. One of the links had gone to get a drink. The rest carried on working. I hoped the guards wouldn't notice.

The link staggered toward the well. I hoped I would find some water already in the pail. It took a lot of energy to drag a full pail of water from the depths of the well. Energy I didn't have.

The door of the nearest barracks flew open. Two men wearing white aprons emerged and approached the well. They had the ruddy and slightly doughy faces of the well-fed. Their ears were well scrubbed, and their shoes were clean. They carried a cauldron hanging from an oxlike yoke wedged between their beefy shoulders. I stopped and watched them from a distance as they effortlessly heaved the winch and filled the cauldron with water. They were prisoners like the rest of us, but they worked in the officers' mess. They didn't like dirty rations anywhere near their clean cauldron. I crept a little closer, not daring to ask them for water.

"Why are you standing there, staring at the pail as if you've never seen one before?" said one of the water bearers. I wanted to tell him I was thirsty, but my tongue wouldn't move. I stood there gawping. His mate understood and poured some water into my outstretched bowl without touching the rim.

"Don't you know you can get malaria from this water? I don't drink this water and look how healthy I am! And look at you!"

I envied the water bearer his good health. How did he manage not to drink water? Didn't he drink water with his meals?

I drained my bowl in one gulp. My gullet felt like I'd swallowed a large piece of meat. Distentio esophagi. The bowl was empty, but I was still thirsty. My mouth and throat were still dry.

"More please," I gulped down another bowl of water.

"Look at this fool. He's downed two liters of water. Don't you know about hygiene? I told you this water can give you malaria. I know this. I am from this region."

I asked for more. The water bearer stared at my emaciated face, muttered something about foolish townsfolk who insist on poisoning themselves, and refilled the bowl for the third time. Some of the water splashed over my hands. It was a shame about the spilled water. How nice it would have been to use it to wash my face. But I didn't want to waste precious water on washing.

"Thank you."

I headed back to the human chain, stumbling on the rough terrain as the water sloshed about in my stomach. I was still thirsty. Muscles burned; joints grated. I turned to the well again, but Milan grabbed me by the sleeve and pointed me to a pile of logs nearby. He motioned for me to sit down.

"Don't worry, I'll tell you if I see someone coming," said Milan.

Every time I got up to go to the well again, Milan pulled me down, some-times roughly.

Later that evening when we were lining up for our potatoes, Milan sidled up to me and slipped a small piece of cheese in my hand.

"From your comrades," he whispered.

The day was nearly over. At night we could rest. But when night came, my double and Biserka reappeared. She ran toward me with her arms stretched out, but my double stopped her. He scolded us for being so shameless.

"She sold you out to the police," he glared at me. "Shame on you! You dirty turncoat, sleeping with a traitor," the double brayed on and on. I went to the barred window to cool my temples. I placed my hands on the iron railings. The double and Biserka skulked in a dark corner, then disappeared.

I wished for daylight. The straw bedding rustled with lice like a giant anthill in a forest. The lice had typhus. They were thirsty, too. They drank our blood to quench their thirst until they burst. We slapped at them, the lice and the prisoners killing each other. They thirsted for our blood; we thirsted for water, big and unbearable thirst. Blood, water, they were all the same . . .

The Twin

I was once a fierce fighter,
They say I was a hero. Perhaps, I said.
Deep inside I'm a dreamer,
In my heart I'm never cruel.

There have always been two of us.
The Quiet One with a few close friends,
The Other One more worldly,
Leader of men.

One was hidden deep inside me,
No suit of armor, soft and tender,
Weeping often for his lost ideals,
Out of view from other people.

The Other fought with all his might,
Raised his fist against the tyrant,
Backed the cause all day and night,
Refused to kneel before the charge.

I am both of these two,
One in tears, the Other in blood.
People around me will never know
When I'm One and when the Other.

Biserka had returned but only as a specter in your nightmares. I wondered, once again, what happened to her. Did you ever try to contact her after the war?

Your poems amplified the horror of the camp. "The Twin" showed you were two people in one: one of you was soft and emotional; the other, strong and determined. Which one did I know?

The orange in your typhus delirium triggered more of my own memories. Memories of a dad unlike the coldhearted twin of your nightmares.

Autumn evening in Belgrade. I am seven years old. You come home from work. You keep your coat and shoes on.

"Shall we go get your orange?" you say.

"Yay! Let's go!"

I slide my hand into yours, warm and firm, the size of a spade. You glide effortlessly along the pavement. I skip and hop beside you, trying to keep up. We sing and hum a garbled version of *"Papaveri e Papere,"* "Poppies and Ducks," mangling the lyrics in our broken Italian. The grocery shop is at the bottom of our cobblestoned road, a few minutes' walk away.

"One orange, comrade Dragan?" says the greengrocer.

"One, please," you nod. "Thank you, comrade Rade."

Oranges are expensive. You don't buy any for you and Mama, just the one for me. You peel the fruit on the spot, golden juice squirting and dripping on the floor, zesty aroma filling the air around us.

"Full of vitamin C," you beam down at me.

"I know," I nod. I have no idea what vitamin C is, but I know it is good for me. You've said so.

I stretch my hand upward with a segment of orange, thrusting it toward your mouth, but I can't reach.

"You're too tall for me, *Tatice*," I address you by the diminutive for *Daddy*. "This one is for you."

"Ooh, thank you. But you eat the rest of it."

We munch on the segments together. Then it's just me demolishing one juicy morsel after another. When I finish, you remove your linen hankie from your pocket and wipe our hands dry. They're still sticky as we hop and skip back home.

Did my daily orange remind you about your emotional twin, the one you left behind in Jasenovac more than twenty years earlier? Or was he safely locked up in the dusty storerooms of your mind by then?

Chapter 9

Comrade Schwartz

Of all the poems you left behind in your secret folder, the one dedicated to Comrade Schwartz was the longest and most difficult to translate from Croatian to English. It came attached with a rusty paperclip to a section of prose separated from the twelve pages.

"Why are you bothering?" I could hear you say. "Poetry is impossible to translate." You told me this years ago. Subtle meanings in poetry are lost in translation. I gave it a try, anyway. I attempted to capture the spirit of your poems, even as I lost their rhythm and rhyme in Croatian.

Who was Comrade Schwartz?

It was nearly lunchtime. We milled around the kitchen, waiting for the cook to signal the food was ready. Will it be turnip soup or pura *today?*

What was this *pura* you were fed on in the camp? It was not a modern word. The shoulder-dislocating dictionary I purchased on a trip to Zagreb defined *pura* as polenta, hard cornmeal mush, or thick hominy pudding. I understood it was some kind of slop made of corn or maize. Perhaps words like *porridge* or *grits* would be suitable. Or maybe something more derogatory, like *gruel*, with all the Dickensian connotations of hunger and poverty, would be better? A *pigswill* you called it in some parts of your manuscript. Never having tasted *pura* myself, I couldn't even describe it in sensory terms. Perhaps best to leave it untranslated. I stuck with the Croatian original *pura*.

A gray silhouette shuffled toward us, his head panning left and right as if searching the ground ahead of him. It was Schwartz. He tapped his way along the walls of the barracks, his right arm slightly outstretched from his emaciated body. What drove him on? Was it the clatter of aluminum rations or the acrid stench of unclean people? But something was different this time. His face was a grim mask of coagulated blood and mud.

"What's the matter with you?" I asked him.

"Nothing. Everything is fine."

"You don't look fine!"

"It happened so fast," he blurted out. *"I was walking along when a shadow approached me. He was gray and dirty, like everyone else in this wretched place. I didn't realize he was a guard until he hit me. How could I have missed him? It happened in broad daylight. Why did I not recognize the uniform?"*

I took Schwartz by the elbow and led him to the water well. He was shaking. I poured water from the pail into his ration bowl and rinsed the blood off his cuts. Schwartz was going blind, I thought to myself. People and objects in his field of vision were amorphous blobs shifting in and out of focus.

"It feels like swimming in a murky pond with your eyes open," he'd told me. *"Storm clouds of fine silt swirling in front of your eyes."*

The dull pressure inside his head was ever present, as if his skull was being squeezed in a clamp, getting tighter and tighter. Comrade Schwartz was losing his sight. But he would not, could not admit to it. We never used the word blindness when we talked about his condition.

"He beat me because I didn't greet him," Schwartz wailed through his swollen lips. *"I didn't greet him because I didn't see him."*

The cook bellowed lunch was ready. Schwartz gave Moses his aluminum bowl. Moses brought his lunch most days. Schwartz suspected Moses ate some of his portion as he walked back from the kitchen. His lunch bowl was lighter than it used to be when he could still fetch it for himself. Moses was also in charge of bringing our monthly parcels from the post room to the barracks. The packages were always half-empty. Maybe he stole some of the contents? We couldn't be sure it wasn't the guards who did the pilfering. Schwartz didn't complain. Moses was a good man. He didn't tell anyone Schwartz was going blind. He could be trusted to keep a secret.

Moses returned with the food. Schwartz waved the bowl up and down in his hand.

"We've got a bigger portion of pura today."

"The cook Joseph gave me some extra for you," said Moses quickly, a slight shadow passing over his eyes.

"How nice of Joseph to remember me. He's a good guy," said Schwartz.

Joseph wasn't a good guy. He used his massive soup ladle to whack people on the head if they pushed too hard to get to the cauldron. He gave extra food only to those who supplied him with cigarettes. Schwartz had no cigarettes to give him.

After lunch we sat in our barracks for a few minutes before the siren called us to our afternoon shift. Schwartz dangled his feet from his bunk bed.

"How nice it is to have legs!" He often said this, as if to remind himself life could be worse. His sister had her legs blown off in a bomb explosion in the English reading room in Zagreb. People reading English newspapers were not tolerated by the Ustaša. They'd taken her legs to make their point. Schwartz had taught his sister how to walk again. When she'd received her prosthetic legs, she was thrilled. Every step was a joy, in spite of the pain.

"She had such a zest for life," he said. He had comforted her, but I suspect she'd been of most comfort to him. She was the stronger of the two.

"How do people find new energy for life when they need it most?" mused Schwartz. "She learned to live without legs. Maybe I can learn to live without my sight?"

She'd woken up on the operating table with her amputated feet in the bucket beside her. He didn't wake up in a hospital bed blind. He was losing his sight gradually. The police had beaten him because they wanted to know everything. As a communist and a Jew, he was in double trouble. Double offenders were punched twice as hard.

They thumped him until he lost consciousness. When he came to, his head hurt but nothing was broken. He ignored the sensation of pressure in his temples. He had more important things to worry about. He didn't know if he would be sentenced to death by firing squad or sent to a concentration camp. On arrival in Jasenovac, he noticed he had blurred vision. He hoped he might be given some spectacles. How naïve he was! Prisoners with glasses soon learned to take them off so as not to provoke the guards. Spectacle wearers were seen as troublemakers and were beaten more often.

"Can anemia cause blindness?" Schwartz asked me.

"Yes," I said without hesitation, although I couldn't remember reading anything about this in my medical textbooks. We were all anemic after subsisting on pura *and potatoes. We weren't all going blind. But I wasn't going to tell him that.*

"Maybe the beating didn't cause my blindness?" said Schwartz. "Maybe all I need is a few vitamins to make things better? If only I could get a juicy, yellow lemon. I could squeeze it on a sugar cube and suck the lemony sweetness into my mouth. If only . . . ! I'll go to Dr. Joshua and speak with him privately, tell him what's happening. Maybe he can help."

Like Biserka's story, your account of Comrade Schwartz ended abruptly, but the poem you wrote about him revealed more emotion than prose ever could. Despite his failing eyesight, he survived in Jasenovac until 1944. When he was finally selected for liquidation, his end stayed with you forever.

Stolen Death

Dedicated to the shadow of Comrade Schwartz, blinded by the police in Zagreb in 1942 and murdered in Jasenovac in 1944

When the wings of history brush past me
And remind me of our days of misery and woe
I ask myself: What happened to us?
Why does the pain refuse to go?

You came to us blind.
The fascists stole your sight

But you still longed for freedom
And dreamed of a good life.

Our nights were hard,
Hundreds of comrades left.
Their deaths were not heroic
But final gasps of slaves in chains.

You called me often from your corner,
Asked me softly:
Where are our boys?
When will they get here?

Across the river, I said . . .
You must wait.
They'll be here any day now.
We will get our freedom back.

Don't waste your words, comrade,
Winter and darkness surround us.
I will never see a rose garden,
Death is my only salvation.

You feared the knife,
You didn't want your throat slit.
In your pocket a vial of poison,
You didn't take it, not yet.

That night . . . Thunder of boots
Outside the barracks.
Someone enters with a list in hand.
We sit and wait in eerie silence.

They call out your name.
You grope for the poison,
Deep in your pocket.
The guard is brutal, he's in a hurry.

Then I saw something I will never forget.
Your hand shakes, you drop the poison,
The boot hits the vial,
Fear pierces your blind man's eye.

In my thoughts, I try to escape,
They tie your pale hands with wire.
I cover my ears,

The chains of the departed jangle.

Why didn't I give you the poison myself?
I am still alive.
What kind of a death did you have?
Whatever kind, I am guilty, too.

The years go by and bring
The fruits of freedom every day.
I still see your bare feet today
Your will to live still haunts me.

You wanted to die your own way.
Instead, I gave you hope.
If by chance I hadn't,
I'd be a happier man today.

Survivor guilt. There it was in plain black and white. Were your poems a form of catharsis for you? A way of consigning painful memories to the past? Your prewar poetry had perished by your own hand in your mother's kitchen stove in 1941. You couldn't risk getting caught with subversive literature at home. You were but a teenager then. By 1952, the only date reference I could find in your secret folder, you were a man of thirty. Your wartime resistance to fascism had paid off. Your side had won the war. There would have been much to celebrate. But your feelings of guilt and shame persisted.

Primo Levi found release in writing *If This Is a Man* after returning from Auschwitz to his hometown, Turin.[1] His recollections, like yours, were vivid and unadulterated by decades of hindsight. In his last chapter, "The Story of Ten Days," Levi described in chilling detail the last days in Auschwitz before the Russians liberated the camp. Arguably the most powerful in his book, it was the chapter he wrote first, within months of returning home. Did you write your twelve pages first?

Chapter 10

The Tower

As I delved deeper into the twelve pages, the stories got shorter, each sentence truncated, as if you were telling them while breathless, gasping for air.

Another morning, another roll call. That morning, I'd stepped on the set of scales in the flour mill, used for weighing sacks of ground corn. My weight had dropped to 49.5 kilograms. I couldn't bear weighing less than 50 kilograms. I'd weighed 85 kilograms when we arrived at the camp. I went to the well, drank three bowls of water, and returned to the scales. I was thrilled. The needle bounced up to 50 kilograms.

"U nastup! Line up, five in a row! Faster, motherfuckers!"

Who would they pick on today?

"Name and occupation! Why are you here?" snarled the selecting lieutenant.

"Dragan Roller. Medical student. For donating ten kuna to the Red cause."

They asked the same question every time. I always had the same answer ready. The officer was so close to my face, I could smell stale brandy on his breath. He stepped back, looked me up and down.

"Medical student, indeed!" he said with a smirk. "Can't be bothered with you! You'll croak here in a day or two. Serves you right for poisoning your own people with your crazy ideas."

"Motherfucking intellectuals!" the lieutenant screamed. "You think you're superior, don't you? Always plotting behind our backs. Traitors! Well, we'll see how much plotting you'll do in building K!"

Building K. K for Komunista.

Maybe weighing under 50 kilograms wasn't so bad after all. If I'd been any heavier, I might have been selected for building K. No one came out of building K alive. No food or water was provided. The prisoners were left to starve to death.

One by one, my comrades were picked off. All the engineering students who'd arrived with us in February 1942 were selected. Milan Špalj, too. Our hero. My guardian angel when I had typhus.

In the chaos of the camp, we managed to smuggle small amounts of food and water to our comrades. But it wasn't enough. Day by day, their cries became weaker.

Milan and his comrades tried to escape. They called a guard over and, under some pretext, persuaded him to unlock the door. They jumped him and ran to the camp gates, which were wide open in expectation of new deportees from Kozara Mountain. They didn't stand a chance. They were shot in the back.

Every day, the gravediggers collected bodies from building K. Later they told us they'd found a corpse with the chest open and the heart and lungs removed.

Building K. K for Komunista. Or was it K for Kanibal?

* * *

Every night in the tower, we heard voices. The voices of women and children. They were housed on the floors above us. Their cries and wails never stopped.

Like the men, the women had to work. We weren't allowed to approach them or speak to them. Sometimes they were taken out of camp to till the fields. Groups of twenty left in the morning but only half came back in the evening. What happened to the women who never returned? We didn't dare ask.

In the summer of 1942, rivers of people streamed in through the gates of the camp every day. Ustaša troops cleared the terrain around Kozara Mountain of Serbs, Jews, and Roma. Croats suspected of collusion with the partisans didn't fare much better. Everything that moved was deported: men, women, and children; cattle and horses; sheep and pigs. Cartloads of furniture and food supplies trundled past us every day. The meat, beans, and potatoes were not for us. They were for the Ustaša kitchens.

There was no room left in our fortress prison. New arrivals from Kozara camped out in the courtyard in the torrid heat. There was one water well. Hordes of flies buzzed around us.

At night, the drunken guards howled out obscene songs and raided the women's quarters. Screams pierced the darkness around us and reverberated against the thick walls of our basement room. After the soldiers left, muffled cries lingered till dawn.

"Something has to be done," the guards muttered the next day. "They can't all stay here."

Germany needed workers, men and women, to service the Third Reich's war machine. The younger women could be traded for hard cash. But many of them had children.

When the guards came to take the children away, the camp swelled with a deafening din. The mothers screamed and fought the armed soldiers with their bare fists. The children screeched. The older ones ran and tried to hide around the workshops. The guards chased them, swearing, beating, clubbing. By nightfall, the children were herded into rooms like ours, lined with hay and not much else.

That night the guards raided our room in the tower wearing gas masks and rubber suits. They looked like aliens from another planet. Were they so afraid of the "flu" epidemic they had to wear masks now? They ordered us all to get up. They took away all prisoners too weak to stand erect.

The next day the gravediggers were busy. They told us they had to clear a chamber stacked full of bodies. Big bodies and little bodies. The corpses of children from Kozara Mountain. There were no wounds on the bodies. The masks protected the guards from Zyklon B, not the flu. One gulp of hydrogen cyanide was enough to stop breathing forever.

For days afterward, not a sound came from the women's quarters.

Christmas Eve 1942 in the Tower

*In my cold cell I think
How happy Christmas Eve used to be
And how gloomy and ugly it is now
As dusk descends over me.*

*I'm not lauding the birth of Christ,
But the joy these festivities bring,
Boughs of oak on the mantelpiece,
Voices of children rejoicing.*

*Light will replace
This long winter night,
Wait for the morning,
The sun will win this fight.*

*On this most festive of nights,
They won't give us food.
In the tower a woman,
Cooks her dead son for dinner.*

The horror of your poem in the tower stopped me in my reading tracks again. Jasenovac didn't run with the Teutonic efficiency of Nazi extermination camps. Attempts to use Zyklon gas to murder children were bungled and eventually abandoned. The preferred mode of killing was one on one, eye to eye. The camp was a haven for sadists. Prisoners were clubbed to death with mallets, knives, and rifle butts in mind-boggling displays of power. The guards were no different from our brutish ancestors. They reminded me of some of the earliest carvings from ancient Egypt showing the absolute ruler, the pharaoh, bludgeoning the brains of another man just because he could. Five millennia of civilization had done little to blunt the savagery of the human race.

When I returned to your manuscript, there was a gap. Your writing skipped from Christmas 1942 to the fall of 1944.

What made you stop writing? In his mission to bear witness, Primo Levi spent a lifetime writing books and essays, speaking to school groups, and giving interviews about the barbarism perpetrated in Auschwitz. He raked over his own torment and suffered from bouts of depression for forty years until, in 1987, he committed suicide. You chose a different path. Perhaps you suspected that writing would not bring consolation, so you locked your memories in a dusty storeroom, hoping to forget the unforgettable. A half-century later, you would find yourself duty bound to unearth them again when you faced the camp commandant in a court of law.

In the fall of 1944, Germany was losing the war. The partisans were getting ever closer to the camp. They were across the river from Stara Gradiška. There was talk of liberation.

September 23, 1944

The guards ordered the evacuation of the old fortress. The nearest train station in Okučani was already under partisan control, so there was no chance of transport. We had to walk. We walked the twenty miles from Stara Gradiška to the main camp in Jasenovac.

We were corralled along the river, three or four in a row. A long column of people. Anyone who collapsed got a gun to his ear and was shot. They didn't bother burying the bodies. Across the river, the sound of gunfire. Was it the Ustaša, or was it our boys?

An old Catholic priest was near the head of the column. He'd been brought to the camp after his brother joined the partisans. But as the day progressed, he fell behind. By the time we caught up with him, he was stumbling. He wasn't going to make it without help. My comrade and I grabbed him either side and dragged him along.

"Come on, a few more steps," we urged him on.

We left a trail of corpses behind us that day. The priest was not one of them.

In Jasenovac, a macabre scene awaited us. Bodies hung from the gallows and lampposts around the camp. Lots of bodies. Some were missing their noses; others had their ears torn off.

"Watch and learn," the guards pointed their guns at the corpses. "Bošković and his bandits tried to escape. This is what will happen to you if you do the same!"

Another winter was coming. Another winter of hard physical work outdoors would finish me off. I volunteered to work as a medical orderly. The camp doctor agreed. It had to be a better way of surviving.

I was paired off with another medic and ordered to take the corpses down from the lampposts and carry them to the gravesite for burial. We took down civilians in threadbare rags and uniformed railway guards, but there was no sign of Bošković himself. Later I was told he'd been shot by the new commandant.

If Mile Bošković couldn't organize a rebellion, what hope was there for the rest of us? The noose was tightening around our necks.
No one could escape from Jasenovac, not even a bird.

Avoiding work while giving the appearance of being able and willing to toil was key to survival in the camps. It was important not to appear useless to the guards, as this could lead to selection for execution. Like Primo Levi, you were unsuited to heavy physical work, so you made yourself "useful." As a graduate in chemistry, Levi assisted in the rubber laboratory. As a student of medicine, you worked in the camp hospital.

Escape from the camp was practically impossible. There had been attempts, but all ended in bloodshed. The prisoners were shot in the back as they tried to flee, or they were caught and hanged for all inmates to see. Your conspiratorial experience might have helped with the organization of resistance, but ultimately, any form of action was made more difficult by hunger, cold, and disease. As Levi noted in his writing, people in rags do not revolt.

Forced labor, hunger, beatings, summary executions, and humiliation were part of everyday life in Jasenovac. Aged nineteen on arrival, you had the physical stamina, the mental resilience, and sheer good luck to survive such conditions. Many did not.

Chapter 11

Homecoming

The Yugoslav partisans liberated the camp in Jasenovac in May 1945. But you were not there.

You'd been traded, like a head of cattle, to the Todt organization, an engineering group that supplied forced labor for the Nazi war machine. You and six hundred other prisoners had been dispatched by freight train to work in Germany. You left on February 18, 1945, three years exactly to the day when you first arrived at the camp. Your three-month sentence had stretched to three years.

It was the last transport out of Jasenovac. The journey probably saved your life. The majority of those who stayed behind perished during the final liquidation of the camp.

On arrival at the holding camp Lanzensdorf near Vienna, the Nazi guards discovered lice in one of the wagons. The authorities were terrified of a typhus epidemic, so the whole shipment was placed into quarantine. You were delighted. You got four weeks off work. The live cargo got a month's holiday.

Quarantine over, you were sent to Linz and then on to work for Herr Grubauer, a farmer in the hills surrounding the town. You were lucky. Others were assigned to the blast furnaces of the Hermann Goering Werke. The work there was hot and arduous, and the site was a daily target for bombing raids by the Allies.

You developed a good relationship with the Grubauers. In an ID photo of the period, your lean facial features had filled out. Despite the war, the farm did not lack food, the one thing you missed most in the camp. You regained some of the weight you'd lost in Jasenovac. Your knowledge of conversational German helped, too.

Years later, when I was about to visit Linz with a school friend, you told me a little more about your time there. With a glint in your eye, you recounted how, in April 1945, you watched a dogfight between Messerschmitts and Spitfires in the skies over Linz, the planes twisting and turning like demented hornets, releasing quick bursts of gunfire at irregular intervals. You were full of admiration for the skills and bravery of the pilots on both sides. I asked you if you were frightened. You assured me that, after Jasenovac, you felt no fear in Linz.

Herr Grubauer's son was at home, recovering from an illness he'd picked up on the eastern front. As soon as he was well enough, he wanted to reenlist. "Helmutt, are you mad?" you said to him. "The war is nearly over. If you reenlist, you will almost certainly die or end up in Siberia and never come home."

"*Ja, Dragan hat recht.*" "Yes, Dragan is right," said Herr Grubauer.

You offered to look out for military police from the hilltop above the farm and raise the alarm in time for Helmutt to hide. You helped him to dig a hole in the forest and bury his uniform and weapons. By persuading him to desert, you effectively saved his life. Your Austrian captors, perhaps ambivalent about Hitler's annexation of their country in 1938, treated you better than your Croatian brethren in Jasenovac.

The American Army liberated Linz on May 5, 1945. It must have been a momentous day for you and the masses of released prisoners all around you. After years of misery, you could go home and start a new life. How did you feel when you discovered you had your freedom back? The question will remain forever unanswered.

Your secret manuscript made no mention of your journey home. Europe was in ruins after the war, and travel would have been difficult. Primo Levi took many months to get back to his hometown, Turin, from Auschwitz. His journey followed a tortuous loop eastward through the Soviet Union, folding back on itself through central Europe and eventually bringing him back to northern Italy. He wrote a book, *The Truce*, about it. Linz was a lot closer to Zagreb than Auschwitz was to Turin, but it couldn't have been easy to get back home. Millions of people were displaced, each individual with their own story of survival and hardship. Your foreigner's ID booklet issued by the German authorities showed the number 1,539,799.

Despite the chaos, I imagined you had much to look forward to. Wartime resistance had triumphed over tyranny. You'd fought for a cause, and your side won the war. You could go home to your country, your language, your culture and help build a new state with lofty egalitarian ideals. Your conviction that the world could be a better place through collective effort could be put into practice, bringing universal health care, public housing, and education to all.

You may not have written about your return home, but others did. Your fellow inmate George Miliša named you in his book *Jasenovac: Torture Chamber from Hell* as one of the two main organizers of repatriation efforts. You'd requisitioned all manner of vehicles—abandoned cars, lorries, and

Figure 11.1. Dragan's ID booklet during forced labor in Linz, Austrian territory annexed by Germany, April 1945.

freight trains—and organized the distribution of food, cigarettes, and clothes donated by the Russian Army.

"We will never forget," you said, according to Miliša, in your address at the last remembrance event for fallen comrades before you crossed the border out of Austria and into the reinstated united Yugoslavia. After four years of terror, the fascist Independent State of Croatia ceased to exist. You were a Yugoslav again, like in your schooldays in Virovitica.

Back in Zagreb, what was it like to meet your mom and dad again, your older sister, Milena, and younger brother, Zlatko? Did you know Milena had joined the partisans after you were taken to Jasenovac? Did you worry about her? I found little about that period of your life in your papers, except for one poem. A poem I didn't know existed until after you died.

The Prisoner's Mother

She had a son, bonny and strong,
In his town he was liked by all.
His parents adored him,
He was their pride and joy.

In the fight against tyranny,
The boy made a bomb.
Others did more,
Gave their lives to the cause.

He started off bravely, knowing full well,
There's no freedom without a fight.
He didn't succeed, ended up in prison,
For the first time in his life.

His mother was frantic.
She searched the city, knocked on doors,
Dared not cry in public,
Her tears were shed at home.

Six months went by until one day,
The postman delivered a card.
It was from the camp,
In the handwriting she knew so well.

From that day on, she sent him parcels
And the twenty words allowed.
His father added cigarettes
A neighbor, her sugar rations.

She could think of nothing else,
She knew he was hungry.
She dreamed of her son,
And the day he'd come home.

The mother doesn't know it,
But there by the wall,
The latrine is full,
A body floats on top.

The son comes home.
Mother is happy, sadness is gone.
Whose body was it, all on its own?
No one to grieve, no mother, no friend.

As in your poem "Comrade Schwartz," survivor's guilt came through forcefully.

In the fall of 1945, you reenrolled at the university in Zagreb. You were an active member of the Communist Party. You were busy building a new socialist system, planning for the future. At the end of a brutal war, the possibilities for change must have seemed limitless. You told me that you spent more time in meetings than studying. As a result, your academic performance plummeted. Your tutor hauled you in for a ticking-off.

"Comrade Dragan, your grades were in the top percentile before the war," he scolded. "Look at them now. They are mediocre."

You were mortified. You'd always been proud of your excellent academic record.

Your heart was no longer in medicine. You were too busy trying to change the world. I imagine the horrors you'd witnessed in Jasenovac didn't help. What of the man with the clawed fingers you'd carried to his fate in the brick kiln? Or the bodies without ears and noses hanging from the lampposts?

That fall, you switched from medicine to economics.

The same autumn, you met a girl. You wanted to look good on your first rendezvous, but you couldn't afford to dress well. As a camp survivor, you had certain privileges, so you applied for a voucher to buy a new shirt. Your student union supported your application.

MEMORANDUM

From: Head of Student Services, University of Zagreb

To: Ministry of Trade, Benefits Department

Re: Dragan Roller, student

Voucher for one shirt

Date: October 22, 1945

I understand your department has recently made funds available to support students with their living expenses, including the purchase of new clothing.

I have approved Dragan Roller's application for funding to purchase one new shirt. Please issue a voucher to the applicant.

Please note the applicant was imprisoned for three years in the concentration camp Jasenovac and later in Germany until the end of the war.

Death to fascism, freedom to the people!

Your sartorial efforts paid off, and your dates became more frequent. By December, you were married. You were twenty-three; she was twenty-one. But it wasn't long before the rows started and became acrimonious. The marriage was short-lived. In your headlong rush to put the war behind you, your decision to marry may have been too hasty. Did your memories of the camp encroach on your attempts at happiness?

You graduated in 1948, started work as a research assistant at the university, and embarked on a PhD in the history of economics. You packed a lot of living into three years, but I had no idea how you felt about any of it. You didn't write about it or talk about it in later life. All I had was a pile of certificates and legal documents, a bare backbone of facts, like a curriculum vitae prepared for a potential employer.

Perhaps you'd decided to abandon your emotional twin back in the camp. The soft, gentle double who plagued you in your poems. The doppelgänger who fought off his aggressive mirror image in your typhus nightmares. You'd decided to be the strongman, to tough it out. The strategy worked, at least for a while.

Chapter 12

Postcards from Dubrovnik

Dragan and Vesna. My mom and dad. You fell in love in Dubrovnik in 1949, that much I knew. But you never told me how you'd met or even the exact date of your wedding. You kept the details to yourselves.

One day when I was in my teens, an unusually opulent bouquet of red roses appeared on the dining room table. It wasn't March 8, International Women's Day, when schools staged special productions and family members gave all women flowers. It wasn't March 21, either, Mama's name day, the occasion she preferred to celebrate instead of her birthday in April so she wouldn't have to reveal how old she was. It was somewhere between, in spring. I jotted "March 11" down in my diary and promised myself I would buy you both a present for your next anniversary. But when the next year came, there were no tell-tale flowers in March. Instead, they appeared on July 30. I was confused. When exactly was your anniversary? What were you celebrating? Was it the day you first met, the actual date of your wedding, or some other significant moment in your life together? When I questioned you about it, your answer was mysteriously vague, as if you didn't want me to know. Whichever date it was, no friends or relatives were ever invited to your private party. It had to be just the two of you together.

In the summer of 1949, you were both researching your dissertations in the city archives, housed in the elegant sixteenth-century Palace Sponza in Dubrovnik. The Renaissance loggia in the atrium of the palace was a perfect setting for the reenactment of the balcony scene from *Romeo and Juliet*. For many years, I imagined you, tall, dark, and handsome, standing on the ground floor beneath the balustrade, reaching up to Vesna, of green eyes and chestnut hair, swooning under the graceful arches of the first-floor loggia. But I never told you about this fantasy, for you would have dismissed it as trite. Hardened by your concentration camp experience, you were bookish and deeply immersed in Marxist economics. Like you, Vesna had a broken marriage behind her. Neither of you was given to swooning. Or did your eyes meet across a room stacked with dusty deed rolls like in a Hollywood movie? "Bah! Another clichéd fantasy," you would have said, for sure.

Vesna was the bubbly younger daughter of a prewar textile merchant and Freemason. The fourth-floor apartment she'd been brought up in was crammed with Biedermeier furniture and Meissen tableware. Her mother employed a cook and a cleaner. As a young girl, Vesna was made to eat with a couple of books lodged under each arm to stop her elbows from disturbing the diners seated either side of her. Her bourgeois background was anathema to the communist principles you'd embraced so fervently. Barely twenty years old, Vesna was a keen art history student, but she wasn't going to let the painstaking archive work get in the way of laughter. Perhaps it was her joie de vivre that attracted you to her. She was the exact opposite of what you were at the time.

By 1949, you were a research assistant at the Faculty of Economics, earning a modest academic salary. You no longer needed vouchers to buy a new shirt. Your pay could stretch to a romantic dinner with Vesna at the elegant Hotel Villa Argentina. No longer an exclusive bastion for the rich, the restaurant offered a vast menu of seemingly delectable dishes. But food supplies were meager that year. President Tito's spat with Joseph Stalin the year before had major consequences for Yugoslavia. Incensed by Tito's resistance to his attempts to make the country a Soviet satellite state, Stalin expelled the Yugoslav Communist Party from the Eastern bloc and imposed sanctions on the country. When you ordered fillet steak with green peppercorn sauce, you got a dry minced-meat patty, no sauce. Undeterred, you ate most of the patty, then called the waiter over.

"This meat is no good. There's a cockroach on it," you said, pointing at a shriveled piece of onion on your plate. The waiter examined the remains of the meat but couldn't establish with any certainty what the charred object on the plate was. He shrugged his shoulders and brought you another full portion of fried patty. Once the waiter was out of sight, the two of you plunged your forks into the meat in fits of giggles.

Like your first wife, Vesna was an impossibly young partner for you. Earlier that year, she'd married a fellow student of art history. But by the time she arrived in Dubrovnik, her marriage was already doomed. Vesna's father was furious.

"Not only have you married against my wishes, but now you're talking divorce three months after your wedding!" he raged. "You are not to get married again until you've graduated with honors! That's an order!"

Despite the distractions, Vesna's archival work that summer had been productive. She'd unearthed volumes of research data for her dissertation. Her academic adviser was pleased with her progress. Maybe her beloved *Tatek*, or Little Daddy, as she liked to call him, would be proud of her again once she showed him how much work she'd done. But what of this new boyfriend? A divorcee and a communist. *Tatek* had made himself perfectly clear: romantic liaisons of any kind were banned until graduation day. Vesna didn't want to risk enraging her father again.

Before you both returned to Zagreb, you agreed to communicate in English. Vesna's estranged husband did not speak any foreign languages, and her parents spoke only French and German, or so you thought.

October 10, 1949

My missed baby,

How are you traveled?
 Remember the Rector's Palace? Can you hear our song: "Tampico, Tampico, little town in Mexico"? I whistle the melody in vain.
 Do you remember your promise? You must put your foot down. Your husband wants whipping badly.

D.

October 11, 1949

Where we used to meet, next to the Giacometti . . .
 Come what may, you must live as woman and not as child. Barking dogs never bite. You have nothing to be afraid.

D.

October 12, 1949

We are at Onofri's little fountain, 9 p.m. . . .
 Tonight is not beautiful. You are not here.
 Joking apart, I hope to find you again young and gay and what is primary—happy!
 Is there any possibility of my being given a crumb of happiness?
 Let me hear from you.

D.

Much later, you discovered Vesna's mother did speak English after all, so she could have worked out something was going on. But perhaps she was too polite to read other people's postcards or too embarrassed to admit she had done so. Maybe she knew but chose not to tell *Tatek*. Maybe they both knew.

Vesna's divorce was granted in the fall of 1949. The two of you continued to see each other discreetly. Vesna stood by her father's wishes and persevered with her studies.

The archival work in Dubrovnik had been productive for you, too. Your first book on the history of Dubrovnik from the thirteenth to the fifteenth centuries was published, a prerequisite for enrolling in a PhD program. The follow-up study on trade relations in the fifteenth and sixteenth centuries was the focus of your doctoral thesis, which would eventually also be published.

At a friend's wedding, you asked the official photographer to take a snap of the two of you. Striking a formal pose, you leaned toward each other, staring intently at an invisible point somewhere to the right of the frame. Vesna wore her favorite gold necklace with the exquisite pearl pendant passed down to her from her great grandmother. It was 1952. Vesna had still not graduated.

You were getting restless. You'd been awarded your PhD, and you expected your post at the university to be made permanent. You'd hoped it would be the first rung on the ladder of your academic career. But three months after you'd applied for and been interviewed for the job, there was still no confirmation of your new role. You'd heard through the grapevine that your loudmouth debating at party meetings had not been appreciated by everyone. Infuriated, you handed in your notice. In February 1953, you left for the capital, Belgrade, to take up a new job in the Foreign Office. Did you take your unfinished manuscript and poems with you, or did they stay in Zagreb?

You wrote prolifically in Belgrade but not about the camp or the war. Instead, you published articles in economics journals. You completed a diplomacy training course and polished your English. Vesna was an overnight train journey away in Zagreb. You missed her. Although you visited each other as often as possible, it wasn't enough. And your new job would entail overseas travel. When your first diplomatic mission to Istanbul was confirmed, you wanted Vesna to come with you. She wanted to come with you, too. Turkey brimmed with archaeological and cultural treasures. How wonderful would it be to visit them in person rather than reading about them in books? You were both itching to go. But diplomatic protocol demanded that couples be married. You wrote a letter to your employer.

MEMORANDUM

To: Department of Human Resources, Foreign Office, Belgrade

From: Dr. Dragan Roller, 3rd Secretary

Date: September 13, 1953

Figure 12.1.　Dragan and Vesna, 1952.

I hereby request permission to marry my girlfriend, Vesna Brovet.

I've known Vesna Brovet for four years. She was born on April 13, 1929, in Zagreb. Her father, Krešimir Brovet, was a textile merchant before the war. He was the son of a watchmaker from Čabar. He moved to Zagreb with his brother Slavko to set up their joint business.

Vesna's mother, Hana Brovet, is from the old Zagreb family Mašek. Vesna's grandfather the university professor Dr. Dragutin Mašek was one of the three founders of the Faculty of Medicine at the university in Zagreb.

Vesna's father was a Freemason before the war. Consequently, he was arrested by the Ustaša and imprisoned in the concentration camp Stara Gradiška for several months. He had a longstanding reputation for his anti-fascist and anti-German views and so was arrested twice more by the Gestapo. During the war, the bulk of his wealth in stocks and shares was confiscated by Nazis. After liberation, he was an employee at the import-export firm Merkur. He is now on an invalidity pension, as he has a serious heart condition. He is not politically active.

Vesna was a child during the war. She was deeply traumatized by her father's repeated arrests. She was fifteen when the war ended. After liberation, she joined several of our more progressive youth organizations. In March 1949, she married Milan Zvjezdić from Zagreb, but they were divorced six months later.

Vesna is a final-year student at the Faculty of Philosophy, reading for a degree in the history of art. She speaks German and is able to get by in English and Italian. Her sister, Dr. Dina Keglević, is a research assistant at the Faculty of Life Sciences at the University of Zagreb. Dr Keglević is currently in London completing a postdoctoral research fellowship at the Medical Research Council Institute in Mill Hill.

I believe Vesna Brovet would make a suitable wife for an employee of our diplomatic service despite originating from a bourgeois family. She loves our country and the Communist Party, and she is sincerely antifascist. She currently lives with her parents in Zagreb. I would like her to come to Belgrade as soon as possible, and this is her wish, too.

Death to fascism, freedom to the people!

When I first read your letter, I was outraged. What business of theirs was it? What right did your employer or the Communist Party have to all these personal details about your future in-laws? And what would have happened if they'd refused permission? I could find no evidence of a reply in the family archive. Perhaps there never was a reply. I imagine it was done on a nod. Perhaps the party bureaucrats were aware a written reply would have been as ludicrous as your letter had been. Did others write such letters? This was more than just party loyalty. It was bordering on subservience, not a sentiment I normally associated with you.

You were married in Belgrade on March 11, 1954. Vesna had still not graduated, so you kept the wedding date secret, lest you provoked her father's ire. Your appointment as commercial attaché at the Yugoslav consulate in Istanbul was confirmed. Vesna finally graduated on July 20, 1954. A few days later, you announced to family and friends that you were traveling to Belgrade, where you would be married in a registry office with your two closest friends as witnesses. You didn't want anyone to make a fuss. The telegram from your new in-laws congratulating you on your nuptials was dated July 30, 1954.

On your return to Zagreb, you were invited to lunch for your first family meal with your new in-laws. I imagine the atmosphere would have been formal, perhaps somewhat strained. At the end of the meal, your mother-in-law, Hana, asked if anyone would like to polish off the dressing in the bottom of the salad bowl.

"Yes, please!" you and your father-in-law shouted in unison.

Krešo picked up the dish, turned toward you with a broad smile, and said, "We can share." You grabbed your spoons and tucked in. The ice was broken.

* * *

After a few months in Istanbul, you were transferred to the Balkan Pact Secretariat in Ankara. The treaty had been an alliance between Yugoslavia, Greece, and Turkey, intended to facilitate trade and cultural exchange between the three countries. It was unusual, as Greece and Turkey were capitalist countries and members of NATO, while Yugoslavia was communist and a founding member of the Non-Aligned Movement, espousing neither of the two major power blocks.[1] Geographically, it made sense for these Balkan countries to cooperate. From President Tito's point of view, it was yet another way of distancing himself and Yugoslavia from the Soviet bloc and the continuing threat of invasion from Stalin. Ironically, one week after the Balkan Treaty was signed, Joseph Stalin died. Replaced by Nikita Khrushchev, the following years saw a gradual thawing of relations between Yugoslavia and the Soviet Union. But that was still in the future. You joined the team tasked with setting up a mobile secretariat staffed by representatives from all three countries. The secretariat rotated between Ankara, Athens, and Belgrade every six months. Your next posting would be to Athens, then back to Belgrade. You would be busy.

Turkey did not disappoint. It was a treasure trove of antiquities. You both indulged your passion for history. While you were at work, Vesna was determined to teach herself how to cook. Her mother had given her a few recipes before leaving Zagreb, but she lacked basic culinary skills. Growing up in a household with servants, there was no need for her to have them. The first time she tried to make pork chops for dinner, she placed the meat in a pan, switched the cooker on and went to the sofa to read her book. When the smell of burning reached her nostrils, she realized there was something amiss . . .

You were thirty-two; Vesna was twenty-five. Nearly ten years had passed since you'd been released from Jasenovac. I imagine your manuscript and poems lingered, almost forgotten, in a folder in Zagreb. Your life was on the up. You refused to allow the weight of history to crush you.

Chapter 13

The Child

It would be absurd to claim that I can remember Athens, the city of my birth, but I'm going to do it anyway.

For starters, there were the balmy nights. Every Saturday evening, the three of us went to the movies at the local open-air cinema, you and Mama in your sheer cotton outfits, me in my Moses basket. Grace Kelly, James Dean, and Yul Brynner loomed large on the silver screen. I am convinced to this day that my love of the moving image started in my baby basket under the Athenian moon.

We left Athens before I could walk, so I couldn't possibly remember any of it, right? My memories are your memories, and Mama's, retold and reinterpreted countless times at family gatherings and reinforced by a dozen black-and-white photographs stashed in a creased envelope marked "Greece 1956." My head has appropriated our collective memories as if they were my own. How else do I explain the uncanny feeling of belonging every time I return to Athens? On a business trip to the city some four decades after my birth, I asked the taxi driver from the airport to stop in front of an open-air cinema. I wound down the window, took a deep breath, and sank back in my seat, eyes closed. My shoulders relaxed away from my ears. The stress of the journey lifted. All was well. I was home.

The Yugoslav Foreign Office confirmed your relocation from Ankara to Athens in January 1956. You and Mama were delighted. Your diplomatic career was progressing nicely. Greece had even more ancient ruins than Turkey. Pediments and architraves, temples and gymnasia, theaters and baths—their graceful symmetry attracted you both like magnets. You'd read about the ancient world in your books; now you had a chance to see these classical wonders for yourselves.

Our Athenian home was in a two-story mansion, located in a leafy southern suburb of the city. Whitewashed to reflect the scorching sun, the house had a flat roof buttressed by angular pillars in neoclassical proportions. Three imposing balconies fringed with intricate, wrought-iron balustrades traversed the facade. Young olive trees in the narrow passages around the house softened the overall look. The French windows on the first floor led from the central balcony into the shady interior of the upstairs apartment, where the landlady lived with her Pekingese dog. You rented the more modest, ground-floor apartment.

The white house, as you liked to call it, was on Odos Naiadon, the address scrawled in your handwriting on the back of a black-and-white photograph. Many years later, I went searching for our Grecian home on Google Earth, but I could not locate it. Perhaps it no longer exists. Instead, rows of six-story concrete apartment blocks stretched all along the street. They lacked the grandeur of the white house, but they were not soulless. Striped awnings perched over expansive terraces strewn with loungers, barbecue equipment, and children's inflatable paddling pools. Along the pavement, a promenade of bitter orange trees lined up like soldiers on parade. The neighborhood was still as leafy in the new millennium as it had been in the 1950s.

I was tempted to book a seat on a flight to Athens and escape the gray gloom of London. Maybe I could visit Odos Naiadon and see it for myself. But then I remembered something you said to me.

"Never revisit places where you were happy as a child. Everything will look small, dingy, and miserable. Your memories will be ruined."

I didn't want to ruin my memories of Athens, real or imagined. I heeded your advice.

The white house was within walking distance of the sea. You made the most of this with long walks in the winter and swimming in the summer. In a photo dated June 1956, you are sitting with Mama on the shingle beach near your home, the seven-month bump underneath her swimsuit barely noticeable.

In September 1956, Mama and I were not doing well. We were both skinny as rakes. I was cranky and not gaining weight. Mama was fretful and not producing enough milk. You suggested a purée of cooked kidney beans for the baby. After all, a similar concoction saved the legendary fourteenth-century Serbian Prince Marko from starvation after his mother died.

"Prince Marko became king and a folk hero," you said. "He was as strong as Hercules. He was so strong he could squeeze water out of desiccated dogwood."

Marko's exploits and bravery were celebrated in many epic poems, learned by heart and recited verbatim by schoolkids. A real Prince Marko did exist, but I've always suspected his alleged feeding regime as an infant was somewhat embellished. Kidney beans were your favorite food. You loved them in every shape and form: smothered with mounds of thinly sliced onions and

Figure 13.1.   Dragan, Athens surrounds, 1956.

baked in a low oven for three hours or with strips of pork belly in a hearty soup or in a salad seasoned with red wine vinegar and olive oil. But kidney beans were not brought to Europe until after Christopher Columbus discovered America, so Prince Marko could not have been fed on them, hero or no hero. Besides, you were rather scrawny, certainly no Hercules. And you definitely couldn't squeeze moisture out of dry dogwood.

Worried by your girls' lack of progress, you decided modern medicine was the only answer. You whisked mother and baby to the doctor, who diagnosed infective mastitis. He prescribed antibiotics for Mama and a newly developed American infant formula for the baby. Within weeks, we were thriving. Mama recovered fully from her infection, and I was getting chubby, like all proper babies should be. Our smiles made you smile.

I imagine you didn't smile when you stashed away your *Spomenica prvoborcima*, the Memorial Medal of Honor for Freedom Fighters of 1941, in an off-white cardboard box labeled in modern Greek with the name and address of an Athenian stationery shop. When I found it fifty years later, I wondered why the medal wasn't in a specially made presentation box. Instead, it was in a container that once held a deck of playing cards. I knew of the medal's existence, for you often referred to it with pride, but you'd never shown it to me personally. Did the medal invoke mixed emotions for you?

I lifted the tarnished black medal out of its incongruously pink cotton/wool cocoon. It felt heavy in the crook of my palm, as if to make up for its diminutive size. I pulled out a silver polishing cloth and rubbed at the radiating spokes. From the dark center of the star, the figure of a young man in a triumphant pose emerged in a high sheen. He lunged forward with his left knee, but his head was turned backward and tilted up toward the fluttering flag held up in his outstretched arms. The medal was never on display in our home. Perhaps it would have reminded you too much of your days in Jasenovac.

By the middle of 1957, we were back in Yugoslavia. That summer, I had my first taste of Grandma Hana's holiday home in the quaint fishing village of Novi Vinodolski on the northern Adriatic coast. The 1930s-style seaside villa stood on a rocky outcrop, lapped by the aquamarine sea and surrounded by pine-scented cypresses. It was the place where family and friends congregated every summer to rest and soak up the sun. The place where my first real memory of you was formed.

I am a toddler. I am clinging to your shoulders, piggyback style, while you swim ahead, your arms making shimmering circles beneath the translucent sea.

"Look, Sibel!" you say, pointing downward into the deep blue. "Starfish!"

I reach my hand down toward the spiny creatures, but they are elusive. You twist around to face me, laughing. Soft bristles of your moustache brush against my cheek.

Figure 13.2.   Dragan's Memorial Medal of Honor for Freedom Fighters of 1941.

Novi was the place we returned to every summer and after every adventure abroad. Those adventures were yet to unfold. The first of these had us heading east, to Iraq.

Figure 13.3.   Dragan and Sibel in Novi Vinodolski, Yugoslavia, 1958.

Chapter 14

Arabian Nights

BBC News

July 14, 1958

Coup in Iraq sparks jitters in the Middle East

Iraqi army officers have staged a coup in Iraq and overthrown the monarchy.

Baghdad radio announced the army has liberated the Iraqi people from domination by a corrupt group put in power by imperialism. From now on, Iraq would be a republic.

Major General Abdul Karim el Qasim is Iraq's new prime minister. King Faisal and his family have been killed.

In the aftermath of the 1958 coup in Iraq, the West fretted over Qasim and his leftist leanings. Meanwhile, President Tito of Yugoslavia wasted no time agreeing a program of cooperation with Iraq. He dispatched a diplomatic team to establish a new embassy in Baghdad. You were part of that team.

Mama had studied Sumerian cultures at university, but now she would get a chance to visit Mesopotamia in person. She was thrilled. You shared her enthusiasm. After the marvels of ancient Turkey and Greece, the cities of Ur and Babylon represented another significant step in your joint quest for historical enlightenment. On the back of a photo of Mama standing enraptured in front of a ruined citadel, you wrote, "Vesna in archaeological trance."

Your embassy work came with parties and dancing. Mama was twenty-nine; you were thirty-six. What better way was there to put behind you the legacy of the camp?

Our arrival in Baghdad did not go smoothly. In the box of memorabilia labeled "Iraq," I found a telegram addressed to you from the commercial attaché at the embassy in Cairo: "I've received your shipment. Have you got mine?" There'd been a mix-up. You were not amused. Invitations to formal receptions and dinners were arriving daily, but you had nothing to wear. Two black tuxedos, one for the winter and another for the summer, and an ivory dinner jacket with satin lapels, tailor-made for you in Zagreb, were now in Cairo instead of Baghdad. Mama was incandescent. Her apricot-pink brocade cocktail dress, off-the-shoulder taffeta ballgown, and black opera-length gloves were missing, too. But once our belongings finally arrived, the new outfits were premiered in style.

You had much to learn about etiquette and customs. You'd been told that social events in Iraq never started on time. When your first invitation to a dinner party starting at 8:00 p.m. arrived, you showed up at, what you thought, was a fashionable half-hour late. The hosts were still getting dressed. Of course, they were perfectly charming about it and pretended not to notice the gaffe. They instructed their butler to keep your champagne glasses topped up while you waited, and they returned to their ablutions. An hour later, the other guests trickled in. Dinner wasn't served until midnight, by which time you slurred your words and forgot the name of the ambassador sitting next to you at the table. Worse still, you weren't sure which country he represented. Mama wasn't much help either. Every time you asked her to remind you of someone's name, she burst into fits of giggles.

The Iraqi hosts had prepared a traditional Middle Eastern meal, eaten with the hands. No cutlery of any kind was on offer. You tucked in and tried your best not to squirt the braised okra into the other diners' laps.

"It was shameful," you said afterward.

"Tomato stains and couscous all over our finery, while the Iraqi ladies got the tips of three fingers dirty," Mama added. "They had such beautifully ornate hands, decorated with an intricate lacework of henna. So elegant! After eating, they swished their fingertips in bowls of water with lemon slices floating in them. Your Tata and I looked like pigs in need of hosing down!"

"We must stop behaving like barbarians and learn how to be civilized," Mama announced. For the next week, she made us eat our family meals with our fingers until she judged us to be sufficiently proficient to avoid any future embarrassment.

* * *

Our home in Baghdad was a stark sandstone cube, one of many lined up along a grid of concrete streets embedded into the flat plain of the desert, not a tree or succulent in sight. The house was surrounded by a high brick wall and closed off by a heavy metal gate, locked at dusk against intruders. The

Figure 14.1.   Party time in Baghdad, 1958–1962.

short, straight drive from the gate led to a carport providing much-needed shade for your all-white, winged Chevrolet with its oval CD plate displayed prominently on the front grille.

A square of yellow thatch in front of the house passed off as a lawn. Mama's attempts at gardening were futile in the arid climate. The only green-ery was at the Yugoslav ambassador's residence. The Dizdarević children had an olive-green lawn, watered daily by a full-time gardener. Judging by the number of photos you took of us in their garden, we went there often. There's the photo of me, aged three and smiling to order for the camera, in a costume vaguely resembling a white rabbit. The bodice had been crudely fashioned from a bed sheet into a sack. A linen serviette with the corners shaped into floppy ears was wrapped around my head. Sewing was not one of Mama's strengths. In other photos, I'm in one of several romper suits, made by Grandma Hana from a pattern cut out of a French magazine, puffed out around the bottom with a cascade of flowery frills in a kind of bloomer effect.

The floors of our house were tiled throughout, a wonderfully cooling tonic for bare feet in summer but freezing cold in winter. There was no heating of any kind in the house.

"I've never been as cold as in our first so-called mild winter in Iraq," Mama complained.

"Perhaps we should insulate our feet from the floor with some rugs," you suggested. Mama jumped at the idea. The two of you set off for Souq Menahim, leaving me with Samira, our live-in maid. You were gone all day, or so it seemed to me.

"What took you so long?" I wailed when you returned home.

"You can't rush these things," you said as you unrolled a maroon-and-indigo Kashan on the floor. "We had mint tea with Mr. Hamid and got chatting." A Qum with a delicate teardrop-shaped motif in swirls of ivory, cobalt blue, and burnt sienna followed a few months later, after an equally interminable day at the souq. At the time, I didn't appreciate what all the fuss was about. It took decades before I learned to cherish the exquisite patterns on the handmade tapestries. That year in Baghdad, Mr. Hamid had kindled your passion for beautiful rugs, a passion that lasted you both a lifetime.

Our kitchen was in an outbuilding at the back of the house. A room next to the kitchen was home to our maid Samira and her young son. I have forgotten his name, but I remember playing with him. We were about the same age. He spoke Arabic to me, and I spoke Serbo-Croat to him. It did not take long before we developed our own language, a mishmash of Slav and Arabic utterings incomprehensible to anyone else.

You were convinced I spoke Arabic fluently. You boasted to your friends that your clever daughter was bilingual. One day, Uncle Marouf came to visit. He wasn't a relation, but in Slav tradition, all children addressed adult males as uncle and females as auntie. You wanted to show off my lingual prowess to your friend, so you asked me to get Samira to bring some tea for the visitor. I went to the back door and shouted out the instructions to Samira in the kitchen. Uncle Marouf burst out laughing.

"Did you know Sibel's Arabic is a long string of expletives?" Uncle Marouf asked.

You shook your head, frowning.

"Lots of mothers' and sisters' organs in action, if you get my drift," cackled Uncle Marouf.

"I guess she must have picked them up from Samira and the neighbors she plays with," you said, raising your eyebrow. Your face feigned concern, but the right corner of your mouth was turning up into a grin.

"Whatever you do, don't let her talk to your Oxford-educated Iraqi friends in Arabic," said Uncle Marouf.

You both guffawed raucously. Mama was mortified. She needn't have worried. The Arabic didn't stick. Not long after we left Iraq to return to Yugoslavia, the words vanished from my brain. A language quickly learned and even more quickly unlearned. Five years later, when we left Yugoslavia for Libya, I had to pick it up again from scratch, this time without the swear words.

* * *

Most evenings, Mama would start getting ready for an outing early. You'd sit in the lounge reading the *Economist* and smoking a cigarillo. Every few minutes or so, Mama stuck her head through the bedroom door to remind you what time it was.

"*Dragane, obuci se*! Get dressed," she said. "We have to leave in twenty minutes."

"No problem! It won't take me more than ten minutes to get dressed. Not like you ladies . . . "

Figure 14.2.   Dragan and Sibel in Baghdad, 1961.

True to your word, you disappeared into the bedroom and emerged, exactly ten minutes later with dinner jacket, cummerbund, and bow tie in place; hair slicked back; moustache neatly brushed; stray hairs from ears and nostrils clipped away; and shoes polished so clean they reflected the ceiling lights.

We climbed the stairs to my room together, clouds of musky Old Spice and densely peachy Femme mingling around us. You tucked me in, brushing your soft moustache against my cheek. No kisses from Mama, lest her lipstick get smudged.

"Sweet dreams," you'd say in English.

* * *

Your visits to the dentist were becoming more frequent. You had gum disease. You didn't explain it at the time, but it was a legacy of the Jasenovac camp, brought about by malnutrition and poor oral hygiene. There were no toothbrushes in the camp. And there was no cure for it. The loose teeth had to come out. Your dentist gave you two options: extract the teeth one by one over a period of many years or several at a time over a shorter interval. You opted for the latter.

As you approached your fortieth birthday, you had six of your front teeth removed and a set of brilliant white dentures made for you. The day of the extractions, you came home tight-lipped and looking tired. You didn't mention the pain you must have felt. I wish I'd been more sympathetic to your plight.

"Why won't Tata play with me today?" I asked Mama. That was all my six-year-old self wanted to know.

Once your new set of teeth arrived, you wasted no time showing them off to the world, grinning like a Cheshire cat at every available opportunity. At the next reception at the French embassy, Madame l'Ambassadrice couldn't help but notice your dazzling smile.

"Which product do you use, Dragan, to make your teeth so white?"

"Bleach, of course!" you replied and watched her closely for a reaction.

She stared back, wide-eyed.

"You gargle with bleach?"

"I take my teeth out and plop them in a glass of Clorox overnight. They're sparkling white in the morning!"

You told me afterward her face was a sight to behold.

You weren't about to let a throwback of Jasenovac ruin your life. The gum disease persisted for a number of years until nearly all your teeth were replaced by dentures. But you never complained about it. Not once.

* * *

Every year on November 29, the Yugoslav ambassador hosted a gala reception to celebrate the Day of the Republic, the national holiday commemorating the formation of the new socialist Yugoslavia in 1943. You and Mama assisted with meeting and greeting esteemed guests and dispatching them on their way at the end of the evening. In the numerous photos of you doing that, you both look gracious. On the back of one photo, Mama wrote, "I may be smiling, but my feet are killing me!" Did you ever get bored with having to be polite with everyone, including the most tongue-tied or awkward of guests?

Iraqi Premier Abdul Karim el Qasim came to one of the galas. In one photograph of you with him, Qasim, dressed in full uniform, is turning toward the camera and waving on his way out of the embassy. He was shorter and older than you, but his slim frame and dark hair and moustache were not unlike yours. He'd received his officer training in the United Kingdom. I imagine his English would have been pretty good. Did you get to exchange many words, or was he unapproachable?

On July 14, 1962, you were invited to attend the president's military parade to celebrate the Iraqi Day of the Revolution, or the day Qasim came to power. The parades started at 6:00 a.m. and finished by midmorning, by which time the heat would have been unbearable for soldiers and civilians alike. No one knew it at the time, but it was to be Qasim's last annual parade. No amount of military hardware could protect him from a coup.

Reuters News Bulletin (Baghdad)

February 9, 1963

President Qasim was ousted yesterday in a coup led by the Ba'athist Party. He was tried and executed today.

Like the Ustaša in fascist Croatia in the 1940s, the new Iraqi authorities wasted no time on protracted trials, juries, or reporting of proceedings to the public. Death penalties were implemented swiftly and without clemency.

Exiled in neighboring Syria for his historic attempts to assassinate Qasim, a young Ba'athist officer was pleased by the news of his opponent's downfall. He would be able to return to his home country and work his way up the military ranks in Iraq. The officer's name was Saddam Hussein.

Chapter 15

Land of the South Slavs

On the day of the Iraqi coup, we were no longer in Baghdad. You'd finished your four-year tour of duty at the embassy, and we returned to Belgrade.

You had work to do. Yugoslavia's President Tito and his allies Nehru, Sukarno, Nasser, and Nkrumah had founded the Non-Aligned Movement. The five heads of state stood up to both blocs dominating the Cold War. Western capitalism and Soviet communism were not for them. The new alliance would forge its own middle ground. The leaders signed lofty pledges to great fanfare at the launch conference in Belgrade. You joined the team tasked with turning those pledges into reality.

You traveled extensively. Trips to Cairo and New Delhi, then Jakarta and Accra, followed each other in quick succession. Your red passport buzzed with visa stamps. Curved-horn gazelles and golden eagles leaped out of the pages, as if competing for the most flamboyant country crest award.

Mama and I joined you on your first trip to Cairo. A single snapshot of the visit, frozen in time, has remained with me.

> It's a sweltering afternoon. I am drifting in and out of slumber on a museum bench. The faux leather sticks to my bare legs. I hear voices—your baritone mingles with Mama's high-pitched whooping. I raise my head to check what all the fuss is about. You and Mama are standing in front of a glass case, facing each other. You are pointing at a brown, shriveled mummy inside the case. Mama's hands are flapping, her feet tapping the ground rapidly. My head feels heavy with sleep. I turn over and carry on napping.

For you and Mama, the Cairo Museum was full of meaning, a welcome step in your joint pursuit of archaeological nirvana. For me, the suspended moment on the museum bench was an observation, a child's perception of the present, unencumbered by reflection or interpretation. I remember such moments with great clarity, but they are disconnected from each other or to my sense of reality at the time.

Once I started school, Mama and I stayed at home. You brought us presents, weird and wonderful mementos of exotic places far away. I waited eagerly for you to return and that moment when you opened your suitcase. From Indonesia, you brought back a pair of sinuous Balinese dancers, carved out of rain tree wood and polished to a rich chestnut-brown gloss. Mama admired the boneless grace of the carvings, oohing and aahing as you removed them from their newspaper wrappings. Today, their improbably rolled-back spines adorn my living room in London, and I appreciate their beauty as much as you once did. But at the time, I preferred the certificate you received from Qantas for crossing the equator on the airline's famed Kangaroo Route. The captain's signature on the document confirmed you'd been admitted to the order of King Neptune Equatorial Air Voyagers. A colorful cartoon of the sea god embellished the front of the certificate. The king wore a crown of four interwoven sardines and spliced the ocean waves on a gilded fish, brandishing his trident and letting his waist-long white beard flutter in the breeze behind him. For weeks afterward, King Neptune gave me bragging rights in school.

The boasting wasn't confined to the school playground. You, too, were fond of telling everyone about your travels. Your favorite was the story of mistaken identity in Indonesia. You'd been in a delegation led by your head of department for Asia and the Far East. As deputy, you were tasked with briefing him on the program throughout the visit, so you practically never left his side. He was a short, tubby man, and his English wasn't particularly good. You towered above him, as well as most of your other colleagues, so the security detail invariably mistook you for the leader. On the first morning in Jakarta, you emerged from your hotel room to find two armed guards in dress uniform standing at attention on either side of the door. As soon as they saw you, they clicked their heels and saluted. Your boss's room down the corridor had been left without a guard all night.

* * *

Accommodation in Belgrade was hard to come by. The city had been heavily bombed in the 1940s, first by Hitler's Luftwaffe and subsequently, when it was under Nazi occupation, by British and American Air Forces. After the war, the communist government promised a roof over every citizen's head. A building boom followed. High-rise apartment blocks rose like mushrooms on the north bank of River Sava in New Belgrade. But it wasn't enough. Chronic shortages of concrete and other building materials hampered progress. To make things worse, the population tripled in size to more than one million by the mid-1960s, mainly due to the influx of migrants from the countryside.

Seventeen years after the war had ended, there was still a housing shortage in the capital.

You added our family name to the long waiting list for an apartment.

"Families with young children have priority, so hopefully we won't wait too long," you said. "I've applied for an apartment in the center, close to my workplace. I don't relish the long commute to the dormitories of New Belgrade."

Meanwhile, we rented a couple bedrooms from Auntie Mila, a widow whose adult children had left home to work in Germany. Auntie Mila was probably middle-aged, but to my eyes she seemed old, most certainly older than you were at the time. She had a head of prematurely gray hair, cut short and lacquered into a stiff helmet that belied the softness inside. Her warm, rounded midriff was at a perfect height for me to wrap my arms around.

Auntie Mila's house was in a distant suburb of the city, on a cobbled street dating back to the time when Belgrade was part of the Ottoman Empire. Surrounded by a sizeable garden, the building was a single-story longhouse, one room deep and five rooms wide, typical of the style found all over the fertile Pannonian Plain north of the city. The three of us lived at one end of the house. Auntie Mila and another couple tenants occupied the other end. The six of us shared the kitchen and the one bathroom. Our communal living was at variance with the glittering salons of Baghdad, but I never heard you or Mama grumble. For me, as the only child in the house, I felt as if I'd gained two extra moms and an extra dad. I had five adults to fuss over me. A few years later, when we moved away, our cohabitants remained our lifelong friends.

Winters in Belgrade were harsh. The fireplaces provided some respite from the cold, but they needed cleaning and topping up with pine logs every day. The water in the toilet bowl froze overnight during the coldest snaps. The first person up boiled a saucepan of water and poured it down the toilet bowl to melt the ice before anyone could have a pee. And your car was difficult to start in subzero temperatures. On waking, you pulled your heavy overcoat on top of your pajamas, slipped your bare feet into your shoes, and waded through the snow to the car parked on the street. You coaxed the frigid engine into action and let it idle while you got dressed for work. By the time you emerged from the house again, the car was cozy, and you could move off swiftly. On those drives in to work, did your life in the Arabian desert seem like a long-lost mirage?

* * *

At the top of the hill, where our cobbled street ended and the tarmac began, was my first school. When Mama and I trudged up the steep slope to enroll me, the headmistress refused to admit me to the reception class because, at age six, I was considered too young. The nationwide admissions policy dictated children had to be at least seven years old to start school.

"Children younger than seven are not mature enough for school," the headmistress explained. "Forcing them to read and write at such a young age can have serious developmental consequences."

"Utter nonsense!" you fumed when you learned from Mama I couldn't start school yet. The next morning, you asked me to choose two of my favorite books, one in Serbo-Croat and the other in English. We walked up the hill together, hand in hand. You demanded to speak to the headmistress yourself.

"My daughter reads every day," you said and nudged me to start reading aloud from my book. I read a few lines, then looked up at you.

"Is something wrong?"

"Nothing wrong at all," you said. "You've read that beautifully." You turned to the headmistress and said, "Would you like Sibel to read in English now?"

"No, no. That won't be necessary," she blurted out and fidgeted with her fountain pen.

"In the English system, children start school at age five," you said, your back as straight as a rod. "Not only that, but Mrs. Davidson in Sibel's nursery in Baghdad was teaching kids as young as four to read." Your lips were smiling, but your eyes were dead serious.

"But she is reading from the Latin alphabet," the headmistress countered. "Here we teach the Cyrillic alphabet first."

"Well then, it's up to you to teach her Cyrillic, isn't it?" your eyes locked with hers.

She blinked first.

The headmistress allowed me to enroll. She wasn't going to argue with a Freedom Fighter of 1941. Your war record still carried some weight in those days.

* * *

In my first year of school in Belgrade, I became a Pioneer, like all the other children in my class. At a ceremony on the Day of the Republic, we stood erect on the school stage, looking down on an undulating sea of eager faces. Moms and dads, grannies, aunties, brothers, and sisters—they watched us, beaming up their high expectations at us, willing us to make them proud. You and Mama were in the crowd, too. I couldn't see you well, as you were at the back of the hall, but I could feel your acclaim beaming in my direction.

Unlike the ragtag of mismatched skirts, blouses, and jumpers we normally wore to school, our new Pioneer uniform was strictly prescribed. It was for special occasions only. The crisply ironed white shirt, topped with a red neckerchief covering the shoulders and tied at the front in a double knot, was tucked securely into my navy-blue skirt. My cotton socks, in brilliant white, were pulled neatly up to each knobby knee. Unused to wearing any kind of uniform, I fidgeted and scratched at the stiffness of the fabric. At least the patent-leather shoes were comfortable. I could wriggle my toes in them easily. You'd bought them one size too big so I could grow into them.

The part of the uniform I liked best was the navy-blue hat, known as the *Titovka*, with its enameled red-star badge affixed to the front. Modeled on caps worn by the partisans in World War II, it was intended to inspire respect for the brave fighters who liberated our country from fascist rule. The hat reminded me of an overturned boat, like the fisherman's *barka* I found washed up on the white pebble beach in front of Grandma Hana's house in Novi. I remembered spending a summer's day playing around the boat with my cousins, imagining it was a beached pirate's ship full of treasure. Happy memories for sure but perhaps not the sentiment the designers of the hat had hoped to elicit.

Like Brownies or Scouts in the West, we swore an oath of allegiance to the Pioneer movement. The head Pioneer in our school read out the pledge, line by line, and we repeated it after him. I have forgotten the exact words, but they had something to do with working hard in school, respecting our parents and elders, and being loyal to our friends and country. Loyalty struck a chord with me. We were loyal to each other as a family. You were loyal to the party. And best of all, Pioneers got to spend a week every year with their loyal pals in summer camp, away from their parents and the sooty haze of the city.

* * *

You didn't talk about the Jasenovac camp in Belgrade, at least not within my earshot. You didn't write about it, either, with one exception. There was a list, or rather a carbon copy of a list, I found decades later in your files. There were 132 names and addresses on the list, arranged in two columns. In the first column, some names were in full, but many were first names or nicknames, like Blackie, your own nom de guerre from the 1940s. Few of the addresses in the second column were complete. They were mainly names of towns or regions where the individuals came from or where they were thought to be working. You'd compiled the list with a fellow camp survivor, Čedomil Huber, in December 1964.

For many years, I failed to grasp the significance of the mysterious list until I researched the history of the era more thoroughly. You and Čedo compiled the list in response to a nationwide call from the Yugoslav government to establish the number of people who died during World War II with the aim of obtaining reparations from Germany. Nearly twenty years after liberation, former inmates of concentration camps were being asked to remember names of people they knew or met during their incarceration. How did it feel to have the past raked up again? You never said, and now I will never know.

For many months, the authorities sought corroborating evidence for the lists. Mass graves around Jasenovac were excavated; their contents, investigated. Total numbers of victims for the country were eventually calculated, but the final list and the thousands of pieces of evidence collected were not made available for scrutiny by researchers or the public. Your original list is to this day languishing in a locked box somewhere in the Yugoslav archives in Belgrade.

You started writing again in the 1960s but not about the camp. You wrote about the economics of Turkey, Greece, and Iraq, the countries you'd lived and worked in after you left Zagreb. I found the reprints of your published articles many years later, their fawn pages as brittle as autumn leaves. I leafed through them with some trepidation, concerned they might crumble into dust under my clumsy fingers. The earlier articles brimmed with facts and figures intended for a narrow readership of professional economists. The impenetrable jargon reminded me of the turgid writing I went on to produce in volumes during my own career in science. When I completed my PhD, you forced yourself to read my thesis. The title alone, "Growth and Osmoregulation of *Escherichia coli* at Low Water Activity," would have been enough to put off the most devoted parent. But you persevered. Several weeks later, you announced you'd finished reading the weighty tome.

"So, what is Sibel's thesis about?" Mama demanded to know, her left lip and eyebrow curling upward. "Summarize in words of two syllables, please."

You mumbled something about bacteria and how important they were for life on Earth.

"Hah!" Mama snorted. "You didn't understand a word of it, did you?"

"Well, hmmm . . . " you grinned, eyes down. "I understood some of it. Maybe not a lot of it, I am ashamed to admit . . . "

I owed it to you to read your articles. I tried hard to understand. But like you, I struggled with the technical minutiae of a subject I wasn't versed in.

The longer we stayed in Belgrade, the more your writing turned to domestic policy. You published in *Ekonomska Politika*. Despite its title, the periodical was aimed at a wider readership, not only economists and politicians. The language you used was simpler, more recognizable. But your articles no longer bore your name. You'd adopted the pseudonym Petar Sabin. You'd told me the surname was an abbreviation of your mother's first name, Sabina. This made me feel all warm inside. It showed me you were loyal to your mother. In my childish brain, I assumed you wanted to honor your mother in your publications. It didn't occur to me at the time to ask why you didn't publish under your real name. In any case, even if I'd asked, I would probably not have understood the answer.

In your articles on Yugoslav national debt, you raised concerns about the state of the economy. The country was becoming increasingly indebted to foreign creditors. Although exports were rising, imports were soaring at a much higher rate. You'd calculated on the basis of statistics available at the time that the outgoings necessary to service overseas loans would exceed income by 1970 unless improvements in productivity were made. You called for urgent economic reforms, the sort of reforms that could not be proposed using your real name.

You continued to be an active member of the Communist Party, attending meetings regularly and participating in debates. Mama never joined the party but went out with you to vote in regional elections.

You and Mama are about to leave through the front door. You are wearing somber clothes, buttoned up to the neck, faces solemn.

"Where are you going?" I ask.

"We are going to vote," says Mama. "We must do our civic duty."

"In a one-party state, dissent must come from within," you say. I have no idea what you mean.

* * *

At the annual conference of 1965, party members were asked to vote for the new leadership of the central committee. By your own account, a list of names was passed around, but there were no new names on the ballot paper. All the names were those of the existing committee members. You couldn't help yourself. You had to speak out. I can imagine the heat rising up your neck to your face. You raised your hand.

"Comrade Dragan, you have the floor."

"This is totally unacceptable," you said, jabbing your finger at the ballot paper. "According to the rules, the makeup of the committee must be rotated. We cannot appoint the same committee members year in, year out. Voting for the same people now would be undemocratic."

Your plea drew a round of applause from the audience.

But when the counting was done, the same committee members had been elected again—by a majority.

"Scared shitless," you raged when you got home. "Spineless gits, the lot of them!"

Years later, when I recalled your account of this episode, I was reminded of a line in George Orwell's *Animal Farm*: "It had come to be accepted that the pigs, who were manifestly cleverer than the other animals, should decide all questions of farm policy, though their decisions had to be ratified by a majority vote."[1]

At your next annual review at work, your own role was "rotated." You were moved to a new job in the cabinet of Prime Minister Petar Stambolić. It wasn't a demotion, but it was certainly not a promotion, either. Someone in the Foreign Office wanted you out of the way. Did you know who it was, or did you merely suspect? Did the grand new title of secretary for international relations sweeten the bitter pill of your sideways move? Did the award of a two-bedroom apartment in the heart of the city help soften the blow?

I can only imagine the whispers behind closed doors.

Too lippy for his own good.

Arrogant.

Insubordinate.

* * *

We had a new home to look forward to.

The previous occupants had left the ground-floor apartment in Jovanova Street in a dire state. Undeterred, you embarked on a thorough refurbishment project. Mama was ecstatic, but you were pleased, too. You'd lived all your lives in parental homes or rented properties decorated and furnished by someone else. This was the first time you had a chance to arrange your home using your own imagination. In went a fitted kitchen with sliding cabinet doors in shiny red-and-black melamine. Up went new glazing over the balcony to make a "winter garden," as Mama called it. And across the walls of adjoining rooms went a series of striped wallpapers to make a trompe l'oeil, a feature making the apartment appear a good deal bigger than it was. When I returned from Novi that summer, my new bedroom was ablaze in canary yellow, my favorite color. Great-Grandma's bulky single bed, intricately hand-carved out of cherrywood and polished to a high sheen, dominated one end of the room. At the other end, a modern desk by the window awaited the paraphernalia that would come with the new school year.

"Your new school, Pero Popović Aga, is on our road, about three minutes' walk from here," you'd written in a letter to me in Novi that summer. "It's the best school in Belgrade. You will have to work hard to do well there. It won't be a walk-over like your old school, so don't forget to practice your math and writing in between your swims."

There was more good news. Mama started a new job as librarian at a foreign language academy directly opposite my new school. It wasn't her dream job. It didn't have anything to do with art history, but it boosted her self-esteem and provided an extra income for the family. There was much to be pleased about.

* * *

By the summer of 1966, change was in the air.

On July 4, you were invited to the grand opening of the newly constructed commemorative park dedicated to the victims of the Jasenovac camp. The marshy fields where the prisoners' barracks once stood had been transformed into manicured lawns and meandering footpaths. In the center of the park, a giant walk-through monument in the shape of a water lily, mimicking the marshland flora, thrust its concrete petals high up toward the sky.

In black-and-white photos of the event, you wore a light suit and tie. Your shades matched the ebony black of your hair and moustache. Sat next to you was Neđo Bartulović, blond and equally smartly besuited. Around you, others wore farmers' caps and workers' jerkins. On the back of one photo, Neđo wrote, "To comrade Dragan, a sad reminder of the Ustaša torture chamber that was Jasenovac," and on another, "Forever friends, in war and peace." Twenty-one years had passed since your release from the camp.

Two days earlier, the country was rocked by the news that Vice President Aleksandar Ranković had resigned. A staunch opponent of economic reform, he was regarded by many as a possible successor to Tito. But he was also in charge of the secret police and had a reputation for abusing his powers over state surveillance programs. When Tito discovered Ranković had authorized the bugging of the presidential study and bedroom, he was incensed. His second in command had to go. Did the resignation give you hope for the future of the country? Whether it did or not, your personal journey had already changed course. You had an offer of a new job abroad.

A few months later, we left Belgrade for Libya. You were forty-four, Mama was thirty-seven, and I was ten years old. I'd completed four years of primary school and learned to read and write in two alphabets. At home and in school, we spoke Serbo-Croat, the official language in Yugoslavia. As loyal citizens, we went abroad not to emigrate but with the full knowledge we would one day return to the mother country. Our identities were firmly rooted in the land of the South Slavs. We could not imagine being anything other than Yugoslav. We were not to know this could and would change over the years to come.

Chapter 16

The Ghibli

Was Libya another fix, like Iraq, to help you forget your wartime experiences? For as long as we lived in Yugoslavia, the reminders of Jasenovac were inescapable. You were asked to help compile a list of victims. You were invited to the opening of the memorial park. Or was our next move entirely down to professional advancement, following your rotation out of the Foreign Office? I shall never know the answer.

In the fall of 1966, we traded the shrill winds of Belgrade for the southerly Ghibli of Tripoli. The wind usually started when the heat was at its most oppressive, a dry, throat-tickling kind of heat that had us gasping for water all day long. We knew it was on its way when the crisp line of the Saharan horizon blurred, thickening and rising like a giant soufflé in the distance. Clouds of fine sand billowed toward us, at first slowly, then picking up speed and turning into an ochre tsunami. The Ghibli devoured every building, every creature in its path. Visibility dropped to less than a yard. You used to call it the "fog of sand." Driving in the Ghibli was treacherous even in daylight with full headlights switched on. Once submerged in the sepia gloom, the faint orange glow of the sun was the only marker of direction. On the wings of the Ghibli came the scorpions, too groggy from their long flight to cause harm, except once, when our dog Rexy got stung in the paw. You and Mama spent all night fretting over him until he recovered. Mama loathed the Ghibli. It killed her precious morning glory saplings and dredged the furniture with a layer of fine powder, like icing sugar on a cake, sending her scurrying around the house, yellow dust cloth in hand.

Villa Granada, our new home in the Gargaresh District of Tripoli, stood in splendid isolation on an arid plateau overlooking the Mediterranean. Driving west out of the city on the main tarmac road, it was easy to miss the house, its salt-white walls camouflaged against the bleached sand around it. An unmade track led from the main road downhill toward the house. Surrounded by a ten-foot wall and a sturdy black metal gate we were advised to lock every night, the building looked impenetrable at first sight. But the bright blue cassettes of concrete latticework set into the wall at regular intervals softened the look and allowed the sea breeze to cool the garden within. A porthole in the north-facing wall, set at eye level, offered expansive views of the sea horizon, straight as a die, disrupted occasionally by the rusty contours of a solitary oil tanker.

The beach below the house was but a few minutes' walk away and nearly always deserted, but we rarely used it. The scalpel-sharp rocks, long skeins of slimy seaweed, and treacherous undercurrents were sufficiently off-putting even for the most confident of swimmers, which all three of us were. We told ourselves we were lucky. Unlike our friends who lived in the city center, we could enjoy the salty air and the soothing sound of crashing waves every day, interrupted only occasionally by the overhead screech of Libyan jet fighters on their training sorties. Whenever you came back from work, you took a deep breath before stepping indoors.

The house came fully furnished. Years later, I could remember little of what the furniture looked like, except for the Italian suite in your bedroom. It was made of white melamine decorated with extravagant swirls of gilded roses on the outside and a coat of bright fuchsia pink paint on the inside. The double bed faced a dressing table with a triptych of mirrors and was flanked by double wardrobes, each with a pair of full-length mirrors mounted on the doors, facing the bed. Mama took an instant dislike to them.

"When I wake up in the morning, I am forced to look at seven ghastly versions of myself before my first coffee," Mama complained.

"Well, how do you think I feel when I'm forced to look at eight ghastly versions of yourself?" you piped in. "It's much worse for me!"

The school year had already started when we arrived in Libya. We had to make a quick decision about my education. There were one American, one French, and seven Italian schools on offer.

"The American school has a bad reputation," you said. "I've looked at the curriculum for your year, and it's pretty weak, especially in languages and mathematics."

"I don't know about the quality of Italian schools, but Italian is not a world language," Mama added.

"But Italian is so musical," I argued. "When Grandma Hana took me to the opera in Zagreb, the singing was in Italian."

"Maybe learning French would be more useful for Sibel? It's spoken in more countries than Italian," Mama said.

"That's right," you agreed. "Vast swathes of Africa, as well as Europe and Canada, rely on French. And it's the most beautiful language in the world, no doubt about it."

You opened your mouth to start your favorite Edith Piaf song, "*La Vie en Rose*," but Mama, inured to your tone-deaf rendition of it, read your mind and interrupted.

"She'll have to learn more than Piaf's words in French."

"We need to ask, is the French curriculum rigorous enough?"

It was.

I enrolled in the Lycée Français. The teachers, used to expat children getting parachuted in midyear, were not in the least perturbed by the fact I didn't speak a word of French. I wasn't too bothered, either. You'd promised to help. Mama didn't speak French, so it was down to you. In the first month of school, we sat down every evening for a crash course in the most beautiful language in the world.

"French has lots of rules, but once you know them, you can't go wrong," you said. "The letter *G* is pronounced as *G* when it is in front of the letters *a*, *o*, and *u*. Repeat after me: Ga, go, gu."

"Ga, go, gu," I parroted.

"As in *Garçon*, boy; *Gomme*, glue; *Gustation*, tasting."

"As in *Garçon*, *Gomme*, *Gustation*," I repeated.

"And when the *G* is in front of the letters *e*, *i*, and *y*, it is pronounced as a *ž* in Serbo-Croat or *zh* in English. Repeat after me: Ge, gi, gy."

"Ge, gi, gy."

"As in *St. Germain*, a district in Paris; *Girafe*, the animal; *Gymnastique*, the exercise you're not so keen on."

"As in *St. Germain*, *Girafe*, *Gymnastique*."

"Again: Ga, go, gu . . . "

And so it went on. By the end of that term, I was getting by in French. Within three months, I was correcting your French, especially your pronunciation.

And then there was the Arabic. The language learned and unlearned. The rough dialect I'd picked up in Baghdad and forgotten during our four years in Belgrade didn't help much the second time around. This time, the learning required more effort. Like all our lessons at the Lycée Français, the weekly sessions in Arabic were thorough. They included reading and writing, as well as the spoken word. Once again, it didn't stick. Beyond a few basics, like *Salaam Alaikum* and *Inshallah*, my Arabic did not follow me into adulthood.

At home we spoke Serbo-Croat, reinforced every Saturday at the Yugoslav club. There were hundreds of Yugoslavs in Tripoli. You were one of the few economic advisors working directly for the Libyan government. Many others were dentists and ophthalmologists. Libya was oil rich but lacked enough medically trained cadres of its own to set up an effective health-care system. Families of doctors stayed for a few years until their savings allowed them to build a house back home. The expat club had enough critical mass to rent a substantial building and offer supplementary education for all the children.

As the wife of a foreign worker, Mama was not allowed to hold down a full-time job, but a part-time post teaching Yugoslav history was exempt from the prohibition. There was a social club, too, and a program of events that included a live band and dancing. You and Mama were always the first on the dance floor, replacing the "tanba" you'd invented in Baghdad with multiple variations on the twist.

Were your memories of Jasenovac finally consigned to a distant past in Libya?

* * *

On the morning of January 1, 1967, when we were still in our pajamas after a New Year's Eve gala at the club, the front doorbell rang. We opened the door to a young shepherd in an ankle-length tunic and a headcloth weighted with rope. He was holding a hessian sack. The bag moved, and every time it did so, it released a cacophony of high-pitched squealing. The three of us stood in the doorway, gawping at the wriggling sack. He smiled, lowered the bag delicately on the floor, and opened it to reveal a mass of chocolate-brown puppies. They squirmed and clambered over each other, falling over on their backs and waving their pink pads in the air. The boy said something in Arabic, lifted one of the puppies out of the pile, and thrust it into my arms.

"Aww, he's so cute!" I said, cuddling the ball of brown fluff in my embrace.

"Wait! We can't take on a puppy," Mama said, averting her eyes. "We don't know how long we'll be here. We had to give Laika away in Baghdad. I don't want to go through that trauma again."

"Well, this is no Gordon setter, that's for sure," you said, your face beaming as you reached out to stroke the fur ball in my arms.

"No. I can see that," said Mama. "More like potpourri of Tripoli!"

"Coochee coochee coo," you tickled the puppy under his chin. "Mixed breeds are so much healthier." The puppy yawned, then licked your fingers with his tiny pink tongue, provoking an "ooh" and an "aah" from you.

We were hooked. It was two against one. Mama was right, but she didn't stand a chance.

We named him Rexy.

* * *

June 1967. You are at work. Mama is in the kitchen, clattering away with pots and pans. I am in my bedroom reading, Rexy at my feet. There is a loud crack outside, like someone popping an inflated paper bag. Then another and another in quick succession. Rexy dives under my bed. I walk over to the window and look out in the direction of the city center. A thin ribbon of smoke undulates toward the sky like a snake charmed out of its basket. Mama crashes into my bedroom, grabs me by the arm, and pulls me away from the window toward the bed.

"Move away!" she screams, ashen faced.

"Aw! That hurts!" I glare at Mama.

The force of her pull is so powerful, we lose our footing and fall on top of the bed. Rexy whimpers underneath. Mama's hand is still clamped on my arm.

"What's the matter, Mama? It's firecrackers."

"Not firecrackers!" she breathes heavily against my face. "Guns! Stay away from the window!"

"OK, OK, I will!"

Mama lets go of me. She creeps up to the side of the window and lowers the blind. Her hands are shaking.

"They're getting closer. Don't move. And don't let the dog out. I'll go and lock all the doors."

The gunshots stop. Mama returns and sits with me on the bed. Rexy shivers even though it's not cold.

"Some guard dog he's turned out to be, eh?" I said, still not fully comprehending what was going on outside.

"It's better this way. We don't want him attracting attention." Mama is calmer now. We sit in semidarkness and wait for you to come home from work.

When you came home that evening, you were reassuring. There'd been no trouble on the main roads from your office. Israel's victory against an Arab coalition in the Six-Day War and its occupation of substantial swathes of territory in Egypt, Syria, and Jordan had triggered riots in the city center. Enraged crowds targeted mainly Western businesses. There was damage to property in the main shopping district but no casualties. The protests fizzled out before reaching the suburbs. Mama was relieved. She'd been a young teenager during World War II. She knew what real gunfire sounded like. I remained oblivious to the potential danger we'd faced. Without a phone in the house and no immediate neighbors, we had no means of calling for help. Mama's strategy of lying low and stilling the dog had been our only option. Like you, she was a survivor.

A few months later, you discovered your American colleagues at work were paid three times as much as you were. You made further inquiries. British economists were getting paid double the amount of your salary. You were incensed. Why did the Brits put up with this? Why did the Yugoslavs put up with it? You queried the discrepancy with your Libyan employers. They had no satisfactory explanation. You looked around for another job. A friend told you the United Nations was recruiting development economists for Uganda. They paid everyone with similar qualifications and experience equally, irrespective of nationality.

In your letter of resignation, addressed to his excellency the minister of industry, you gave a month's notice of your intention to leave and requested politely that you be paid pro rata for the accumulated annual leave. The minister was not happy. He wanted you to work the remaining six months of the contract. We prepared to leave anyway. The outstanding holiday allowance was never paid.

"I wonder how long King Idris will last," you said as we packed our bags. "Western-backed monarchies don't survive in these countries. Look what happened in Iraq."

Not long after we left, a young colonel seized power while the king was conveniently out of the country. The new military head abolished the monarchy and proclaimed Libya a republic. No one was sure how old the newcomer was. He came from a poor family of goat and camel herders. As illiterate Bedouins, they did not keep birth records. The colonel's name was Muammar Gaddafi.

You'd survived Jasenovac and avoided a disastrous regime change in Iraq and now in Libya. Was it coincidence, or was there a pattern emerging? You were a survivor.

Chapter 17

Paradise

Uganda in the late 1960s, filtered through the rose-colored glasses of my adolescence, was our Garden of Eden. Cobalt skies and leafy greens never gave way to the misty grays of autumn. In the land of perpetual spring, hibiscus bushes flowered daily in flushes of pink and magenta. Candy-sweet scents of frangipani blew in on gentle breezes. And the people were friendly, easygoing folk. Years later, when I read V. S. Naipaul's *In a Free State* and Joseph Conrad's *Heart of Darkness*, their gloomy visions of Africa held no resonance in my memories.[1] If there was poverty, I did not see it; if there was misery, I did not feel it.

On our first flight from Zagreb to Entebbe, you and Mama could barely contain your excitement. We were heading to a country no family member, friend, or acquaintance had ever visited. During our stopover in Rome, you bought a new 35mm camera in the duty-free shop.

"It's expensive, but it will be worth every Italian lira, you'll see," you said, your voice bristling with anticipation.

"We'll be living on the equator," said Mama. As was her habit, she'd read up as much as possible about our new destination in advance. "But it won't be hot like in Libya because Entebbe is at an altitude of 4,000 feet."

"They have the big five in Uganda: elephant, rhino, lion, buffalo, and leopard," you said, turning toward me.

"Why do they call them the big five? Other animals, like giraffes and hippos, are big, too."

"It's something to do with hunting and how difficult these animals are to shoot. I guess a hippo wouldn't have a sporting chance of escaping."

"You're not going hunting, Tata?" I said, my voice rising an octave. You'd always been an animal lover. I couldn't imagine you hurting a living being.

"No, no! Don't worry! I wouldn't do that! We'll be shooting with our new camera, not guns."

True to your word, you went on to take dozens of snaps of wildlife, many in black-and-white, a few in color. You allowed me to use the camera occasionally, too, especially when we were home, where I was less likely to drop it than on safari. In one photo, you are sitting on our couch with your arm around Mama, both of you beaming at the lens pointing at you. You are wearing a white linen shirt and loose khaki slacks, while Mama dons a sleeveless floral house dress. Her bouffant hairdo is teased into a perfect halo around her head. On the back of the photo, you wrote, "Family idyll in Entebbe." You were happy in Uganda. You often said so. Had you finally left your wartime memories behind?

The climate in Entebbe was never too hot or too cold. Summer cottons filled our wardrobes. A jacket was rarely needed. In the dry season, it rained twice per week; in the wet season, it deluged every day. But even in the wet season, there was always a morning or an afternoon dry enough to go swimming at one of the two pools in Entebbe. Lake Victoria was off-limits. Dangers lurked, big and small, from the occasional hungry crocodile looking for a meal to the tiny bilharzia parasite waiting to jump ship from freshwater snails to humans. I was annoyed with you for not letting me join the local children frolicking on the lakeside beach. I often sat watching them with envy from a nearby hill. It wasn't until many years later, when I enrolled in a parasitology class at Johns Hopkins, that I learned how debilitating bilharzia could be. The kids' distended bellies were not caused by an oversized lunch.

The bigger of the two pools in Entebbe was at the Lake Victoria Hotel, a sprawling double-story brick building with a red-tiled roof set in several acres of lush tropical gardens. The central courtyard of the hotel was laid to lawn, with elephant grass cropped methodically by a family of tortoises. The fine, downy turf of an English garden would not have survived here. Mildew and a multitude of insects would have put an end to it in a matter of days. We lived at the hotel for the first month in Uganda, while you and Mama searched for a suitable home to rent.

"Would you like a four-bedroom house with a half-acre of garden or a two-bedroom apartment with a terrace and maintained grounds?" you asked Mama.

"We don't need so many bedrooms," Mama said. "We won't have any visitors from Europe, like we did in Baghdad and Tripoli. It's too far and too expensive to get here. Two bedrooms are enough."

Mama didn't want a large garden, either. Her futile attempts to grow roses in the Iraqi desert and morning glory on Libyan sand dunes had exhausted her gardening ambitions. A few potted plants would be enough to satisfy what remained of her land-tilling instincts.

Our home was on the ground floor of a two-story rectangular block on Kampala Road. The unmarked tarmac roadway, cuffed by strips of earth the color of burnt sienna, meandered gently up the hill from the lake's edge, where the airport was, to the center of town and on to the capital, Kampala.

Our building was whitewashed and flanked on either side with garages, where you parked your white Peugeot 404 at the end of each working day. Beneath the living room and bedroom windows, all facing the front, neat rows of amaryllis and canna flowered in blood-red and orange profusion all year long. The approach to the glazed front door was via a tiled patio where we once found a green mamba basking in the morning sun.

The apartment came fully furnished with cream-colored walls throughout. Undaunted by the bland décor, it did not take long for you and Mama to personalize the space. The prized Qum and Kashan rugs you haggled over in Baghdad got pride of place in the middle of the room, softening the polished concrete floor underneath. Bright, mass-produced table covers with a geometric motif hid the gouges and scratches left behind by the children of previous tenants. And everywhere there were ashtrays made of brass, glass, crystal, and ceramic.

You and Mama chain-smoked your way through the day, lighting every fresh cigarette with the tail end of the previous one. The two forefingers of your right hand were stained ochre yellow. This didn't bother you until the Yugoslav ambassador's doe-eyed daughter questioned you about them with a look of disgust on her face. Piqued, you decided to do something about it. You persuaded Mama her yellowing teeth were as revolting as your discolored fingers and you both ought to stop smoking. She agreed. The ashtrays were banished to the cupboard under the bar. Mama lasted about a week, resorting to lighting up in the toilet when you were not around. But even with the window open, the smallest room in the apartment reeked of stale tobacco, and tell-tale butts floated in the toilet bowl, resolutely refusing to be flushed down. You lost your temper. You shouted and mocked her. She shouted back, accusing you of getting her hooked on cigarettes in the first place. I sat in my bedroom with my hands over my ears until the storm blew over. A month down the line, you gave up, too. The ashtrays came out again.

* * *

There was only one school in Entebbe at the time: the English-speaking Lake Victoria School. A Lycée Français did not exist, not even in Kampala, twenty-five miles away. My francophone education ended abruptly. The new school wasn't the baptism of fire the French school in Libya had been. I'd learned some English at school in Belgrade, so I didn't start off as a tabula rasa. But the English way of doing long division was different from the method used in continental Europe. It slowed me down in the math test I had to take before admission to the school. When I was told I'd have to join the class below my year, I burst into tears.

"Don't worry," you said when you came home that evening. "We can prac-tice math at home, and you will soon catch up." For the next two months, you gave me division exercises to do every evening for twenty minutes before dinner. You relished our sessions together. You wrote out the exercises on two sheets of paper. You worked on one sheet, and I worked on the other. You always finished first, lit a cigarette, and hummed "Ochi Charnye."

"Nothing easier than math," you said, your face beaming. "The answer is either right or wrong. No maybes. No ifs, no buts, no gray areas. Nothing to argue over."

I groaned and moaned, but the sessions worked. The following term, I was moved up a class.

But there was another problem. The English school did not offer French as a subject. Concerned about forgetting my French, you made inquiries about private lessons. Sister Marie-Berthe Robillard, a French nun at the Catholic Sisters of Mary convent in Entebbe, came highly recommended.

My French lessons took place once a week on a bench in the pineapple garden of the convent. Sister Marie-Berthe wore her pale gray habit wrapped tightly around her tulip-shaped face, accentuating her sky-blue eyes, which invariably lit up on my arrival. We always addressed each other with the polite *vous*, never the more familiar *tu*.

Each week, Sister Marie-Berthe introduced a new biblical theme: Noah's ark, the parting of the Red Sea by Moses, or Jesus walking on water. She encouraged me to borrow her colored storybooks to read at home. It did not strike me as odd at the time that the daughter of a Communist Party mem-ber was receiving Bible lessons from a nun. But our friends in the Yugoslav embassy noticed.

"Hey, Dragan, I hear you're letting a Catholic nun teach Sibel French. Aren't you worried she'll indoctrinate her with religious mumbo jumbo?"

"Well, I think it's important to maintain her French," you said. "A brain is like a wet sponge. If you don't keep topping it up with water, it dries out quickly. She's forgotten her Arabic twice already. It would be a shame if she lost her French, too."

"Yes, but the nun could be filling her head with all sorts of nonsense about Heaven and Hell. She may turn your daughter into a God squaddie."

"I don't think that will happen. Scenes and characters from the Bible fea-ture in great literature. It will do her no harm to know about them. References to David and Goliath, for example, make no sense if you don't know the background to their story. It's all part of a good education."

"Art, too," Mama piped in. "So many paintings and sculptures have bibli-cal themes. And music—often inspired by faith. Bible stories are part of our civilization and culture, whether you believe in them or not."

"Be careful. Ask Sibel if Sister Marie-Berthe has told her about deathbed confessions."

She had. She told me it was possible for nonbelievers to ask God for forgiveness on the point of death. The Almighty was magnanimous. People who recognized God on their deathbeds were forgiven and went to Heaven.

You asked me what I thought about this.

"How is it that you can spend your life not believing in God, doing as you please, not going to church, not doing what the scriptures tell you to do, and then when you are about to die, you turn around and say, 'Please, God, I'm sorry I didn't believe in you earlier. I've changed my mind. Please let me into your Heaven.' Isn't that a bit dishonest?"

You didn't answer straight away. You sat and nodded.

"You know, when I was in the Jasenovac camp, I looked after sick people in the hospital there," you said. "When they didn't look like they were going to get better, we asked them what their last wish was and tried to fulfill it. We offered what we could: a cigarette or a bowl of soup or a priest, if they were religious. My dying Catholic friend did not want a priest. Nor did he pray to God. He asked for walnuts. For two days, he kept asking for walnuts. But we didn't have any to give him."

"That's so sad, Tata. All he wanted was a few walnuts."

"Yes, walnuts. We couldn't fulfill a dying man's last wish," you said, your mouth curving downward. "But let's not talk about that. Tell me how your school day went today." For a fleeting moment, your wartime memories had bubbled up, but you were not about to let them disrupt our African idyll.

The French lessons with Sister Marie-Berthe continued uninterrupted. Years later, after I'd moved to Vienna and then New York, Sister Marie-Berthe continued to write, always in impeccable French. *Trop heureuse de votre jolie carte et de votre bon petit mot . . .* She always inquired about my *chers parents* and wanted to know what subjects I was studying. Her last letter came from a convent in Paris, where she'd moved in 1972 after Idi Amin changed Uganda forever.

* * *

Like all expatriate and many better-off local families in Uganda, we employed a houseboy, David. Larger families often had teams of servants: *ayahs* to look after the babies and toddlers, houseboys to cook and clean, gardeners to keep the teeming vegetation in check. I couldn't understand why he was called a boy when he looked older than you, then in your midforties. Maybe the network of decorative ruts in the Kikuyu tradition crisscrossing David's broad face made him look older? He'd left his extended family in his village in Kenya to find work in Uganda.

We were never sure how many children David had. We guessed he probably didn't know, either. When you asked him about the size of his family, he shrugged his shoulders and said, "No matter, Bwana. All chil'ren welcome." And after every visit to his home village, he reported on the latest new arrival, another son or a daughter, smiling broadly.

On the first morning in our household, David came into our dining room wearing a starched bleach-white jacket buttoned up to his chin over a pair of neatly ironed black trousers.

"Would you like some eggs?" he asked us all. Mama and I declined.

"Yes, please, David. Two please," you said.

"How would you like them done, Bwana?

"Scrambled, please, David."

"Certainly, Bwana Mkubwa," said David.

A little later, David came back carrying a prewarmed plate piled high with mounds of milky white clouds, dotted with specks of yellow.

"These look a bit strange," you said. "They are pale. Maybe the eggs had tiny yolks?"

You raised a tentative forkful to your lips.

"The texture is odd, as if the whites have been whipped separately. More like blancmange than scrambled egg," you said.

Mama and I picked up our forks and tasted the eggs for ourselves.

"I think he's added milk to the mixture," Mama said. "I'll have to watch him when he makes the eggs next time."

"Yes, please, Vesna. And please show him how to make scrambled eggs properly. A little finely chopped onion or bacon would be lovely. Definitely no milk. I am not an infant."

David's cookery training by his former English employer was wasted on us. Mama spent the next month teaching him the cuisine of Mittel Europa. All our favorites were on the menu: chicken paprika, schnitzels and dumplings, boiled tongue, and a roasted pepper salad seasoned with olive oil, vinegar, and finely chopped garlic. Our meals often started with soup made from scratch with a chicken carcass or chunky beef bones. We picked the marrow out of the bones, spread it on thick slices of crusty bread, and sprinkled it liberally with salt and pepper. And after we left Uganda, David had to go through the cycle again. Only this time, he had to master Japanese cooking, the preferred cuisine of his new employer, Professor Hashimoto and his family.

The learning wasn't one-way. We learned from David, too. Mr. Patel's Aladdin's cave of a grocery shop wasn't good enough for David. He tolerated it when Mama bought Lux soap, Pond's cold cream, or cans of Carnation condensed milk from there. Mr. Patel's fresh fruit and vegetables bore the brunt of David's scorn. When he saw our first batch of bananas, David smirked and spat out a torrent of words in Swahili.

"This no good, Memsaab. No fresh. David bring fresh."

He disappeared into the neighboring village and returned bearing a sheaf of bananas on his shoulder. He lowered the bundle and turned it so we could see the stem where the plant had been cut with a machete minutes earlier. A milky white fluid oozed from the gash.

"This fresh!" said David, pointing at the cut.

When in season, David brought us mangos and papaya, guava and custard fruit, dripping with sweet, mellow juices. He showed Mama how to cook matoke, sliced and gently fried in a little chili oil or simmered in a well-seasoned goat-meat stew. And he dealt with the snakes, too. If one happened to make an appearance on the footpath or terrace, David brought a thick stick he stored in his room and incapacitated the serpent with one powerful whack on the head. Sometimes he disposed of the limp body in the ditch by the road. At other times, he took it to the servants' quarters. We did not ask him for the recipe.

Not long after David joined us, you noticed he had a persistent dry hack.

"What's wrong, David? Your cough seems to be going on and on." you said.

"Nothing, Bwana. David good."

"You should see a doctor, David."

"No, no. David good."

After a few weeks of this, you insisted on driving David to the doctor. David reluctantly agreed. Always eager to hitch a ride in our white Peugeot, I went along with you. We waited for David at the clinic, but when he finally emerged from the lengthy consultation, he looked crestfallen. You demanded to know what was wrong.

"It white disease, Bwana. You fire David now, Bwana?"

"What white disease? Oh, you mean TB? Of course, I won't fire you. What nonsense! Did the doctor give you a prescription?"

"Yes but medicine expensive, Bwana."

"Never mind that! Give it here!" you said. "I'll pay for it. We'll pick it up from the pharmacy on the way home."

David did get better, but his illness remained chronic and required lifelong treatment. When David went to Professor Hashimoto, you forewarned his new employer about the illness, but the good professor wasn't fazed. He continued to pay for the medicines David needed.

* * *

Unlike some of the more established safari parks in Uganda, the Kidepo Valley National Park lacked a lodge to stay in. Our friends the McCourts suggested we explore it together and offered to share their camping equipment with us.

We drove northeast from Entebbe in a convoy of three cars. Brick and concrete housing gave way to mud rondavels roofed with bamboo canes and grass. Beneath the tires, red earth jagged with ruts made by rainstorms replaced the asphalt of the main road. Large lorries ahead of us swayed and rocked, avoiding the deeper potholes and sometimes stopping altogether. Progress was slow.

Kidepo was in the lowlands of Karamoja, near the border with Sudan. Savannah scrublands stretched for miles in an ocher-yellow haze, peppered with thorny acacia and baobab. The crowns of these colossal trees were almost entirely devoid of leaves, as if a playful giant had turned them upside down, revealing their roots to the skies. Dark, lean warriors herded their scrawny cattle across the parched land. The men wore capes made of antelope skins across their shoulders and nothing else. Some carried a diminutive wooden stool wrapped around their forearms with a leather skein. Others bore metal shields and spears.

Four punctures, two wrecked mufflers, and one leaking fuel tank later, we arrived at the camp in Karamoja. The men set up the tents; the women lit a fire to prepare dinner. A park ranger arrived to brief us on safety.

"Bananas must not be kept in the open or in the tents," he said. "You must wrap them in several layers of newspaper and canvas and lock them in the boot of a car. Better still, eat them up before nightfall. Monkeys love them, and elephants simply adore them. They will smash into a tent if they can smell a banana in it."

That night, we sat around the campfire and watched comets falling out of the black African sky. Pairs of eyes circled around us as the fire dwindled to a red glow. After we retired to our tents for the night, we listened to hippos munching away nearby. Later you told me with a gleam in your eye that an elephant had visited while I was asleep. It passed by our tent, lifting its feet like a ballerina to avoid the pegs and guide ropes, and swished its trunk along the canvas roof, sniffing for bananas. You were awestruck by the agility the African elephant demonstrated to you that night.

The following morning, we woke to a sweet smell of vanilla. Mrs. McCourt stirred something in a cauldron over the campfire. The others stood around her, mugs of coffee in hand, chatting. I ran up and looked inside the pot. A gray mass gurgled and popped like a volcanic mud pool on a photo in the *National Geographic* magazine.

"What is this, Tata?" I asked you. "It looks like the pot of glue we use for our craftwork in school."

"I have no idea," you said. "It reminds me of the *pura* they fed camp inmates with. Only thicker. And it smells nicer."

In the middle of the African savanna, your memories occasionally crept up on you. A throwaway comment, the mention of *pura*. A word you used in your secret manuscript. A word that I puzzled over a half-century later.

"It's called porridge," said Mrs. McCourt, amused by our perplexed faces. "Try it!"

She doled out ladlefuls of the steaming mass into bowls and topped them with slices of fresh papaya. You declined the porridge, politely, but you asked for double portions of papaya.

* * *

I come home from school. You are sitting in your armchair with your back to the window. You are not usually home before me. The bright backdrop makes it difficult to see your features clearly. Your face is in shadow.

I come up closer to give you a hug. You are silent. You return my hug, but your eyes are full of sorrow.

Alarmed, I run to the kitchen, where Mama and David are preparing dinner.

"What's wrong with Tata? Is he ill?"

Mama turns toward me, face solemn.

"We've had a telegram from Zagreb today. It's bad news. Grandad Dragutin has died."

"What happens now? Do we fly home for the funeral?"

"No. There's no point. The funeral is tomorrow and the next flight to Europe isn't until next week. And it's fully booked anyway. We've checked."

"What should I do, Mama?" my voice quivered. "Tata is sad."

"Go give him a big hug and sit next to him."

I return to the salon and put my arms around you. "Don't cry, Daddy." Your eyes glisten, but you don't cry.

It would be another thirty years before I saw you this sad again, not for the loss of a relative, but for a memory snapshot from Jasenovac.

Figure 17.1.   Dragan in Entebbe botanical gardens, 1970.

Chapter 18

Paradise Lost

There were no secondary schools in Entebbe in 1969. Kampala had several, but the city was an hour's drive away by car. The basic tarmac road was pockmarked with potholes resembling the footprints of a giant mastodon. Maintenance crews could not keep up. A profusion of tin-roofed bars along the roadside offered *waragi*, brewed and home-distilled from cassava, to passing motorists. Their hallmark colors, yellow and green, painted in horizontal stripes across the facades, brightened the journey but cast doubt on the sobriety of the drivers. The last straw came for you when you had a head-on collision with another car overtaking a lorry traveling in the opposite direction. Catapulted through the windshield onto the grass median, you woke up concussed in hospital. No one died in the accident, but all three vehicles were insurance write-offs. The Volvo Estate, which you'd borrowed from the Ministry of Planning while our Peugeot was being serviced, was least damaged. The solid steel mainframe of the vehicle saved your life, as you were fond of pointing out. From then on, you praised the wonders of Swedish engineering to anyone willing to listen.

A daily commute to school in Kampala for your daughter was a risk too big to contemplate. It would have to be a boarding school. I agreed. A school in Zagreb was not an option. Grandma Hana had her hands full looking after Grandad, who'd suffered a series of debilitating strokes. Perhaps more importantly, I wanted to go to a "proper" boarding school in Europe. I had an inkling teenagers had more fun there. They listened to the latest pop songs on the radio, wore the coolest outfits, and danced their nights away at rock concerts. On the verge of turning thirteen, I wanted to join them.

For the first few weeks of that year, large envelopes stuffed with thick brochures arrived from Swiss and English boarding schools, crushing all the other letters in our post box. We sat around our coffee table and looked at all of them together, deliberating the pros and cons of each one.

"Grandma Hana went to a Swiss boarding school for a year when she was about your age, Sibel," Mama said. "She made many new friends there."

"I've been told some of these Swiss establishments are finishing schools for daughters of oil barons and movie stars," you said. "They teach their girls to become good hostesses, in several languages of course, and to know the difference between solid and plated silver, but they don't provide a good education. And they are eye-wateringly expensive."

"Ok, so what about Headington School in Oxford?" Mama said. "Dina's chemist friend who works at the university there says the school is academically rigorous."

"Doesn't it drizzle all the time in England?" I queried.

My question remained unanswered. Neither of you had ever visited Britain.

"Can't I go to an English school somewhere near Yugoslavia? That way, I could spend Christmas and Easter with Grandma Hana in Zagreb and the summer holidays in Novi?" I was taller than Mama, but I was still, in many ways, a child. Grandma Hana let me lick her mixing bowls with my fingers after she tipped her cake mixtures into a tin. Mama never baked cakes. You didn't like them, and she was always watching her figure.

"And if it's close enough, maybe Auntie Dina and Uncle Kegla can come and visit me there between the school holidays," I added.

You fetched a map of Europe and spread it out on the coffee table. I brought my ruler from my bedroom, and we measured the distances from major cities to Zagreb.

"Vienna looks the closest as the crow flies," I said.

"There are good rail connections between Vienna and Zagreb. I believe you can travel overnight by wagon-lit," you said.

"Can you find out if there is an English school in Vienna?"

There was.

* * *

Mama and I spent much of August 1969 getting ready for our long sojourn to Europe. I had a place at the English School Vienna on Grinzingerstraße, in the hilly nineteenth Bezirk of the city. The German-speaking boardinghouse where I would live was about ten minutes' walk from the school. The boarding headmistress, Frau Dr. Paula Popp, or Poppina as we rechristened her, had requested that we embroider the number 11 on all my items of clothing, including socks, tights, and underwear. We procrastinated until the week before we were due to travel.

"It's now or never," Mama said sternly. "Let's get down to it."

We piled the mountain of clothing on the coffee table in front of us and attempted to get on with the stitching.

"Aw! I've pricked myself," I yelped and sucked a droplet of blood off my middle finger. There was no sympathy coming from Mama. Her fingers were already pockmarked with red spots. And you weren't much help, either. You'd never sewn a stitch in your life, and besides, it was not the manly thing to do. Your chunky fingers would have struggled with a needle and thread.

You made yourself an instant coffee, black, no sugar, and sat down to watch us work. You complained there was no room on the coffee table for your cup. We snapped back. You sighed.

"Come on, girls. Let's keep calm. When you've finished, we can all go to the pool to cool off," you said. You sat with us, drinking your coffee, not reading, watching us, not smiling. It did not occur to me at the time you were dreading our imminent departure. You were staying in Entebbe. You had to work. We were flying off into the blue skies above. We would not see each other again until the Christmas holidays, when the family would regroup in Zagreb. Mama would return with you to Uganda in the New Year. I would not return until the following summer. Yet all I could think of was the adventure ahead of me. I spared no thought for your feelings.

* * *

"*Grüß Gott! Willkommen in Wien*! Greetings! Welcome to Vienna," said Poppina as she opened the door to us. Within minutes, she thrust a postcard from you into my hands. It was the first of many that fall. You wrote two or three times a week. Your letters were always upbeat. You were not one to complain. There was never a hint of sadness in them.

September 15, 1969

Dear Sibel

I was thrilled to get your first letter today. I've heard about the famous Prater, and I'm glad you enjoyed riding on the Ferris wheel.

I'm pleased you've made new friends already, especially the Yugoslavs in your school and boardinghouse. You see, we Jugovićs get everywhere! The boy who was worried he'd have to translate everything for you made me laugh. How sweet! He must have had some bad experiences in the past with other kids who didn't speak English. Let me know the surnames of your Yugoslav friends. I might know their dads if they work in the embassy.

You'll have to get used to living in a boardinghouse now. When I was eleven, I went to a boarding school in Slavonia for a short while. I lived in a convent with six hundred boys, not like your home of fifty girls. Mine was a more modest school than yours, and the food was terrible. But now, looking back, I realize they were happy days. Of course, boys will be boys. We were constantly fighting each other. I hope you don't have to fight in your boarding school, but you never know. If somebody hits you, hit them back.

Your friend Seka keeps asking about you. She's complained she's had just one postcard from you. Do write to her if you haven't already.

All is well over here. It's been raining a lot, but the swarms of flies pestering us before you left have disappeared. That's until the next wave completes its incubation period . . .

Now you're back in school, it's time to knuckle down to work. If you study hard, maybe you can skip a year? Practice your French whenever possible. Your new friends from Canada and Thailand may speak French.

How are you getting on with the German? It's not difficult, is it? Many words are not dissimilar to English. Reading German is easier than English, which seems to follow no rules.

Lots of love,
Tata

Many years later, on rereading this letter, your advice to hit people if they hit me gave me a jolt. I'd never seen you use violence against anyone. Perhaps you wanted me to stand up for myself and not let my peers push me around. We didn't fight physically in Vienna, but we bickered plenty. Sometimes, relations got so acrimonious that we had to be reshuffled into different bedrooms to avoid World War III breaking out. We became experts at standing up for ourselves.

"It's been exactly one month since the two of you left and a fortnight since you've arrived in Vienna," you wrote in another letter a week later. You were counting the days you'd been on your own. At the time, I did not appreciate how much you missed us. And my friend Seka wrote, too. Her first aerogram had something to say about you.

URGANT [sic]

To: Sibel Roller
Mittelschülerinnenheim
Hohe Warte 46
A-1190 Wien
Austria
Europa

Kampala, September 17, 1969

Dear Sibel!

I got your letter. I have to say your address is impossible. What's with the Mitttelssshhh . . . ? Why must this name be so long? It's taken me ages to write it out.

How are you? I'm enjoying life. It's not bad here, but as usual, there's nothing to do. I bet you have lots of fun in your boarding school. Have you made new friends yet?

I've been to see Where Eagles Dare *with Clint Eastwood and Richard Burton. They were supposed to rescue someone from imprisonment in a German castle. There was lots of shooting. So loud!*

I'll tell you something funny but true. The week after you left, your dad fell fully clothed into the swimming pool. But don't tell him I've told you this. He asked me not to tell you or your Mama.

I heard you've had to get your new bell-bottoms dry-cleaned after you spilled tomato sauce on them. Send me a drawing of your bell-bottoms. I don't want some rough sketch, though. A proper picture. Use your colored pencils. And no tomato stain, please!

Did you know that Paul McCartney died a few years ago? The photos on the new Beatles LP covers are of his double. I think the double looks like the real Paul. There is a telephone number on the Magical Mystery Tour *cover, but you can only see it if you look at the album in a mirror.*

I'd like a quick reply. Chop, chop! Get writing!

Lots of love,
Seka

Seka never could keep a secret. The whiskey sodas must have got the better of you when you fell into the pool. I wanted to know how you got home dripping wet, but I couldn't ask you without betraying Seka's confidence.

* * *

By January 1970, you and Mama were back in Uganda. You had a state visit to get excited about. Yugoslav President Josip Broz Tito was on a month's tour of Africa promoting the Non-Aligned Movement, which he'd cofounded to give smaller nations a voice against the bully boys of NATO and the Warsaw Pact. But there was a snag. There'd been an assassination attempt on Uganda's President Milton Obote in December. The bullet had penetrated Obote's tongue and dislodged two teeth. He was finding it difficult to speak. There would be no point in Tito meeting Obote if they couldn't talk. To your dismay, the visit was canceled.

A few days later, the event was back on. There would be no pomp and ceremony, as Obote's health was still fragile. Instead, Tito would make a brief stopover in Entebbe on his way from Kenya to Sudan. The two statesmen would spend a few hours together in the State House in Entebbe. You were elated again.

Years later, long after you passed away, I found a clip of Tito's visit to Uganda in the British Pathé archives. I watched it with bated breath. Would I recognize any faces in it? Would I see you?

Friday, February 22, 1970. The camera pans across the welcoming crowd, standing in rows on the tarmac in front of the whitewashed airport terminal in Entebbe. A guard in a short-sleeved khaki uniform, seemingly unarmed, watches the crowd. Security was so much more relaxed in those days, despite the attempt on the president's life.

In the next frame, Milton Obote stands at the head of the crowd, looking slender in his dark, open-necked shirt. His gold watch gleams in the sun. Next to him, his wife, Miria, is in a figure-hugging sleeveless ensemble in red and black, sporting a tall black turban, red clutch bag, and matching gloves. Behind them, two rows of Ugandan dignitaries and politicians, then a row of Europeans, crane their necks. And yes, there you are, head above the rest. No need for you to crane your neck. Silvery strands on either side of your temples accentuate your black hair and moustache. You are looking intently straight ahead of you, your mouth upturned in a demismile. Familiar faces mill around you, our Yugoslav friends, the ambassador and his wife.

Next, Tito and his wife, Jovanka, descend the front staircase past the red-white-and-blue insignia of the Yugoslav Airlines plane, twin propellers jutting out from the wing. Tito is in a formal dark suit and delicately rimmed glasses; Jovanka, in a dusky pink two-piece and a matching pillbox hat in sharp contrast with her obsidian-black hair. They sport the tubbiness of people who enjoy their food. They smile expansively. Obote and Miria greet them at the foot of the stairs. The foursome face each other in a circle. Beyond the ring of Ugandan hosts surrounding them, cameras raised high on besuited arms click away.

Two children, a boy and a girl, both blond and wearing red Pioneer scarves, approach Jovanka to hand over bouquets of flowers. The hosts line up to shake the visitors' hands, first the civilians, then the military. The chief of the Ugandan Army, Idi Amin, a former heavyweight boxing champion, towers above his compatriots.

The clip jumps from the airport to the State House in Entebbe, showing Tito and Obote sitting together on a couch. Tito waves his favorite Cuban cigar, a gift from his friend Fidel Castro, as he talks.[1] The footage ends.

I replayed the newsreel many times, frame by frame, noticing more details in every rerun. But the moment you remembered most vividly wasn't caught in the Pathé clip. It was the point at which the Yugoslav welcoming party had a few minutes to greet Tito.

"Did you get to talk to him?" I asked you the next time we met.

"There wasn't much time, barely enough to introduce ourselves. I did get to look him in the eye though. He is surprisingly short, so I had to look down at him. Then we shook hands."

"Druže Tito, ja sam Dragan Roller, ekonomski savjetnik Ujedinjenih Nacija u ministarstvu planiranja u Ugandi. Comrade Tito, I am Dragan Roller, United Nations' economic advisor in the Ministry of Planning in Uganda."

"Neka si. Be it so," Tito said. He smiled and shook your hand with vigor. It was an encounter you talked about for years afterward.

* * *

In the summer of 1970, I returned to Uganda for the long holidays.

After the interminable journey from Vienna, I dropped my suitcase and handbag in my bedroom. Nothing had changed in the ten months I'd been away. The familiar rosy haze of bougainvillea streamed in through the window to bathe my battered old desk in a pink glow. Jim Morrison still pouted with a sultry gaze from the poster on the wall, the top right-hand corner flopping forward.

I returned to the salon in search of Fanta and company. Mama clattered around in the kitchen. You sat in your favorite chair with your back against the window, your dark shape outlined by the rays streaming in from outside. With your head looking down, you whispered something into your navel. You looked up and grinned.

"Surprise!" you said, pointing at your lap. The tiniest of creatures shivered as it stared at me, unblinking. A pair of brown eyes bulged out of an incongruously small, apple-domed head set on a creamy white body. The winglike ears were on full alert, straining to point up to the ceiling. The right ear had a kink in it, like the Morrison poster in my room. What was it? A bush baby from Madagascar?

"Meet Malenki van der Sprenkelhaar, otherwise known as Kiki," you said.

I reached out to stroke him, but before I could touch him, he leapt to the floor and yapped furiously, his feet tapping the ground beneath him like a drummer in a solo crescendo. He jumped around me, lunging forward occasionally to snap at my feet.

"What's the big noise?" Mama dashed in from the kitchen, tea towel in hand. We burst out laughing.

"Don't worry. He needs a little time to get used to you," you said.

"We got him after Tito's visit from a Dutch family in Kampala," said Mama.

"He is a Chihuahua," you said. "They are refined dogs, you know. Imperial stock, nothing less. Kiki has a proper pedigree certificate showing three generations of ancestors. His great-granddaddy was a Crufts champion."

"Chihuahuas used to guard Mexican gold in Mayan times," added Mama. "They are fierce little dogs, especially when there are two to three hundred of them guarding one temple."

"Yes, I can believe it," I giggled as I dodged the snappy jaws chasing me around the room.

"Take a seat," you suggested. "He'll calm down once he realizes you're not a threat to him."

I sat down in my usual place on the sofa. Kiki remained on the floor, his eyes following my every move. Minutes later, he jumped up and settled next to me. It wasn't long before I was allowed to stroke him. We would be friends for life.

* * *

The Guardian
January 26, 1971

Curfew in Uganda after Military Coup Topples Obote

Uganda's army has seized control of the country and appointed its commander, Major General Idi Amin Dada, as head of a military government. Troops moved in on Entebbe Airport and principal buildings in Kampala early this morning. Sporadic firing of automatic weapons and a few mortars continued until about midday. Then Radio Uganda gave the country the news of an apparently successful coup. President Milton Obote, who was flying home from the Commonwealth Conference as the coup was taking place, arrived in Nairobi tonight.

You and Mama were in Entebbe on the night of the takeover. I was 3,500 miles due north in Vienna, oblivious to the events unfolding in Uganda. The only TV set was in Poppina's private sitting room, a no-go area for us girls. Radio was for pop music, and daily newspapers were for boring old people. Singularly uninterested in global current affairs, I didn't register anything untoward until your letter arrived. Your words were reassuring. In your usual matter-of-fact style, you wrote there'd been a coup, but you and Mama were well, and there was nothing to worry about. If you'd heard shots from the airport like the ones we'd witnessed in Tripoli after the Six-Day Arab-Israeli War in 1967, you didn't mention them.

"Did you notice anything different after the coup?" I asked you when we met again, months later.

"Not straight away," you said. "The changes came gradually, at least for us. It took some time for the new regime to review all governance structures. When it was our ministry's turn to be scrutinized, one of Amin's generals came to visit me unannounced in my office. He wasn't a real general. He was one or two notches below that rank, but I addressed him as general anyway."

I didn't know it at the time, but you were using a survival skill learned in the Jasenovac camp. You always addressed military men by a rank or two higher than they were. The skill had served you well during the war. Now it was proving useful again.

"What did he want?" I asked.

"He knew my contract was coming up for renewal."

"How did he know that? Had you met him before?"

"No, but I met Amin once at an Independence Day celebration. Some Ugandans in the room snubbed him; one or two were openly hostile. I carried on chatting with him, being friendly, like I am with everyone else. Perhaps he remembered that."

"Anyway," you continued. "He offered me a new contract for three years. I'd be employed directly by the Ugandan government, not the UN. The job came with a generous salary, too."

"Sounds great!"

"No, not great. Amin is dangerous. There will be trouble ahead. When his general came to see me, I'd already applied for a job at the UN headquarters in New York, but I didn't have an offer. So, I made up a little white lie and told him I'd already signed my new employment contract and could not renege on it."

A few months later, you and Mama packed your bags and left Uganda for good.

Chapter 19

Manhattan

Christmas 1971. It would be a holiday to remember.

The jumbo dipped its nose almost imperceptibly, signaling the start of our descent toward Kennedy Airport. We cut through the thick, wintry cloud cover, seemingly weightless, for a good fifteen minutes. I fidgeted with my earphones and stared at the black porthole next to my seat, willing the show to begin.

And then it happened. A checkerboard of bright lights flashed up from below us like the opening to a Hollywood science fiction movie. I gasped. The lights twinkled red, yellow, and blue in a manic crescendo, disappearing into the distance to form a hazy golden globe over the city. Broad boulevards snaked their way across angular blocks of low-slung suburbs as far as the eye could see. I'd never seen anything so bright before.

"Welcome to America," the lights screamed.

And I did indeed feel welcome, despite the long lines at JFK and the gruff border guards you'd forewarned me about. Not long afterward, there you were, on the other side of the barrier, shouting my name, and Mama waving frantically. We threw our arms around each other. I was in a new country, but it felt like coming home. Home was wherever you and Mama were. A sea of brightly dressed people rippled around us.

"Everyone wears such colorful clothes here," I breathed. "In Europe, we dress in funeral garments all winter."

"That's right," you said. "Isn't it fun? Mama is eyeing up a red coat in Macy's already."

You hailed a taxi from the curbside. The three of us clambered into the back of an improbably wide yellow Cadillac and sank into the softness of the seats. There was plenty of elbow room to spare.

"This taxi is enormous! Are they all like that?"

"Oh, yes," you said. "Everything in America is big. Bigger than anywhere else. Americans build the biggest cars, the tallest skyscrapers, the widest bridges. America first." You paused and watched my face for a reaction. "Or at least that's what the Americans say," you added quickly with a smirk.

The cab weaved and swerved through dense, rush-hour traffic. Two hours and a dozen pothole jolts later, each one triggering a torrent of Hispanic swear words from the cabbie's mouth, we emerged out of the midtown tunnel under the East River into the cavernous streets of Manhattan. We stopped in front of a maroon awning at 300 East Forty-Sixth Street. A man in burgundy livery trimmed with thick gold braid around the cuffs and shoulders opened the door.

"Good evening, Mr. Roller!" he said. "Is this your beautiful daughter? Welcome!"

The doorman grabbed my suitcase and carried it into the building.

"Would you like me to bring your luggage to your apartment, Mr. Roller?"

"No, thank you, Danny," you said, pressing a dollar into his hand. "Just to the elevator, please."

"We live on the thirteenth floor," you said as you pressed the button marked 15 in the elevator. "But Americans call the ground floor the first floor and they omit the number 13 from buildings as it supposedly brings bad luck. So, on paper, we live on the fifteenth floor."

The front door of the apartment opened directly into an L-shaped living room with double-aspect windows overlooking Second Avenue. Below us, seven straight-as-a-die lanes marshalled an army of tooting cars, lorries, and buses from Harlem in the north to the Bowery in the south. Strips of headlights shimmered up from street level. Pedestrian WALK/DON'T WALK traffic lights blinked their red and white duets, mirroring the front and back lights of cars. The more familiar red, yellow, and green trio of traffic lights was reserved for vehicular traffic.

The views from the apartment kept me mesmerized for the rest of my maiden visit to America. You'd chosen the apartment for its location. It was a short stroll from your office on the twenty-third floor of the UN Headquarters building on the East River. On arrival in New York, old friends from Uganda had invited you to stay with them in Queens while you searched for a place to rent. The daily two-hour commute to and from work on the efficient but less-than-salubrious subway system was a baptism of fire for you. Not even a book or the daily newspaper could relieve the tedium of the experience. You dreaded the city commute and pitied everyone who had to do it because they had no choice. You wanted to live within walking distance from your work, but this came at a price. Rent in midtown Manhattan was astronomical.

Undaunted, you reached for your calculator. You worked out your hourly pay rate, multiplied it by the number of hours you would spend annually commuting, and added it to the average annual rent in the suburbs. You also added the cost of purchasing and maintaining a family car, an essential mode of transportation in the suburbs but an unnecessary luxury in Manhattan.

After the number crunching was done, the differential between the cheaper suburbs and the heart of the city didn't seem great. You discussed it with Mama, and she agreed with you. She wanted to be near the museums and galleries for daytime visits and within striking distance of Broadway for the evening shows. Kiki didn't complain either. He didn't need a garden. The Dag Hammarskjöld Plaza, a leafy enclave one block from the apartment, was more than enough for him. Scores of pooches of all shapes and sizes made their appearance there at all times of day and night. Kiki had no trouble swapping the African bush for the American metropolis.

Inside the apartment, things looked familiar. Bows and arrows and the shield we bought on our trip to Karamoja adorned the russet feature wall in the salon. A Makonde carving in the shape of a demon wearing a skirt made of armadillo scales bared its teeth near the front door to ward off evil spirits. I remembered how we'd haggled for it on an Indian Ocean beach in Tanzania on our last holiday together as a threesome. Great-Grandma's Biedermeier secretaire with its graceful cabriolet legs stood in pride of place against another wall. Two paintings hung on either side of it. Great-Grandma's nineteenth-century oil portrait in a gilded frame jostled for attention with the modern pastel of Mama that she sat for when we lived in Baghdad. You insisted on hanging them side by side. They demonstrated, in your view, that the "potato-shaped" nose was a familial trait passed down the maternal line from generation to generation. Great-Grandma had it, Mama had it, and I had it. The evidence was there for all to see.

On my first full day in New York, we sat down to brunch. "It's a great idea for weekends," Mama said. "Two meals rolled into one."

"Yes, a quick cup of coffee in the morning, when you're not hungry," you said. "Then, as you're getting peckish around 11:30, brunch is served, and you can take your time eating it until midafternoon."

You'd been shopping the day before. You bought a side of thinly sliced smoked salmon and a hunk of Roquefort cheese from the Swedish deli on Third Avenue. The terrine of venison pâté garnished with tangy cranberry jelly was from Tony, the Italian butcher a block away on Second. Thick slices of dark rye bread topped with crunchy poppy seeds filled a basket lined with a starched linen serviette. Mama brought in bowls of lemon wedges, radishes, and olives, while you opened a chilled bottle of white wine from Gallo.

"We've been trying out some wines from California," you said. "They are delicious. Would you like some? This one makes decent spritzers, too."

"You know, you can buy foods from all over the world in New York," you continued. "The city is a melting pot of world cuisines. Shopkeepers bend over backward to get the right ingredients for their customers."

"At a price, of course," Mama said. "Whenever I let your Tata out to shop, he spends much more than the household budget allows."

"Well, yes. Who can resist these scrumptious goodies?"

You stacked three slices of bread in alternating layers with the salmon, pâté, and blue cheese. As the towering concoction was about to keel over, you pierced it with your fork and cut it in half with a serrated knife. You made your way through it slowly, methodically, savoring every mouthful, lips smacking.

"Tata, you're mixing it all up here. You can't distinguish between the subtler flavors. You've killed off the flavor of the salmon with the pâté and blue cheese."

"Never you mind telling me what I can and can't eat!" you said, glaring at me in mock anger. "I like it this way. And besides, it all gets mixed up together in the stomach, anyway." Mama shrugged her shoulders and looked up at the ceiling. We burst into laughter. It was great to be home again.

You speared the last morsel of bread with your fork, wiped the plate clean with it, and placed your cutlery parallel on the plate. You were always last to finish your food. You sat back and sighed, wiping your lips and moustache with the linen napkin. It did not occur to me at the time that perhaps you savored your food even more because you'd endured genuine hunger in your youth.

"*Trebam oprati kljovalo.* I need to clean my mandibles," you said as you stood up from the table. "There's a poppy seed stuck underneath." By the time you moved to New York, you had full dentures, top and bottom, a lasting legacy of the Jasenovac camp. But you never complained about the demanding cleaning regime or the frequent check-ups at the dentist. It was a small price to pay for all the enjoyment you got from eating well. Enough to banish all thoughts of *pura* forever?

Sometime later, you returned holding a booklet with cerulean-blue covers. You handed it to me with a big swing of the arm and a bow, like a courtier delivering an important message to the queen.

The words *United Nations* shimmered from the leather cover in gilded letters. Embossed in the center of the cover was a map of the globe, as seen from the North Pole. This view of the world made Europe and the United States look much smaller than I was used to from my schoolbooks. I passed my finger across the map, fascinated by its difference. You noticed me looking intently at the design.

"The vertical line is the Prime Meridian, the one passing through Greenwich in London. It becomes the International Date Line on the other side of the world in the Pacific Ocean," you explained, pointing at the grooves on the emblem.

"Africa looks much bigger than the United States on this map," I said.

"Yes, that's because it is. Three times bigger," you said. "The problem is with the standard Mercator projections we normally use. Flattening a sphere makes landmasses further away from the equator appear bigger than they are."

"The sheaves of wheat around the globe remind me of the ones in the Yugoslav coat of arms."

"They're not wheat. They are olive branches, symbols of peace."

Underneath the emblem were the words *LAISSEZ PASSER.*

"Allow passage. Is that what this means? Is this your new passport?"

"Yes," you said. "Let the bearer pass. But it gets better. Look inside."

I opened the passport, expecting to see lots of exotic country stamps of the sort that filled your Yugoslav equivalent, but the pages were blank. All I could find inside were your name, date of birth, height, hair and eye color, and a photo.

"It's empty," I said, looking at you quizzically.

"It is now. I haven't started my official trips yet. But look again. It doesn't say anywhere what my nationality is," you said, your face beaming. "No place of birth, either. Isn't that great? I am an international civil servant, and it is irrelevant where I come from. It says to the border guards: 'I am here for my technical expertise in economics. Don't ask me about my nationality because it's not important, and besides, it's none of your business.'"

"I guess if the border guards knew something about European names, they might guess someone called Dragan is Yugoslav."

"And if they look at my surname, they might mistake me for a German. But they wouldn't know for sure."

"Cool. When can I have my blue passport?"

"Ha, ha! You can't have one. This is for UN work only."

"Aw! I want to be a citizen of the world, too!"

"Dream on, sunshine," said Mama. "Now give me a hand with the clearing up."

You remained sitting in your carver chair. You rarely helped with cooking, serving food, or clearing up. That was Mama's job. Mama often said you didn't know one end of the frying pan from the other, a claim you hotly disputed.

"Come and look at this," Mama pointed to a cupboard door in the galley kitchen and pulled the handle toward her. The door swung open from the top down. Inside was a machine with racks. Our first-ever dishwasher.

"No washing up!" Mama said, grinning broadly. "This machine is a lifesaver. Now I can invite ten people for dinner and not worry about the dirty dishes." She showed me how to load the plates and cutlery into the appliance. "But it can't do sticky pots and pans. You still have to scrub those by hand." She reached for a box of tissues and blew her nose, the familiar foghorn sound reverberating against the kitchen walls. She opened another cupboard and dropped the dirty tissue in the swing-out bin. "Oh, and we don't use our cloth handkerchiefs anymore. Out with the boil-washing and ironing! We use disposable paper tissues. So much more hygienic."

"Let's get back to the table," she continued. "And grab the bottle of wine from the fridge. We need topping up." I opened the fridge door and lingered for a few seconds, letting the chilled air tumbling out of the wardrobe-sized appliance cool my cheeks.

"We're invited to a Christmas party tonight," you said when I returned to the table.

"I think I will wear my black palazzo pants and silver lamé sleeveless top," Mama said. She reached for her Dunhill lighter and lit up a cigarette. You were already halfway through yours, sending the picture-window views of the Manhattan skyline behind you into a hazy mist.

"We've been to loads of parties since we've arrived here," you said. "We seem to be particularly popular with native New Yorkers. They see us as exotic curiosities."

"We're a kind of social trophy here," Mama said. "How many American hostesses can boast about knowing a real, live communist who doesn't bite?"

"Indeed," you said. "A commie bastard who knows how to use a knife and fork, no less."

"Yeah, and one who laughs a lot and enjoys rock and roll!"

"We're destroying our American hosts' preconceptions."

"Talking about preconceptions, we're shedding some of ours, too," you said. "At party meetings back in Belgrade, we argued that Americans couldn't possibly be patriotic. A nation of immigrants, after all. Their allegiances would be with their family roots in Europe or Asia or Africa. Well, we were wrong. Mama and I spent a long weekend in Washington, DC—"

"Fantastic trip," Mama interrupted. "A planned city. Vast boulevards. You can't walk anywhere. We took the tour bus around all the monuments."

"You should have seen the faces of the guides when they spoke. They beamed with pride."

"And the tourists, too," Mama added. "We were the only non-Americans onboard. The rest came from all over the United States, from Alaska to Florida."

"At one point in the tour, they all sang the national anthem. They were proud. Proud to be American."

"Let's go out now," you said. "There's a lot for you to see and learn."

And so there was. I spent the rest of my visit gawping at the marvels around me. I craned my neck up from street level to stare at shiny glass towers soaring above me. I looked down at traffic and people the size of ants from viewing platforms atop vertiginous skyscrapers. I learned to recognize the distinctive landmarks around us. The art deco Chrysler building, three blocks from our apartment, served me well as a useful indicator of distance. But the bulky Pan Am building straddling Park Avenue was deceptive; it looked close from fifteen blocks away, but the distance was not easily walkable. We watched skaters gliding past us at Rockefeller Center, the gilded statue of Prometheus overshadowed by a dazzling seventy-foot Christmas tree. We admired the windows at Tiffany's and mooched through Saks Fifth Avenue without buying anything. We eavesdropped on other people's conversations on the pavements and in the subway, trying to guess what languages they spoke. On the way home from a performance of *Jesus Christ Superstar*, two months after it had opened on Broadway, we hummed Mary Magdalene's "Everything's Alright" and crunched through the nuts and creamy marshmallows in rocky road ice cream.

This, then, was the Big Apple. Brash, insolent, loud.

By the end of the fortnight, I was hooked. When you asked me if I would rather do my A levels at the Headington School in Oxford or join you and Mama in New York, there was no contest. It had to be New York.

Figure 19.1.   Dragan and Vesna taking a cigarette break on an excursion from New York to Washington, DC, 1971.

Chapter 20

The Americans

Choosing New York over Oxford was the easy part. Finding a suitable school for me to enroll in was a little less straightforward. There were no British schools in New York in 1972. I had to adapt, once again, to a new education system. Naturally, you had a strong opinion about this. You'd decided, way back in Libya, that American secondary schools were "too fluffy." You made inquiries about other options. A colleague at the UN told you some American colleges admitted students without high school diplomas into the first year of their degree program on a trial basis. If they passed all their first-year exams with grades B or better, they were allowed to progress to the sophomore year as regular, matriculated students.

"Don't you have to be eighteen to go to college?" I asked you.

"Apparently not," you said. "They offer a liberal arts program in the first year that all students must take before specializing in a chosen subject for the next three years. I guess the first year is a catch-up with everything the students missed out on in high school. So you might as well go straight to college and not bother with high school."

In the autumn of 1972, I enrolled in my freshman year at Hunter College, majoring in biology. At age sixteen, I was probably one of the youngest in my class. Our first-year lectures were delivered in a cavernous hall packed with four hundred students. The lecturers, looking not much older than us, stood in semidarkness in the middle of the stage and dragged their thick, colored felt-tip pens across rolling acetate sheets, magnified and projected onto a white screen behind them. Key concepts and diagrams had to be copied into our notebooks at speed. The lectures were in stark contrast with lessons at the Viennese school, where the biggest class numbered no more than twelve. Even the science practicals at Hunter, lasting six hours each, three times a week, took place in laboratories big enough to accommodate up to sixty students.

You and Mama studied the course list carefully, perplexed by the myriad of subjects and choices on offer. This was nothing like the highly specialized European university programs you'd both attended in your youth.

In the first semester of my freshman year, all students were required to take Expository Writing. Progression to the sophomore year was dependent on passing this course.

"Why do I need to take an English-language course? I want to study science, not languages," I whined.

"Never you mind!" you said, glaring at me. "You will need to communicate your science to others. It will do you good."

Expository Writing was different. With fewer than fifteen of us in the classroom, it was impossible to escape the pitch-dark gaze of Dr. Dash, our tutor. Her petite frame and the silvery glints in her boyish haircut belied an inner energy that had us sitting at attention throughout her class. She whirred around the room and between our chairs like a human dynamo and expected us to maintain the same relentless state of alert. She tested us continuously, probing and prodding with quick-fire questions. In the first week, she assigned us an essay to write in class, on the topic of New York. In the second week, she returned our essays to us, fully annotated and marked. I was aghast. My essay was covered in red spider marks. Worse still, she'd given me a C, a bare pass. That evening, I went home incensed. It was the lowest mark I'd ever achieved for a written piece of work.

For the next ten weeks, Dr. Dash bombarded us with writing assignments. I loathed her for making us work so hard. I slogged away at my desk, facing the window of my bedroom, barely noticing the green on Roosevelt Island across the East River turning gold and then tawny crimson. Expository Writing was harder than plotting graphs from my chemistry and biology experiments. But my grades crept up gradually, and by the end of the course, I emerged with an A. I was ecstatic. I ran home to break the news to you and Mama.

"Dr. Dash. Great teacher," you said. "You will remember her in the future."

You were right. Two decades later, when I was firmly established in my career in science, I could no longer recall the names or the faces of my biology lecturers at Hunter. But I never forgot Dr. Dash.

* * *

Every two years, the UN paid for our family home leave, covering our return air fares from New York to Zagreb. Our periodic visits to the family home had started in the 1960s, when we lived in Belgrade and you braved the four-hundred-kilometer drive along the Brotherhood and Unity Highway, the busiest and deadliest trunk road in the Balkans. Back then, we made the journey three or four times a year, until December 1965, when a patch of black ice caused our car to spin into the oncoming traffic. We came to a standstill a hair's breadth away from an articulated lorry. You swore you would never subject your family to so much danger again and refused to drive to Zagreb in the winter months. By the following year, you no longer had to choose between a perilous journey and a winter break with the extended family. We'd moved to Africa and then on to the United States. Our visits home became less frequent but all the more treasured for their scarcity.

Grandma Hana's fourth-floor apartment in Zagreb was always our first stop. It was where Mama had grown up. Grandma's home was our home, however brief our visits. With parquet flooring throughout and Biedermeier furniture in burred walnut, the apartment exuded an air of faded grandeur reminiscent of a bygone age. A faint scent of quince jelly pervaded the apartment. In preparation for our arrival, Grandma Hana cleared her treasured lace doilies and silver bonbon dishes off surfaces to make more space for us. She always took out her best china for us and our guests. Uncles and aunties, cousins and friends—they all came to see us, feast with us, exchange gifts, and catch up with all the gossip. But for me, the best part came when we set off for the holiday home in Novi. The sea beckoned.

On the winding road from Zagreb through the pine-scented mountain range of Gorski Kotar, I sat back, closed my eyes, and conjured up the thujas and oleanders swaying in the *maestral* breeze in our seaside garden. In the days before the six-lane motorway connected the city with the coast, our journey took the best part of the day. We always stopped at one of the roadside inns for lunch and ordered lamb roasted whole on the spit and sold by the kilo. The succulent meat, served with strips of crackling, fresh young onions and vine-ripened tomatoes, was so tender that it melted in the mouth. Back in the car, we descended along a series of hairpin bends and looked out for the first glimpse of the Adriatic. Once we reached the coastal road, we wound down the windows, letting the salty air and chorus of cicadas assault our senses.

Every morning at the villa, we wolfed down doorstop-sized slabs of freshly baked, crusty bread spread thickly with chicken liver pâté or butter and rosehip jam. When my cousins and I were younger, we played cowboys and Indians after breakfast, hiding behind the gnarled olive and almond trees, trying to evade an imagined enemy. Enchanted by the portrayal of loyalty and friendship in our favorite books by Karl May, we all wanted to be Winnetou, the heroic Apache chieftain, or his pale-faced blood brother Old Shatterhand.[1] After the inevitable squabbling, we drew straws to decide who would get the two favored roles. By midmorning, we flip-flopped our way down the sloping garden path along rows of tamarix and rosemary, clipping their spiky leaves with our snorkels and fins, releasing clouds of fragrance. At the bottom of the garden, the creaky iron gate, set in the dry-stone wall

surrounding the property, opened out onto a narrow stony path and the coast-
line directly beneath it. The seashore in Novi was jagged with cliffs, softened
with tiny white-pebble beach coves. Beyond the rocks, the expanse of azure
sea stretched all the way across the Bay of Kvarner to the massif that was the
island of Krk, hazy on a hot day or breathtaking in its clarity after a few days
of the gusty *bura* wind.

We swam and snorkeled all day, interrupted occasionally by an adult
bringing down platefuls of tree-ripened peaches, fresh figs, or bunches of
deep purple grapes to gorge on. When the sea was mirror smooth, we ran
stone-skipping competitions across the limpid waters. When it was turbulent,
we body-surfed the white-crested waves. We collected limpets and starfish
and made necklaces from the pearly white teeth of sea urchins.

As we left our childhoods behind us and grew into teenagers, our daytime
frolics gave way to nighttime play. We waited eagerly for the first chords of
Carlos Santana's "Samba Pa Ti" to waft across the harbor from Terasa Leut,
the open-air venue where we danced to a live band every night. From the
first-floor balcony of the house, we could see the necklace of lights strung
along the shore in the shape of a giant smile. The smile beckoned. When the
music ended after midnight, we took our last swim in the sea, still tepid from
the afternoon sun. With every stroke forward, the sparkling plankton twisted
and turned behind us, like Tinker Bell's trail of pixie dust in a Disney movie.
We dried off on the rocks and looked out for shoals of fish following the fishing lights suspended from traditional *barka*s. On moonless nights, we laid
on our backs and counted the stars in the velvety black sky above us. Time
meant nothing then.

On those trips back home, you and Mama spent the bulk of your time
socializing with family and friends. You tried to catch up with domestic politics. The country was changing and not for the better, as you often remarked.
You snorted as you read the papers cover to cover every day, wiping your
inked hands with a tissue after each session.

"Can't they use indelible ink for this newsprint?" you said with a look of
distaste on your face. And then you kicked off.

"Any country that routinely prints money to pay off debts is heading for
ruin," you fumed. Yugoslav national debt was rising at an alarming rate, like
you'd predicted it would in the 1960s when we lived in Belgrade and you
called for economic reforms. "Mark my words: it will end in disaster."

Salaries were low, but education and health care were free at the point of
use. In 1970s Yugoslavia, many adopted the maxim "I may be paid little, but
I can always work even less." Productivity plummeted, and Yugoslav companies found it hard to compete with those in the West.

You told everyone at home how lucky they were. Jobs in Yugoslavia were
for life. It was almost impossible to get fired, even for incompetence.

"There is little job security in the West," you pointed out to anyone prepared to listen. "My contract with the UN is renewed every two years, but renewal is not automatic. It is dependent on my performance, which is rigorously assessed. If I make mistakes or get lazy, I'll get the sack."

"I'm lucky compared with many Americans. They have no job security at all. Our friend Vince is an architect with ten years' work experience. He's lost his job three times in the last four years simply because the companies employing him did not win enough new building contracts to work on. It's a case of 'last in, first out.' Vince has been told not to take it personally. He's been lucky enough to pick up a new job within a few months every time. The building trade in New York is booming now, but it won't necessarily stay that way. It means he can't make long-term plans for his family. And between jobs, he has no health care, which often comes as a fringe benefit of employment. Yugoslavs have no idea how privileged they are. The system takes care of them from womb to tomb."

Some agreed with you; others shrugged their shoulders and sighed in resignation. Your pearls of wisdom did not always go down well.

"It's a bit rich for Dragan to stand there with a bundle of dollars in his pocket and pontificate about how badly we're running the country," I overheard an acquaintance say when you were out of earshot. "He's not here every day to deal with the problems. Arrogant git!" Others were less polite.

Of course, no one ever told you this to your face. Some people still had respect for decorated war veterans, however abrasive their comments. But during our first home leave from New York, family and friends called us *Amerikanci*, the Americans. It was a name that stuck for the rest of your eleven-year stay in New York. It mattered little that you were employed by an international organization, not an American company. You were paid in American dollars, and that was enough to convince some people you were filthy rich. After all, everybody knew money grew on trees in America, and all you had to do was reach up and pluck the cash off low-lying branches. We were considered the lucky beneficiaries of easy pickings. It was the first time I understood we were somehow different, or at least that's how we were perceived by many Yugoslavs whether we liked it or not.

"These low rents people pay for their subsidized housing are uneconomic," you raged on regardless. "How much longer can the government afford to carry on like this? People complain about their low salaries, yet so many have enough disposable cash to build a *vikendica* or holiday home in the countryside or on the coast. The average American family spends more than half their income on housing and can only dream of owning a second home. Only the superrich can afford one."

You railed against what you saw as an increasingly corrupt system. You'd given seminars and led discussions at the UN about corruption in Africa, but you were appalled it was so widespread in your home country, too. Corruption and apathy stifled the economy. A year after you arrived in America, you were incensed enough to write to the man at the top, President Tito.

New York, October 7, 1972

Dear comrade Tito,

I don't know if you will ever receive this letter. I am acutely aware it may be disposed of by your cabinet apparatchiks who know best what you are allowed or not allowed to read.

Your recent speech about millionaires and the campaign against "excessive enrichment" has prompted me to write.

I know of several millionaires in Yugoslavia, and you probably know them, too. One of them is Vladimir Dedijer, your biographer, who has earned his substantial royalties by honest means. My point is: if someone has legally earned their income and has paid their taxes promptly, then it is no one's business how that person chooses to spend their money. Targeting a small fry, like people who build their own vikendica *in their spare time, while ignoring the big fish is not going to solve the problem of disproportionate enrichment. Instead, we need to start from the top. For example, how is it that some of our political leaders now own vast collections of fine art? I am not suggesting they have acquired these collections by dishonest means. I suppose they must have purchased them at a reasonable price. I am wondering why I have never been offered an ancient icon or an oil painting by one of the masters at a price I can afford?*

The current campaign against the so-called filthy rich could have serious unintended consequences for our country. As you know, there are nearly one million Yugoslavs working abroad. The money these Gastarbeiter *have sent home in the last few years has prevented economic meltdown in Yugoslavia. This income has also helped to maintain our country's independence by reducing our debts to the great powers who would otherwise demand political concessions.*

A vague campaign against enrichment could scare off our workers abroad who may then keep their hard-won earnings in overseas banks despite the more favorable interest rates in Yugoslav banks. No one likes being called a thief if they've worked hard doing an honest job. They like it even less if much richer people at the top are spared scrutiny for political reasons.

Comrade President, I am ashamed I have not signed this letter. When I fought against repression in Yugoslavia in the 1960s, I was subjected to a lot of unpleasantness. After you made Ranković resign at the Fourth Plenum, things changed for the better, but the damage was done. Once bitten, twice shy.

I will always remain your sincere and loyal fighter,
X.

I puzzled over the letter for years after I found it in your files. The typeface was clean, immaculately presented on lightweight airmail paper and devoid of a single typing error. I couldn't tell if it was the original or a carbon copy. Did you ever post your letter, knowing it might never get to the intended recipient? Even if you did, you could not have had a reply, as you signed it with the anonymous *X*. Or was it a form of catharsis for you, a way of letting off steam by writing down your frustrations? I had so many questions. Questions to which it was now impossible to get answers.

* * *

"They don't do revolutions in America," you said as you stretched your arms to their full length to fold the front section of the *New York Times* back into a semblance of neatness. Earlier that day, doorman Jack delivered the Sunday papers to our apartment by reinforced trolley. It wasn't the first time he'd been obliged to resort to mechanical aids to complete his newspaper round. In the long, hot summer of 1974, the media fired copious salvos of print, first in reaction to the ongoing Watergate scandal, then to President Nixon's resignation, and finally to the unpardonable pardon granted by President Ford. But Jack loved delivering papers to our apartment, however heavy. Your tips were always generous, and whenever a delivery required a trolley, you doubled his reward. The bowl of coins and single dollar notes on the sideboard near the front door needed constant topping up.

"Yes, they do," said Mama. "What about the American War of Independence in 1776? That was a revolution." She looked up from her culture supplement and gave you one of her disdainful "Don't you know anything?" looks.

"Tz!" you said and rolled your eyes skyward. "If you'd only let me finish. What I was going to say before I was so rudely interrupted, once again, is: They don't do revolutions in America; they shoot or impeach the president instead."

You drained the last of the black coffee from your cup. Behind you, the steely frame of Queensboro Bridge arched its way across the East River into Queens. The great cantilever arms shimmered in the midmorning haze. Twelve floors below, JFK Drive hummed steadily. Another sultry day in Midtown Manhattan.

"Is there any more coffee?" you raised your cup and saucer with your eyebrows arched. "And anyway, the American War of Independence wasn't a revolution. It was a war, and it was all about throwing off the imperial yoke."

Mama stood up and refilled our cups from the shiny new percolator she'd bought at Macy's. The stainless steel gleamed so much we could see ourselves in it, our images warped by the curve of the pot.

The cups perched unsteadily on top of the stacks of newsprint.

"It *was* a revolution," Mama said. "Anglo-Saxon settlers revolted against their Anglo-Saxon masters back in the mother country. Native Americans didn't have a say in it. It wasn't the same as an African colony demanding independence from its imperial masters."

You took a long, loud slurp of your coffee and relaxed back into your seat.

"Ah, nice hot coffee!" If there was one thing you hated, it was tepid coffee. Or tepid soup. Coffee and soup had to be piping hot.

"Yes, lovely," I said. I poured a dash of skim milk into my coffee, followed by a sachet of Sweet'n Low. "Less bitter than the coffee from the prehistoric contraption we used to have."

"Nixon is lucky. He hasn't been shot, and he hasn't been impeached," Mama said. "He's just got to learn to live with the shame and disgrace of being forced to resign, pardon or no pardon."

"And the shame and disgrace of losing power," you added. "Now that Ford has pardoned him, he'll never be punished for Watergate. He got away with it. But history will remember him for his shameful deeds. Interesting."

"Even more interesting is this new exhibition at the Guggenheim," said Mama, pointing at an advertisement in the paper. "It's had rave reviews. We could go this afternoon."

"Do we have to?" you yawned. "I wouldn't mind having a nap after brunch. I've got the Comoro Islands trip next week. Possibly Khartoum, too. I need to conserve my energies."

"You might learn something."

"Like what? That a bunch of crazy New Yorkers consider tan canvases drizzled with spaghettilike threads of black and white paint as art? I know that already. I don't need to go to the Guggenheim to learn that."

"You mean Jackson Pollock? I think he's at the Museum of Modern Art, not the Guggenheim."

"Oh, well," you shrugged your shoulders. "Let's go instead to the *Let My People Come* show in the Village. It's meant to be raunchy," you beamed across the table at Mama.

"Tz!" I said, rolling my eyes. "Behave yourself, Tata!" We all laughed at the same time. "I've got to work on my subject choices for next semester." I stood up and left you and Mama to get on with your revolution.

* * *

As a biology student in my late teens, I had no interest whatsoever in politics or the economy, whether Yugoslav, American, or African. I was vaguely aware of the war raging on in Indochina, not so much from the daily news headlines, but more through hearsay in student canteens and cafés. My lab partner, Dino, a Greek immigrant, was a Vietnam veteran. He'd been drafted into the army within days of being granted his American citizenship. Like you, he never spoke about his war experiences except to state simple facts, like dates and places. And to be fair to you and Dino, I didn't ask too many questions. The certainties of science were infinitely more attractive to me than diatribes about historical events or current affairs. A thermometer was neither capitalist nor socialist. A temperature reading had no feelings; it was not up for debate.

Were the demons of your past silenced in America? In the four years I shared with you in New York, I don't ever remember you talking about Jasenovac or World War II. You'd put your memories behind you for good, or so it seemed. You were determined to live in the present. When your younger brother Zlatko died suddenly from a heart attack at the age of fifty-two, you dropped everything and booked yourself a flight home to support the grieving family. In a letter to Mama, you wrote that you got drunk after the funeral in Zagreb, then cried your heart out, but we never witnessed the tears. By the time you returned to the United States, you were determined to make the most of your life. You were not one to dwell on tragedy. You stopped smoking and started a strict regime of Royal Canadian Air Force exercises. Within months, your fitness levels soared. Tar stains disappeared from your fingers forever. And after a holiday in California with Mama, you brought back a sticker for your bedroom door. It read, "I am not a dirty old man. I am a sexy senior citizen."

After I left the parental home for the last time, you stayed in New York for another six years. You and Mama had a love-hate relationship with the Big Apple. You loved the buzz of Manhattan as much as you hated the restrictions that inevitably came with living crammed with another five million people on a granite rock in the middle of the Hudson. You had friends from all over the world, and you mixed readily with native New Yorkers, too. You loved the Broadway shows and the galleries and the shopping. But sometimes it all got on top of you. The noise, the grimy subway system, people's rudeness, and the nagging fear of getting mugged would escalate from being a mere irritation to being unbearable. But every time your contract came up for renewal, you and Mama conferred, weighed the pros and cons, and decided to stay just a little while longer.

Chapter 21

Home

You returned to Yugoslavia for good in January 1983. You'd turned sixty in the previous year, and according to UN rules, it was time to retire. Staying on in the United States was not an option. Your UN pension was modest by US standards. Calculator in hand, you balked at the cost of American medical care, which you figured would escalate as you and Mama got older. The same pension would stretch much further in your home country, where health care was free. You had family and childhood friends in Zagreb, an apartment to live in, and the use of a seaside holiday home on the Adriatic. It made perfect sense for you to retire in Yugoslavia.

After eleven years in New York, how would a couple of change junkies adapt to a small city where many people lived out their lives in their parents' homes? You'd moved twenty-one times in your thirty years away from Zagreb. Some of the moves were within a city, but more often they were between countries and continents. You and Mama relished the excitement every move entailed. The prospect of meeting new people and learning about new places and cultures was always thrilling, never worrying. It didn't matter if you didn't like it somewhere; you could always move on. It didn't matter if you were offered lucrative jobs by unsavory dictators; you had the option of refusing. Sometimes, when you weren't due to move for a year or two, you rearranged the furniture and rehung the pictures in your home, "for a change," as you often said. This time it was different. Your twenty-second move was your last. There would be no going back.

The home country was still in one piece, just about. President Tito, the glue binding the Yugoslav federation together, had died three years earlier. In May 1980, we'd watched his state funeral on TV—you and Mama in New York, me in London. With more than a hundred heads of state, royalty, and other dignitaries present at the funeral, the world media descended on Belgrade. Coverage was exhaustive. Margaret Thatcher, Britain's premier, and Leonid Brezhnev, the Soviet president, were there. The American president, Jimmy Carter, sent his mother and the vice president. The Soviet Union had invaded Afghanistan a few months earlier, and Carter did not want to be photographed next to Brezhnev in case it affected his chances of reelection. Carter's absence was noted but did nothing for his chances—Ronald Reagan won by a landslide.

Like many Yugoslavs at home and abroad, we watched the funeral with some trepidation, wondering what lay ahead. The chords of Chopin's funeral march brought tears to my eyes as the procession made its way through the streets of Belgrade. I didn't know the man personally. I'd missed my one chance of grabbing a glimpse of him in a cavalcade in Belgrade in the 1960s. I remembered standing with my schoolmates along a wide boulevard in our freshly laundered Pioneer uniforms, holding bunches of flowers. We would wish President Tito a happy birthday by throwing the flowers onto his car. But when I flung my red carnations on the lead car in the motorcade, they rolled down the bonnet and into the path of the limousine tires. Dismayed, I watched my offering transformed into a smear of red sludge on the tarmac and forgot to look up when the smiling face of the president flashed past.

I didn't know him, yet I was sad he was gone. He'd been a symbol of unity and solidarity for the Yugoslav people. It must have been worse for you. Tito was the leader of your movement, your hero who galvanized the fight against fascism in your country. You'd shaken hands with him at Entebbe Airport all those years ago. When you wrote to him in 1972, you signed your letter, "Your sincere and loyal fighter." Loyal to the end.

Others were loyal, too. When Tito's Blue Train carrying his coffin from Ljubljana to Belgrade stopped for a few hours in Zagreb, the crowds stretched out for a mile from the train station to the main square and sang in his honor. They sang "The Internationale" and the Yugoslav national anthem. But more poignantly, they also sang the traditional melancholy love song "Fala," "Thank You."

In the hope of holding the country together after his death, Tito had devised a complicated system of governance based on a presidium and a presidency that rotated annually between the six federated republics. On the day he died, all media outlets across the land proclaimed everlasting allegiance to his memory and his mantra of "Brotherhood and unity." Privately, many people worried how long the system would hold without a strongman on top. Did you have doubts, too?

Your first few months back flew by like a whirlwind. You were so busy, you didn't get a chance to write to your expat friends back in New York until April.

Zagreb, April 1983

My dear friends,

The first three months of retirement have been manic. Now things have settled down a little, I thought I'd drop you a line, not least to inform you of what to expect on your return home to the mother country.

Our flight home in January went without a hitch. Customs at Zagreb Airport were polite and helpful, well beyond our expectations. After I told them what I was doing at the UN, they didn't bother opening any of our suitcases. They made a note of my new camera, which I wore across my shoulders, in my passport and advised me to clear it through customs together with the main shipment of our belongings, due to arrive from New York a few weeks later.

So far, so good. We got going with our new Yugo life. We learned quickly that coffee and washing powder are sometimes available, sometimes not. You can buy fresh meat everywhere, but if you want good quality, you must go to a private butcher and spend a fortune. Contrary to rumors we heard in New York, stationery and other paper products, such as toilet paper, are generally easily available. In any case, I doubt that lack of toilet paper would become an issue here in the Balkans. We can always revert to our ancestral customs and use dried corncobs to wipe ourselves, n'est-ce pas?

As soon as we got back, we started organizing Sibel's wedding, arranged for the end of March. Fortunately, wedding venues here are still relatively cheap, especially if you consider the weakness of the dinar against the dollar. Indeed, our Yugo currency is hurtling like a bobsled into oblivion, but it hasn't stopped our government from pouring bucketloads of freshly printed banknotes into the new Olympic stadium for next year's winter games in Sarajevo. The Olympics will bring in so much hard currency, we are told, that all our problems will be solved and the devaluation threatened by the IMF will be averted.

Anyhow, throughout our wedding-organizing mania, Vesna kept fretting the container with our belongings would arrive from New York on the day of the wedding. Of course, I dismissed her comments and told her she was being silly. The wedding was on a Saturday and customs were closed at weekends, so it was impossible for the two events to coincide. Still, she insisted our shipment would probably arrive at the worst possible time.

Well, what do you know? Vesna was right! The container arrived in Zagreb on the Monday before the wedding. I spent two days wrangling with customs officials before they finally released our goods to us on Wednesday afternoon. The groom's family and best man were due to arrive from London the following morning. Happily, the bride and groom were in Zagreb already, so we had two extra pairs of hands to help. The articulated lorry delivering our stuff was so big that it blocked all through traffic in our street. You can imagine how popular we were! Our neighborhood busybodies were treated to a fine spectacle from their windows. I hired a team of students from University Services, and they shifted 175 boxes into the apartment block and up the elevator to the fourth floor. Not everything fit into the elevator, so the bigger pieces had to be carried up nine flights of stairs. Fortunately, the lads were all young and strong, including their foreman, who happened to be a fellow graduate in economics. Zagreb is full of graduates doing manual jobs.

I know some of you are thinking of retiring in the next year or two, so here's a word of warning about customs procedures here. The rules are a bureaucratic nightmare and are designed to maximize the amount of money going into state coffers. As the country is on the verge of bankruptcy, I suppose we shouldn't be surprised. We've had to pay hefty import duties not only on the new kitchen appliances (which I was expecting) but also on used goods, such as the IBM Selectric I'm typing this letter on (I wasn't expecting that!). We bought this machine way back in 1972. We couldn't produce the original receipt, so the customs officials in their wisdom decided to value it at 50 percent of the cost of a new typewriter. They used the same principle to value all our used belongings. To make matters worse, they slapped on the cost of transport from New York and charged duty on that, too. It's a good thing we weren't traveling from Fiji! And finally, they added another 6 percent to the bill using some byzantine "balancing formula," supposedly to even out takings across the six republics. So beware, you will be fleeced!

To add insult to injury, I was accused of trying to smuggle my camera in without paying duty and was threatened with a fine of several million dinars. When I pointed out the note in my passport, stamped and signed off at Zagreb Airport on arrival, the official relented but didn't apologize for his mistake or the foul language he used when addressing me. In this country, you are presumed guilty until you can prove you are innocent.

To get back to the nuptials, they turned out to be a bit of an emotional roller coaster. After several days of bright spring weather, we woke up on the morning of the wedding to a snow blizzard. We had to scramble around in our wardrobes and still-to-be-unpacked boxes for coats and scarves for the wedding party. The ceremony in the Old Town Hall was splendid, but all photos had to be taken indoors. We've ended up with loads of snapshots of family and friends wearing odd combinations of fine silk on top and heavy boots or galoshes on their feet. Afterward, the reception in the Esplanade Hotel was the epitome of elegance. Vesna wanted to wear a black gown, but Sibel vetoed it because it was, in her words, "more suitable for a funeral." For once, Vesna listened to her daughter and wore a turquoise dress with a white lace bolero instead. I stuck to my dinner jacket and bow tie, topped with the Stetson I bought in Texas on our last trip there. We danced until the early hours of the morning. Vesna and I were the last to leave at around 5:00 a.m. We walked home singing "Glory, glory, hallelujah . . ." and got some strange looks from the good burghers of Zagreb.

At home, we found our Kiki shivering and barely breathing. He'd been unwell for some time. We wrapped him up in a blanket, but a few hours later, he stopped breathing altogether. At least he died naturally, without interference by a vet's injection. So we went from being on top of the world at our daughter's wedding to grieving for our doggy, all within a few hours. Kiki arrived in our home in Entebbe after Sibel went to boarding school in Vienna, and now he has left us just as she's establishing her new home in Britain. Life is full of ups and downs, whichever country you live in.

As far as finding consultancy work goes, it's all up in the air now. My friend Jakov at the Academy of Sciences has suggested I join one of his projects as an advisor on Yugoslav relations with developing countries. He's put my name forward to the appointments committee. The problem is, there are always more candidates for these positions than there are vacancies, and my thirty-year absence from Zagreb is viewed by some as politically suspect. It beats me how you are supposed to acquire experience of the developing world if you stay at home? The work could potentially be interesting, so I've told Jakica I'd be willing to forfeit my consultant's fee provided I could have an honorary title of some sort. Since the academy pays its consultants less than we pay my mother-in-law's cleaning lady, it's not much of a sacrifice to work on a voluntary basis. We'll see if it helps.

Overall, my impression is, our Yuga has not changed much in the last three decades. Paradoxes and contradictions still exist, like earlier. They're neither better nor worse than they were before, but they are more visible. Zagreb is as provincial as it's always been. If anything, it seems less cosmopolitan now. Migration from rural areas to the city continues apace. Previously, the migrants were disciplined, hardworking farmers. They brought fresh energy and vitality to the city. But now, the influx of people is from ever more remote and impoverished regions with little to offer in the way of skills or willingness to learn. They arrive with high expectations, demanding the same standard of living as everyone else for little effort. "Anything but hard work" seems to be the motto.

As you can see, I am still the same old cynic. But despite all its problems, our Yugo home is still the best place to retire. The cost of living is less than half of that in the States, and health care is free. My UN pension means we can live here comfortably.

Looking back on the last thirty years, my overseas work has cost us dearly as a family. We've lost our daughter to a job and husband, Marek, abroad, Vesna has given up her career prospects and become a homemaker (although I have to say, an excellent *homemaker), and my hometown has forgotten me as a professional economist and political worker. But we have benefited in one important way: we are financially secure. And if things get on top of us, we can always travel. Our Yugoslav passports open doors East and West. So would I recommend coming home to retire? Yes, I would, provided you, too, are financially secure.*

Lots of love from your friends,
Dragan and Vesna

Years later, I puzzled over your letter and the mixed feelings it revealed. You'd played down the incident with the customs official who accused you of smuggling. He'd rattled you much more than your correspondence implied. I still remember your face, dark as thunder, when you returned to the apartment at the end of your second exasperating day with Yugo officialdom. You told us you'd never been so insulted in your whole life. Your anger was palpable.

"He swore at me like a semiliterate shepherd up a mountainside. Unbelievable!"

You remained silent when Auntie Dina remarked that he most probably was a semiliterate shepherd before he became a customs officer. But when Uncle Kegla suggested that the official was probably expecting a bribe, I watched you closely, waiting for your inner core to go into meltdown and explode. But you kept yourself together somehow. You turned around, stepped to the bar, and poured yourself a large whiskey.

Later in the week, you rejoiced at my wedding, welcoming guests with the broadest of smiles and dancing the night away with Mama. It never occurred to me you might feel sad at "losing" your daughter to a life abroad. If you had mentioned it to me directly, which you never did, I would have dismissed such sentiments as trivial. After all, you'd spent half your lifetime living away from home and family, often in places much less accessible than London. I was a two-hour flight from Zagreb, and we'd be visiting each other several times per year. Floating in my capsule of self-absorption, I would not have understood your sense of loss even if you'd told me about it. Several decades later, I'm more appreciative of how you must have felt.

The day after the wedding, you asked me if I wanted to see Kiki one last time. I did, so you brought out his body wrapped in a blanket. He was stretched out on his side, his eyes closed, as if napping after a good meal. I reached out to stroke him but recoiled with a start. His body was cold. When I looked up, your eyes were sad but dry.

* * *

How long would it be before you and Mama got itchy feet again? By the summer of 1983, I detected a sense of ennui in your letters.

Novi Vinodolski, July 1983

Dear Sibel and Marek

It's been a while since we've been in touch. It's entirely down to your illiterate mother, who keeps promising to write and then never does. To be fair, we have been busy traveling to Belgrade and Ljubljana, rekindling old friendships and looking up distant relatives we haven't seen for decades. Now we're settled into a routine in Novi. Most mornings we work in the garden, chopping up fallen branches and dead trees for me and planting new exotics for Vesna. She's disappointed her poppy seeds haven't germinated yet, but she's pleased with her cactuses from our trip to Phoenix last summer.

Late mornings, we go for a refreshing dip in the sea, followed by lunch and a siesta. After that, we go for a walk along the promenade or into town. We spend most evenings reading, as the TV set is malfunctioning again.

Vesna wanted to come down to Novi earlier because Grandma Hana and her housekeeper Julka monopolize the kitchen in Zagreb and won't let her come anywhere near it. After being boss of her own kitchen for thirty years, Vesna is not taking to playing third fiddle gladly. Now that we're in Novi on our own, she's gone mad cooking all kinds of delicacies. The other day, while I dug a hole for a young cedar tree, she prepared stuffed calamari, Wiener schnitzel, and a salad of red, ripe tomatoes with lots of thinly sliced onions. Delicious! Supplies of meat and fish in Novi seem to be better than in Zagreb, possibly in anticipation of a good tourist season.

Vesna is on her fourth Carlos Castaneda and is dropping heavy hints about checking out his separate reality by visiting Mexico again. It hasn't taken long for her to tire of our idyllic domesticity . . .

Puno pusica, *lots of kisses,*
Dragan and Vesna

Later that year, you told me the consultancy role at the Academy of Sciences didn't come off. Your friend Jakica couldn't push the appointment through. The two of you had studied medicine together before the war, and you both switched to economics after the conflict ended. He was now president of the academy, but he was also part of the old guard gradually losing its grip on power within a system, which was itself unraveling. The new generations didn't remember or care about the war or the *prvoborci*, the Freedom Fighters of 1941. They cared even less about development economics, your area of expertise. Yugoslavia was turning inward. Why look beyond the garden fence when your house is on fire?

For you, looking beyond the fence had become an unshakable habit. You took on short-term consultancy assignments with the World Bank and your former employer, the UN. On your way to Lusaka, Zambia, you and Mama stopped over in London. You spoke with exasperation about the galloping inflation, bureaucracy, and corruption back home. Officials undertaking the most mundane of tasks expected presents. You were in unknown territory— you had to ask friends and family what types of gifts were considered appropriate. Yugoslav-produced Maraska liqueur in a decorative straw-wrapped flagon was not deemed suitable for the registrar who'd married us, but a bottle of imported Johnny Walker Red at three times the price was. Health care was free at the point of use, but doctors and nurses received presents, too, nominally as expressions of gratitude from their patients. Country folk brought whole legs of smoked ham, home-distilled spirits, and rounds of cheese. Urban patients slipped *plave kuverte*, blue envelopes, containing a few banknotes into the doctors' and nurses' pockets. Some medics refused them, but many didn't. When you inquired how this custom of blue envelopes started, no one had a satisfactory answer.

When the invitation came from Alma College, Michigan, to teach two courses in contemporary economics in the spring term of 1986, you and Mama were delighted. You'd visited Alma, a small town in the heart of rural America before. You'd met Fred, a full professor at the liberal arts college, several years earlier when he spent a sabbatical at the UN in New York. You became the closest of friends, even though you never got each other's names right. His name wasn't Fred; it was Frank. Fred got your name slightly wrong, too, calling you Dragon. You didn't correct him. You'd already had a test run at the college with a guest lecture comparing capitalist and communist systems around the world. It was well received by both faculty and students. They wanted more, so Fred persuaded the board of trustees to offer you a visiting professorship. Here was your chance to return to an academic environment, the sort of workplace you first started your career in. It may have been five thousand miles away from Zagreb, but it was academia nevertheless. Your American students called you Professor Dragon, and you got to wear the ceremonial gown and mortar board with tassel at commencement.

You traveled far and wide for business and for pleasure. The Yugoslavia you returned to was still home, somewhat shaken but still built on solid socialist foundations. Those foundations would stand firm, come rain or shine. Wouldn't they?

Chapter 22

War, 1991

I didn't see it coming. My view of *moja Jugoslavija*, my Yugoslavia, the land of the South Slavs, was fogged by a veil of illusions. By 1990, I'd been living abroad for twenty-four years, having left at the age of ten. Regular visits to Zagreb and the Adriatic, once or twice per year, only served to reinforce the mirage. The mother country was a state of mind rather than a real place. Ten years after Tito's death, it never occurred to me the union might not last. After all, it had been in existence since the collapse of the Austro-Hungarian Empire in 1918, first as a kingdom, then as a republic. It survived the tragedy of World War II. In my mind, the federation stood firm. Brotherhood and unity would prevail, like we were taught in primary school. Occasional spats and skirmishes between neighbors were only to be expected. Common sense would triumph, or so I kept telling myself.

Looking back through the prism of hindsight, the signs were there for all to see. Across eastern Europe, change was afoot. Free elections were taking place in countries previously dominated by one-party politics. The Soviet Union was imploding. When the Berlin Wall fell on November 9, 1989, crowds danced on the ruins all night and took home pocketfuls of masonry as souvenirs of the tumultuous event.

In my cozy cocoon in London, my focus was on the imminent unification of the European Community into a borderless single market. On May 5, 1990, the Eurovision Song Contest brimmed with entries celebrating friendship and togetherness. It was an unusually hot day, so we wheeled out our TV set into the garden to watch the competition with friends and neighbors. With our scoresheets firmly attached to clipboards and freshly sharpened pencils in hand, we awarded our *Nul Points* with glee and laughter. When Toto Cutugno took to the stage, we all agreed Italy was in with a chance. Toto's smoldering gaze, dark curls cascading down to his shoulders, the white suit set against his olive skin, and the catchy sing-along tune—they were a winning formula. We took bets on whether the entry could overcome the regional bloc voting that Eurovision was well known for. Our instincts were right. His song

"Insieme: 1992," "Together: 1992," won the contest. We danced late into the night, turning our threadbare lawn into a mud bath under our feet. Amazed at how fluent our Italian had become after a few glasses of wine, we threw our arms up in the air and joined Toto in celebrating the European Union.

Ironically, the contest was hosted in Zagreb, in a country rapidly running out of togetherness. Two days after Insieme's triumph, the second round of parliamentary voting put an end to single-party communist rule in Croatia. The overwhelming majority of seats went to the nationalist Croatian Democratic Union, with Franjo Tuđman at its head. The divisive electoral campaign, buoyed by ethnic rivalries, came to an end, but the war of words between Serbs and Croats intensified. Croatia was still part of the federal Yugoslavia but only just.

You renewed your travel pass in 1991. It wasn't any old travel pass; it was issued exclusively to Freedom Fighters of 1941. Small enough to fit inside my palm, the first page in the booklet listed your entitlements in Serb, Croat, Slovene, and Macedonian, printed in Latin and Cyrillic alphabets. You qualified for one free return ticket per year anywhere within Yugoslavia by train (first class), boat (first class), coach, or airplane (economy). You could make a further four journeys by train, boat, or bus with a 75 percent discount and take two additional flights at a 50 percent discount. When I found the diminutive pass many years later, it looked brand new, its stiff, red covers in pristine condition. The inside pages, intended for recording your journeys, were blank. The pass was valid for five years, but the country that issued it lasted less than six months from the date of issue.

Yugoslavia was in nationalist meltdown. Right-wing parties grew in strength. It was no longer taboo for mainstream politicians to speak warmly of historic nationalist movements, Serb and Croat alike. Revisionist historians were given free rein in the media. They worked hard to belittle Tito's legacy while rehabilitating the image of previously discredited fascist leaders. Expressing admiration for Ante Pavelić, leader of the ultranationalist Ustaša in World War II, was no longer considered heretical but a sign of courageous thinking. An ill wind was threatening the Yugoslav fortress, riddled as it was with yawning historical cracks. Friends and family watched developments with a growing sense of alarm. A thousand miles away in London, sheltered from the daily stings and barbs of life in Zagreb, I still believed the fissures could be repaired.

You traveled abroad for a respite from the chaos at home. Your postcards were always upbeat. Roadrunners from the American Midwest, ancient pyramids from Mexico, and sea lions from Ushuaia adorned our mantlepiece in London. But on your return to Zagreb in spring 1991, the political situation was even more precarious. Hate crimes and violent clashes became daily events. Repeated attempts to negotiate a looser federation for Croatia within the Yugoslav state had failed. When we visited in early May, preparations were underway for an independence referendum. The radio and TV were on all day, blaring out the latest news and interrupting regular programs for special bulletins. The tsunami of change was rolling inexorably toward you.

"I'm surprised you've come to see us in this shaky country," Grandma Hana said when Marek and I arrived from London. "But I am pleased you've made it. Thank you for visiting us." Aged ninety-seven, she was still reading books in several languages, but she now needed a magnifying glass, as well as her thick glasses, to see the print. Whenever I entered her bedroom to wish her goodnight, she'd look up from her reading and tap the bed next to her with her hand. Once I was seated, she'd grin mischievously, open the drawer of her night table, and extract a box of chocolates. Our favorites were the Griotte, dark chocolatey domes wrapped in shiny red foil, each filled with a sour cherry soused in brandy. One evening, I noticed she had a pile of photographs next to her. They were architectural shots of Zagreb focusing on renaissance and baroque landmarks defining the look of the city center. No friends or family featured in the photos.

"What are these, Grandma?"

"Ach," she waved her hand in the air dismissively. "Uncle Kegla has taken them. I'm not sure why." It wasn't until many months later I realized why he'd taken them. He was afraid the city would be bombed.

On June 25, 1991, Croatia and its northerly neighbor, Slovenia, both declared independence from Yugoslavia. Two days later, the tanks rolled in. Serbian leader Slobodan Milošević wasn't about to let a referendum result get in the way of military power. Slovenia got off lightly. Not many Serbs lived there, so Milošević quickly lost interest. The tanks pulled out ten days later. But Croatia was different. A substantial minority of the population was Serb. Milošević was determined to follow through with his policy of "Wherever there is a single Serb, that's Serbia."

Amid the turmoil, Grandma Hana died in July 1991. I was in Singapore at the time delivering an invited lecture at a scientific conference. The news of her passing did not reach me until I returned to London. By then, she had already been buried in the family grave. Having lived through two world wars, perhaps another conflict was too much for her to bear. I looked again at the photos of her from our May visit. I remembered taking the last one, from street level looking up toward the windowsill of her fourth-floor apartment. She was leaning forward, her pale face surrounded by a halo of white hair, her delicate hand raised in a regal wave goodbye. Did she suspect we might never meet again?

The war marched on at full throttle. Milošević stopped pretending he was defending the sacred Yugoslav federation. His ambition to carve out a Greater Serbia was out in the open. New borders were drawn. Swaths of Croatia with

Serb populations, large and small, were sliced off by force. Dominated by Serbian officers, the Yugoslav Army unleashed the full might of its military hardware on a Croatian volunteer force armed with hunting knives and rifles. Demotivated conscripts of all nationalities, including some Serbs, deserted the army in droves, refusing to shoot at their supposed enemies. "They want me to kill my buddy. I shared a desk with him in school. No way!"

Back in London, images of refugee columns and burning villages filled our TV screens. I dreaded watching the evening news for fear of learning about new horrors. Grisly massacres of Croatian civilians and policemen increased in frequency. Revenge attacks on Serbs followed soon afterward. I was ashamed—ashamed to be part of a species capable of committing such atrocities.

"But Zagreb is OK, right?" I asked you during every one of our weekly telephone conversations.

"Yes, don't worry," you said, but your voice was less reassuring every time we spoke.

"They've cleared out the air-raid shelter in the basement," you said during one conversation. "It was filthy. It hasn't been used since World War II. People have been storing their junk in there."

"Isn't it a bit dark and damp?"

"Yes. There are wooden bunkbeds . . . like in Jasenovac. There's no way I am going down there. If there is an air raid, I'd rather take a direct hit in my own bed on the fourth floor than be buried alive in the basement."

"It won't come to that?"

"Let's hope not."

It nearly did come to that. By the fall, Yugoslav MiG jets roared over Zagreb, threatening the population with their flybys. On one occasion, they fired at the city's main TV transmitter, damaging the tower and temporarily interrupting programming. In October, rockets rained on Croatian government headquarters and President Franjo Tuđman's residence. He wasn't at home when the missile struck, but the message was clear. For several weeks, it became more difficult to connect with you, the phone line hissing like an angry feline.

"They're messing with our communications," you said. "They don't want us to talk to Belgrade, but they don't know how to block the lines selectively. The whole network is affected. Our friends are getting through anyway. Auntie Mila was worried about us. Their propaganda machine is spreading all sorts of rumors about the numbers killed in air raids."

Zagreb remained relatively unscathed, but other cities fared less well. Serbian heavy artillery shelled the border town of Vukovar in the Northeast of Croatia for three months, razing its center to the ground. Dubrovnik sustained heavy damage, too. I never did ask you what you thought of the shelling of

Dubrovnik. It was the place where you and Mama met, the city you focused on for your doctorate. Perhaps you'd hoped its modern-day citizens inherited the resilience and independence of spirit characterizing their ancestors in the ancient Republic of Ragusa. The city had endured and survived sieges before, not least against the Napoleonic army in 1814. Would the UNESCO World Heritage site survive the heavy weapons of the twentieth century?

At home in London, I carried on watching the reporting with disbelief, but my mind was drifting elsewhere. I was expecting a baby. My focus turned inward, toward the new life inside me. The war was somewhere else, in another place, another country. When friends asked me to explain what was going on in Yugoslavia, I deflected and told them I didn't understand what was going on, either. By the time our son was born in 1992, Croatia was recognized internationally, and a truce of sorts was in place. A long trail of unfinished business remained. A third of Croatian territory was still occupied by Serb forces and would not be retrieved until three years later. Meanwhile, the war moved southeast to engulf Bosnia and Herzegovina and eventually Kosovo. Clamped between the horseshoe-shaped Croatia to the west and Serbia to the east, Bosnia's ethnic mix of Serbs, Croats, and Bosnian Muslims sank into a blood-soaked quagmire marked by the four-year siege of Sarajevo and the massacre of more than eight thousand Muslim boys and men by General Ratko Mladić's Serbian Army in July 1995 at Srebrenica.

When we next visited Zagreb, you casually mentioned, almost in passing, that you'd given up your membership in the Communist Party. Stunned into silence by your news, I didn't ask you what made you take such drastic action. You'd been a loyal member since you were a teenager, and you spent three years in Jasenovac because of it. Hoping to be given a clue about your reasons, I waited until you were out of earshot and asked Mama what happened.

"They've released some classified party documents recently. Tata discovered some people who he thought were his friends betrayed him. It all goes back to the 1960s when we lived in Belgrade . . . "

I didn't want to open old wounds. I remained silent, and now I wish I hadn't.

At the time, I didn't know your departure from the party was only half the story. The other half was another secret you kept from me. Unlike your unfinished book, cast away in a dusty storeroom, you hid this secret at the back of a filing cabinet in an elegant, leather-trimmed silk folder the color of indigo. Years later, its contents astonished me almost as much as your post-camp writing. Buried inside a sheaf of papers in the folder, I found two heavy, beribboned badges and a certificate bearing a square-and-compass emblem with the letter *G* at its center. I didn't recognize the emblem at first, but a quick internet search revealed it was the symbol of Freemasonry. Like your father-in-law, Krešimir, before you, you'd joined the secretive brotherhood of men and become a Freemason. You'd finally come over to his side.

What would Grandad Krešo have said? Would he have recoiled with horror? I'd like to think that he would have welcomed you into the fold like he did when he invited you to share the salad dressing at your first meal together.

Within the precepts of Freemasonry, you kept your membership discreet. Looking back at the mid-1990s, I am glad you never told me about your new affiliation. My thirty-something self would have been mortified. Exclusive men's clubs, whether on Pall Mall or in Covent Garden, made me bristle.

There was something else in the indigo folder, a six-page script for a talk on inequality in an interdependent world, a theme you'd been grappling with since your youth. You'd delivered the lecture to the brotherhood of your lodge prior to your promotion from initiate to master. In your essay, you expounded on the growing chasm between the rich and the poor all across the world and the corrosive role of corruption in both developed and developing nations. You concluded with a personal anecdote:

> *The other day I watched horrific images of starving children in Africa on the evening news. They reminded me of something that happened to me a long time ago.*
>
> *It was 1942 in the Stara Gradiška concentration camp. I was recovering from typhus, and I weighed less than fifty kilograms. I sat on the straw-covered floor of our cell in the tower, where we were locked up. A couple prisoners I didn't know sat next to me, eating heartily from a package their families had sent them. I didn't beg them for food, but I guess my eyes must have been pleading. One of them saw me staring and said, "Whatcha gawping at? You're not getting a crumb. Look at you. You'll croak in a day or two anyway." I didn't cry like the African children on TV, but for a brief moment, I loathed them with the intensity only the have-nots can muster against the haves.*
>
> *Today I am one of the haves. Some of the have-nots probably hate me even though they know nothing about me.*

Chapter 23

The Inquest

Easter week in 1998 should have been like every other. Terminal 2 at London Heathrow Airport thronged with travelers eager to get away for a spring break. We moved sluggishly through the crowd, laden with bags, coats, and duty-free shopping like modern-day beasts of burden. Even five-year-old Max had a bottle of perfume stuffed into his Pokémon rucksack. We heaved our way to the departure gate and dove for the three seats facing the runway. Our sleek jetliner awaited, attached with its umbilical cord to the terminal building.

No sooner did we sit down when Marek tapped my forearm with some urgency.

"Hey! Did you see that?" he said.

"See what?"

"The newsflash," he pointed at the screen in the corner of the waiting room.

"No. What was it?"

"Something about a Croatian war criminal. Dinko something or other. Bragging on Argentine TV about being a great patriot."

"Weren't they all? That's why they escaped to Argentina. To avoid getting lynched at home. Big patriots. Where are those flipping keys? Don't tell me I've lost them," I said irritably as I rummaged through my hand luggage.

"He said no one died in Jasenovac during the war."

Oblivious to his words, I removed items from my bag one by one, piling them onto the seat next to me. Johnnie Walker for you, Benson and Hedges for Mama, a couple paperbacks from the best-seller list, a plastic sleeve with some work papers, a triple pack of strong mints, hairbrush . . .

"Wahaay! Here they are!" I extracted the house keys from the bottom of my bag and jangled them in front of his face. "End of panic."

I crammed everything back in the bag, but the zip wouldn't close.

"Why is it that stuff never seems to fit back in once you've taken everything out?" I muttered. I slouched back into the seat. Exhausted already, and we hadn't so much as left London yet.

"The newsreader said Dzasenowak. It's Yasenovatz, not Dzasenowak? Right?"

"Correct. Yasenovatz."

"The Beeb would have gotten it right. They train their newsreaders to pronounce foreign names properly. Anyhow, wasn't that where your dad was?"

"Mommy, can I have some crisps?" Max pulled at my sleeve and pointed to the vending machine at the end of our row of seats. The new Game Boy had failed to distract him from noticing the shiny metallic wrappers beckoning from behind the glass.

"Aw, gawd! Did we have to sit down so close to the machine?"

"Pleeeease! Mommy dearest! Daddy dearest!"

"Oh, well," Marek muttered as he dug around in his pocket for some change. "They're savory. Not as bad for his teeth as sweets."

The two of them stood up and walked over to the machine hand in hand, Max chirping and skipping alongside his dad. So much for being strict about snacks. They returned to their seats with armfuls of crisps, big grins on their faces. They sat crunching away.

"So, what exactly did he say? That no one died there?"

"I don't know what he said. They didn't show the original interview. Would have been in Spanish, I suppose. He claimed people died of natural causes. No one was killed."

"That's absurd. What about the mass graves? The shattered skulls? The guards took photos of each other in the act of . . . "

"Oh, I can't remember exactly. He's being extradited to Croatia to stand trial. Maybe they'll show the news clip again."

A loud chime over our heads heralded an announcement. Finally. We boarded the plane. Within a half-hour, we were sipping our complimentary vino. Our Easter break had begun.

* * *

"Right a bit!"

"No, no, too far! Left a bit!"

"That's it. Stay still! Smile!"

Max stood askew, an impish grin on his face. For once, his blond tresses were behaving themselves, washed and brushed smooth under duress. His bow tie and waistcoat stayed put, but his white shirt was determined to escape the confines of his trousers. I snapped away.

Auntie Dina's finest damask tablecloth, monogrammed in one corner and ironed to perfection with spray starch, stretched across the huge dining table between us. An embroidered runner cascaded down the center of the table. Ten place settings flanked the runner like soldiers. Plates of fine bone china framed by double sets of silver jostled for space with the delicate crystal wine glasses, each perched incongruously on an African felt and straw coaster, a gift from our stay in Uganda in the 1960s. Rickety wooden stools, requisitioned from the kitchen, alternated between the upholstered dining chairs, their faded fern-green fabric harking back to a more genteel age. An oblong platter with thick, hand-sized slices of country ham arranged in a fanned pattern graced the center of the table. Plump, red radishes and spring-green onions glistened in bowls on either side of the platter. And then there were the trays of stuffed eggs, Auntie's pièces de résistance. She'd spent hours painstakingly filling the white globes with the creamy crush of egg yolk, finely chopped gherkins, and mayonnaise, topping each one with a caper. A tiny chick fashioned from yellow feathers and a couple brightly colored eggs sat on top of a yellow napkin in the center of each plate. There were place names for each guest.

Auntie Dina breezed into the room carrying a basket lined with a linen serviette and piled high with freshly sliced crusty bread. She turned toward her guests, took a bow, and announced, "First course is served."

Every Easter, I took the same pictures of family and friends. Max, the only child in the room, grew taller every year, but no one else seemed to change much. Congregated around the table, the ladies' heads were a little grayer, and the men's hair, a little thinner, but their eyes were still shining. But that Easter, something had changed. Your eyes had lost their gleam.

That evening you told me you'd left a copy of the weekly newsmagazine *Globus* in our bedroom for me to read. You'd been interviewed by a journalist from the magazine for an article published in the latest issue. You didn't say what the article was about. You remarked, nonchalantly, that it might be of some interest.

When we got back to our room, I glanced quickly at the magazine cover. Headshots of politicians vied for attention with a topless blond model pouting to the camera. A jumble of headlines screamed about the latest corruption scandals. Corruption? That had been the hallmark of the communist regime, now banished. It seemed not. The new government, barely seven years in office, was continuing the tradition. *Plus ça change* . . . Near the top of the cover but in much smaller typeface, a headline read, "The Case of Dinko Šakić," next to a black-and-white photo of a youthful officer in a peaked cap. I flicked impatiently through the magazine. On page 17, a double spread of color photos showed you and Šime Klaić, your old friend from Jasenovac, flanked by a headline-sized quote: "In all our misery, filth, and disease, Dinko Šakić strutted around the camp looking like a fashion model."

"Hey, Mommy, that's Grandad! Is he famous?" Max piped up next to me.

"No, darling, he's not famous. It's some work Grandad was doing. Now it's time for bed!" I was continuing the family tradition of avoiding difficult conversations. How do you explain a death camp to a child? He's not even six yet. Maybe when he's a bit older . . .

Later that evening, I looked more closely at your photo. Taken indoors, it projected an image of a dignified older gentleman with neatly trimmed dark hair and moustache, wearing an open-necked white shirt and a softly undulating cardigan of black cashmere. Your reading glasses dangled on a string around your neck. The photo editors hadn't bothered to airbrush the bloodshot from your eyes. The caption underneath read, "Dragan Roller: Some prisoners ran to the barbed-wire fence on purpose so the Ustaša guards would shoot them and put an end to their unbearable suffering."

How different it had been a few months earlier in London. You and Mama were on your way back from an extended tour of Australia and New Zealand. We'd decided to meet you at the airport, expecting a couple exhausted gray hulks to emerge from the luggage hall after the thirty-six-hour traveling ordeal. Instead, you strode out beaming, tanned, a couple of suave seniors stepping off their luxury yacht expecting a welcoming party and a brass band. Mama's pale blue muslin trouser suit, embroidered along the edges with delicate pastel flowers, fluttered gently behind her as she walked. It was her favorite outfit, getting softer after every wash. You were her silver-fox companion, tall and still dark, despite the streaks of gray. The jacket of your cream linen suit, pulled over your floral shirt, strained a little around your middle. You made a grand entrance. A belly laugh of an arrival. That day at Heathrow, your eyebrows were bushier, your moustache, inkier, than in the *Globus* photo. The article did not bode well. It raked up the past, forcing you to remember what you'd been trying all your life to forget.

* * *

Two months later, the Argentinian government delivered Dinko Šakić to Croatian authorities to stand trial for war crimes committed during World War II. The first step was an inquest to establish if there was sufficient evidence for him to stand trial. You were the first witness called to testify. It was June 30, 1998, a hot day in Zagreb.

You stepped out of the courthouse into the blazing sun. You blinked a few times to let your eyes adjust to the glare.

"Mr. Roller! Mr. Roller! Can we ask you a few questions please?" Voices clamor for your attention. "You promised you'd talk to us after the inquest!"

Across the road from the District Court, the crowd of journalists surged toward you, seemingly oblivious to passing traffic. Cars screeched to a halt, their drivers hurling torrents of swear words out through open windows. A sea of fresh, youthful faces jostled around you. They thrust their microphones and camera lenses toward you. They'd spent the whole morning waiting for you in the shade of the mighty plane trees in Zrinski Park, where you'd been shot at by a plainclothes policeman way back in 1941. You dodged the bullets then by bolting like a startled colt. This time you stood still and faced the demons of memory.

"Yes, I did promise," you said, looking down at your watch. The questioning had taken four hours. "You've all been very patient."

"Mr. Roller, when were you in Jasenovac?"

"Did you see Dinko Šakić there?"

"Did you see Šakić murder people?"

"What did you tell the judge?"

"What did the prosecutor ask you? And what about the defense?"

"Please, one question at a time. I can't hear you when you're all shouting at once." You raised a hand to rub at the bags under your eyes, puffed up into gray crescents like the neck pillows you used for your long-haul flights.

"Quiet, everyone! Let the man speak."

"Thank you. I arrived in Jasenovac on February 18, 1942. Some officers traveled on the same train from Zagreb. Dinko Šakić was one of them. I was in the cattle wagon, shackled at the ankles with chains to my fellow students of medicine. I was sentenced to three months in Jasenovac for being a member of the Communist Youth League. They kept me there for three years."

"Mr. Roller, did you see Šakić murder anyone?"

"No, I haven't seen him strangle anyone with his own bare hands. But in my opinion, that is not important. Adolf Eichmann didn't kill anyone personally, either, but he was still guilty of murdering millions of Jews in extermination camps. While Šakić was in charge, he was responsible for the starvation, the beatings, the torture, and the murder of unarmed prisoners in the camp. I saw Ljubo Miloš slit the throat of a prisoner eating potato peels out of the dump. Miloš was the murderer, but his supervising commander was equally responsible."

"What was Šakić like?" someone in the crowd shouted.

"He was a fine dandy. His boots were always polished to a high sheen. He didn't walk much around the camp. He was worried he'd get dirty in the Jasenovac mud," you said.

"Was Šakić the commanding officer throughout your incarceration?"

"No, he wasn't in command to start with. But he had been promoted to commandant when the orders came to liquidate the camp near the end of the war."

"What happened in the camp during liquidation, Mr. Roller?"

"The Ustaša came to our barracks at night and selected people from a list. By 1944, they selected people by name. Prior to that, their recordkeeping was so poor, they selected people at random. They tied the prisoners' hands with wire. Those who left at night never came back. They were killed . . . "

"How did you know they'd been killed? They might have been moved to a different camp or released?"

"We knew they were dead when their clothes were returned to the recycling workshop. The gravediggers told us how they died. They'd been bludgeoned to death with sledgehammers, or their throats were cut."

"Were there mass executions in Jasenovac?"

"Yes. When Šakić was commandant, several group executions took place in front of the prisoners. Dr. Mile Bošković and his group had planned an escape, but they were caught. Their bodies hung on lampposts for several days for everyone to see."

You took a handkerchief out of your pocket and wiped the sweat off your brow.

"I saw several hangings. Some were railway men still in their uniforms. As a medical orderly, I had to take the bodies down and load them onto a cart. The gravediggers took the bodies away and buried them in mass graves. Šakić didn't hang these men personally, but he was in charge. He was responsible for these murders as much as the hangmen themselves."

"Mr. Roller, how can you be sure you remember these things correctly? It's been more than a half-century since World War II ended."

"These are not things that are easily forgotten, young man. Believe me, I have tried hard to forget. But you cannot forget. I may be old, but the scars are still there."

Your favorite cream guayabera shirt belied the heat of the day. On your head, your hair stuck sweatily to your scalp. You looked exhausted, yet you carried on, answering the journalists' questions, slowly and deliberately.

"Hang on a minute!" I imagined you saying. "How do you know all this? You were in London at the time."

I thought you might ask. I was, indeed, in London at the time. The day after your testimony, you were quoted extensively in all the national papers. Photos of you standing on the doorstep of the courthouse were reproduced in all national media outlets. The same head-and-shoulders shot, taken from different angles, a cluster of microphones thrust toward you. TV news programs showed clips and soundbites from the scene. Years later, it wasn't difficult to reconstruct a scene from the available footage. So I used artistic license. Perhaps you would not approve. What else was I supposed to do in the absence of details from you? All I got was a brief, dispassionate letter on onion-skin paper listing the numerous national and international dailies and TV channels that interviewed you. A whole day filming at the Jasenovac

Memorial Park with the BBC got a single sentence in your letter. And at the end of your brief missive, you casually mentioned that your cardiologist had told you that you had a sick heart. You would be seeing him again as you were having some breathing difficulties at night.

The pressure of those months was unrelenting. You had a sick heart. Or were you sick at heart? Yet when we arrived from London for our family holiday later that summer, you said not a word to us about your ordeal.

Chapter 24

The Shoah

The family archive, jumbled together without rhyme or reason and crammed into cupboards, erupted every now and then with new surprises, like the intermittent discharge of a Yellowstone geyser. The revelations in the tissue-thin sepia pages of your unfinished book, hidden for decades, had been the beginning of my journey of discovery about you. My periodic clearing-up stints occurred in bursts of manic activity squeezed between the demands of career and family. With time, I stopped dreading the sort-outs as chores and approached each boxful of mementoes like a magical mystery tour. What secrets would I uncover this time?

When I first picked up the letter from Steven Spielberg, addressed to you personally at the Zagreb address, I thought it had come from a namesake, someone coincidentally bearing the same name as the film director made famous by blockbuster movies like *Jaws*, *E.T.*, and *Jurassic Park*. Or perhaps it had been a practical joke played on you by one of your more mischievous friends. But words like *survivors*, *Shoah*, and *history* stood out in the short letter. Such words would not have been used by a prankster, but I remembered Spielberg was Jewish, and he'd made another film, *Schindler's List*. A quick search on the internet revealed he'd also started the Shoah Foundation, an organization dedicated to the recording of oral testimonies of Holocaust survivors. I reread his letter, this time with more care and attention:

Survivors of the Shoah
Visual History Foundation
Los Angeles, California

March 12, 1999

Dear Mr. Roller

Your testimony as a survivor of the Holocaust is giving future generations a direct link with history.

> *Your interview has been carefully preserved as part of the biggest library of survivor testimonies ever collected. Well into the future, people will be able to see the faces and hear the voices of survivors, learn about their life stories, and remember them forever.*
>
> *We thank you for your participation, your strength, and your generosity of spirit.*

Steven Spielberg
President

What interview? Why didn't I know anything about this? You'd never mentioned recording an interview for an American foundation. The letter was not a prankster's joke. It was serious. I felt ashamed that I hadn't heard of the Shoah Foundation before. Perhaps there was a private copy of the recording somewhere in these boxes. But the testimony wasn't intended for broadcast, or at least there was no mention of one in the Spielberg letter. It had been shot for an archive, not a TV company. The tape was made for posterity. Another quick flick through the internet told me the recordings were housed at the University of Southern California in Los Angeles.

I searched through the box sheltering the letter again. Maybe the foundation had provided you with a copy, as a matter of courtesy. I was not disappointed. There it was, a VHS cassette, neatly labeled with the Shoah Foundation emblem, your name, the date October 12, 1998, and the epithet "So generations never forget what so few lived to tell." I sat there staring at it, overwhelmed by a sense of déjà vu.

Like your secret manuscript I'd uncovered years earlier, the video remained in a drawer, ignored but not forgotten. The usual excuses cropped up again. A busy life. Family and career took precedence over everything else. Maybe I preferred not to know, not to see. Maybe I was compartmentalizing, much like you did most of your life?

Many months later, I dug out our creaky old VHS player from the pile of donations waiting to be taken to the local charity shop. I plugged the machine in, switched it on, and inserted the tape. The player whirred into action.

There you were, in the frame, breathing and blinking into the camera. I was thrilled. Here's my daddy! I wanted to reach into the screen and hug you. The video recording brought you back to life, twelve years after your funeral, in a way no still photograph could compete with.

Next to you, a woman in her thirties with short brown hair and almond-shaped eyes introduced herself as the interviewer, Jasminka Domaš, and stated the time and place for the record. You sat bolt upright in the chair next to her, wearing a pin-striped, short-sleeved shirt with the top two buttons left undone. You had your fingers interlocked in front of you on your lap, your thumbs twitching. Your expression was serious, impassive.

Jasminka moved out of the frame to leave you sitting on your own. The camera zoomed in on your face and shoulders, cleverly editing out the twitchy thumbs. The hair around your temples was gray but still thick, thinning out a little on top, like I remembered it. The moustache, as always, neatly trimmed, a shade darker than your hair. The lighting accentuated the bags under your eyes.

In the room behind you, a 1930s radiator beneath the windowsill and the sheers covering the window were in the style of the fourth-floor apartment in Zagreb you lived in, but this was not the family home. Next to you, an imposing mantlepiece clock with alabaster columns stood on a brown sideboard covered with an embroidered doily. On top of the clock, a brass eagle stretched out its wings. The black numerals and clock hands stood out against the white clockface at 6:35.

Jasminka invited you to introduce yourself and followed up with a few questions about your childhood and family.

"I had a happy childhood," you said.[1] "When my mother was expecting me, we lived in Zagreb, but in June 1922, the city was flooded. My mother was Slovenian, so we took shelter with her family in Malenca in Slovenia, where I was born. After that, we moved often with my father's job. He was a sawmill manager. I went to secondary school in Virovitica."

"My parents were pleasant people. They didn't try to correct my political views, but they worried I might get arrested."

At first, your answers were a little hesitant, but after a few more minutes of gentle coaxing by Jasminka, your memories tumbled out. They echoed the tiny print of your unfinished manuscript, written five decades earlier. You talked about your political activism, the arrest, and incarceration in Jasenovac. You spent the next hour of the interview recounting your life in the camp, the hard physical labor and the beatings, the starvation rations and weight loss, the humiliation and the fear, the murders of your comrades.

"We knew Jasenovac was bad, but we didn't realize it was this bad. We knew Jews and Serbs were killed there. We didn't know about the Croats, though."

You spoke about the roll calls, the so-called hospital, the recycling of the dead prisoners' clothes in the workshops, the selection of prisoners for the kilns.

"The makeshift kilns didn't work properly, and the camp stank for days afterward. The villagers living around Jasenovac complained to the authorities about the smell, so they had to stop using them in this way."

Perhaps the complaints were heeded because the village of Jasenovac had become an Ustaša garrison. Ordinary villagers would not have dared complain.

"In April 1942, Jasenovac was flooded, so the whole camp was evacuated to Stara Gradiška, where there was an old prison with a tower, a fortress from Austro-Hungarian times."

Jasminka asked if Šakić was the commanding officer at the time.

"No, Orešković was commandant in Stara Gradiška, but he wasn't around much. He was out on Kozara Mountain, raiding Serb villages. Dinko Šakić was deputy commandant. When Šakić was acting up, the selections were at their worst. In June 1942, at one of the roll calls, they selected my comrades from the Faculty of Technology. They were locked up with other prisoners in barracks without food or water. Their deaths by starvation took several weeks."

Jasminka inquired if you were aware of any cases of cannibalism while you were in the camp.

"The gravediggers told us they found a dead man with his chest open and his heart and lungs removed. On another occasion, they told us they found pieces of human flesh in the pockets of an inmate who had been shot."

Jasminka asked you how you overcame such horrors.

You took a deep breath.

"Look, when your life is in the balance, your resolve to survive gets stronger. Your will to live grows. If you lost your will to live, you were done for."

You carried on. You said 1943 was the "golden period" in Stara Gradiška camp. I listened again to the phrase you used: "*zlatno doba.*" Maybe I'd translated it badly. A gilded era? How can there ever have been a golden age in a concentration camp? But then you explained it was a kind of joke between prisoners. The golden era was when "not too many" people were murdered. People died of exhaustion or disease, but there weren't "too many" public executions. At one of the roll calls, an officer addressed a group of Croats and said in a mock friendly voice, "You are children of the Croatian people. You've made a mistake, but you will one day return to your home nation."

How many is "not too many" when referring to people dying? A pause in the killing spree. Gallows humor, I supposed.

"By mid-1944, everything changed again," you continued. "The partisans and the Russians were getting closer. The fascists were losing the war. The camp authorities panicked and moved everyone from Stara Gradiška back to Jasenovac, where the conditions were much worse."

Jasminka asked you if you ever heard of or witnessed the killing of children in the camp.

I held my breath. I recalled the Zyklon gas scene from your manuscript. And the poem about the hungry mother in the tower. You sighed.

"When I was in the tower one night, the guards came into our room wearing gas masks. They selected the weaker prisoners for liquidation. We thought they wore masks because they were afraid of catching typhus from us. We heard them going into other rooms, too, where there were women and children from Kozara Mountain. There was a lot of screaming that night. The next day, the gravediggers told us they had to clear hundreds of tiny bodies from a room where they'd released the Zyklon gas. The guards didn't try to hide what they'd done."

"Did you see the bodies of the children killed in this way?"

"No, I didn't see the bodies. But the gravediggers told us the children had been aged from two to twelve years old. It took them several days to bury all the dead."

Throughout the interview, you retained your composure, speaking slowly and deliberately. You described beatings and summary executions of your friends and comrades and your personal battle with typhus without a tear in your eye. You were in full control. In the preceding months, you'd testified at the Šakić inquest and given countless interviews to national and international media in person and over the phone. It didn't surprise me you didn't break down in public. You were never one to feel sorry for yourself. I'd never seen you cry. So when Jasminka asked you what your most horrific experience in the camp was, your answer caught me off-guard.

"I saw a mother with four young children. They'd just arrived in the camp, deported from their village on Kozara Mountain."

You paused, then swallowed hard.

"At that time, we were given turnip soup to eat. It was a sickly, sour soup. She didn't have a container to put the soup in for the kids. She picked up her apron . . . "

Another pause. Silence. A long, cringing silence.

"They poured four portions of the soup into her apron. The liquid seeped through. The children knelt on the ground and sucked the soup from the apron, like piglets . . . "

You looked down and coughed, spluttered. You seemed to be choking, letting out a strangled sound. Were you sobbing? Your face screwed up.

How could this be? My big, strong dad, brave, proud like a rooster—you sobbed.

When you looked back up, for a split second, I saw an ocean of sadness in your eyes.

"I am still emotional about this," you said apologetically.

You pulled yourself up in the chair, took a deep breath, and squared your shoulders.

The clock behind you still showed 6:35, as if willing time to stop.

"Well, you know, we had to get used to it," you said calmly and looked straight ahead with a determined expression. You carried on describing the horrors of the camp.

I stopped the tape. I could not bear to watch any more. Watching you testify was harder than reading your words.

* * *

Many more months passed by before I played the recording again. The interview had moved on to more general themes. Your composure had returned in full. You were calm again, determined to bear witness.

"Are you aware Franjo Tuđman, the Croatian president, wrote in his book *Wastelands* that the Jasenovac camp was run by Jews?"

"The Ustaša authorities delegated some of their work to so-called trusted prisoners," you explained. "The Nazis had *kapos* in their camps. In Jasenovac, we called them *logornik*. In return for doing some of the guards' work, these people got better food. The *logornik* in my barracks was a Croat. He'd been a member of the Communist Party. The Serb barracks had their own *logornik*, and so did the Jews. Some *logorniks* who survived the war went on to become high-ranking officers in the Yugoslav Army. Others went into the professions. Every morning, the *logorniks* assigned the prisoners to work groups. It mattered a lot whether you were sent to log trees in the forest or were given a job inside camp. More people were shot in the forest than anywhere else. Sometimes, forty people left to work outside the camp in the morning, but only thirty returned in the evening. So what happened to the missing ten? No one knew. Or no one wanted to know.

"Some of the *logorniks* were nasty individuals and took advantage of prisoners. They beat us with clubs if we didn't work fast or hard enough. Some, like Diamantstein and Spiller, set up a racket extorting gold coins from newly arrived prisoners. They were caught eventually by the guards and executed. But overall, the Jewish *logorniks* were no better or worse than Croatian or Serb *logorniks*.

"Sure, the *logorniks* had some indirect power over life and death. But they did not kill other prisoners, as Tuđman suggested in his book. And they were certainly not all Jews. I've noticed he deleted the contentious allegations from later editions of his book."

"Mr. Roller, why do you think Šakić isn't being tried for genocide?"

"I think this is a deliberate mistake on the part of our government. I told the judge this during the inquest," you responded.

The comment made me smile. It was entirely within your character to point out mistakes made by others. Rank or prestige never stopped you from speaking out. Not everyone appreciated your honesty. I wondered what Judge Tripalo thought of your candor?

"It's a big mistake," you continued. "Šakić is being tried for war crimes and crimes against humanity, which is a different category. In Croatia, the maximum penalty for both genocide and crimes against humanity is the same: twenty years. But more importantly, he was commander of a camp that was genocidal in principle, and therefore he should stand trial for genocide."

"You were a political prisoner, Mr. Roller?"

"Yes. But there weren't many of us. In Jasenovac, we politicals had one barracks out of eight. The other seven barracks were Serbs, Jews, and Romani people. There were a lot more of them. What does it mean to be a political prisoner? We communists were certainly political enemies of the fascist state of Croatia, as it was then. But the Serbian smallholder from Kozara or the Jewish merchant from Zagreb—they were not political enemies. Their deaths were down to genocide."

"What do you think about the numbers of victims? How many people were killed in Jasenovac?"

"We will never know the exact numbers. They were undoubtedly shockingly high. But exact numbers are irrelevant. If they killed one, ten, or ten thousand people simply because they belonged to a certain group, then they have committed genocide."

"As a witness in the Šakić trial, were you ever threatened in person or over the phone?"

"No. I've had some annoying calls from journalists, but they were not threatening. I didn't get the feeling there was an organized hate campaign against witnesses. On the contrary, a man stopped me in the street the other day and congratulated me for testifying against Šakić. I asked him why. After all, I simply told the judge what happened. The man insisted on shaking my hand and told me I was brave. I laughed and said to the man, 'If I wasn't afraid of them in 1942, why would I be afraid of them now?'"

"Mr. Roller, what do you think will be the outcome of the trial?"

"I don't think Šakić can be set free. It would be a scandal. There are still a lot of antifascists in the ruling party in Croatia. They wouldn't stand for it."

"Thank you, Mr. Roller, for your testimony."

"*Hvala*. Thank you," you smiled and bowed your head.

* * *

Incredibly, you had to do it all over again when the trial proper started in March 1999. You were first in the witness box. This time, the accused, a man barely a year older than you, was in the courtroom.

During your testimony, Dinko Šakić sniggered. You sat in the witness chair facing the judge. The defendant sat behind you, so you would not have seen his face, but you would have heard him laughing.

"Mr. Šakić, don't laugh," Judge Tripalo warned him several times. "This is not funny. Stop laughing!"

Šakić ignored the judge and carried on laughing. It wasn't personal. He laughed at other camp survivors and the expert witnesses, too.

You were called back in for a second day to continue your testimony. And then you were cross-examined. The defense lawyers questioned the veracity of every one of your statements and made every effort to minimize their client's culpability. I suppose they were simply doing their job, but it must have been an ordeal to listen to them demolishing your testimony.

The trial dragged on for months. Six months to be exact. At the end of it, on Wednesday, September 29, 1999, Šakić was given one last opportunity to make a statement in his own defense. You were not in the courtroom to hear his last words, but they were widely reported in the media afterward. You would have read his statement in the daily newspapers, or did you avoid doing so for your own peace of mind?

Šakić claimed that he didn't make the decisions but carried out orders because they were in the Croatian national interest. He felt that his actions were necessary to ensure the biological survival of the Croatian people, threatened by invaders from the East. His conscience was clear, he said repeatedly. He accused the witnesses of telling lies and the prosecutors of succumbing to political manipulation by Belgrade. He claimed that his extradition from Argentina was based on falsified documents and testimonies from unreliable witnesses. He considered the trial a sham designed to perpetuate historical lies about the Independent State of Croatia of the 1940s and reinforce the myth about the Jasenovac camp.

I can only imagine what it felt like to have your testimony dismissed as a lie or manipulation by foreign states. If you were upset by his words, you did not show it, at least not to me.

The panel of seven judges withdrew to debate the verdict. It came three working days later. Dinko Šakić, aged seventy-eight, was found guilty of crimes against humanity and sentenced to twenty years in prison, the maximum penalty under Croatian law.

Judge Tripalo said in his summing up that Šakić was at the top of the commanding hierarchy with ultimate responsibility for everything happening in the camp. The killings were not occasional excesses. They were systemic and occurred with his full knowledge and approval. The verdict was a warning to other perpetrators of war crimes, which never date: perpetrators would be brought to justice for as long as they lived.

"The victims of Jasenovac have found closure," said one newspaper headline. But had they? Did you find closure with the guilty verdict? Šakić expressed no remorse for his behavior in Jasenovac at any point during or after the trial. His conscience was clear. He didn't think he'd done anything wrong. On the contrary, he was proud of his past, believing he'd acted in defense of the Croatian nation. Like so many fascists and Nazis guilty of war crimes, he claimed that his actions were guided by a clear conscience and a sense of duty. Like Franz Stangl, commandant of Sobibor and Treblinka, or Rudolf Höss, commandant of Auschwitz, Šakić believed he'd acted out of a sense of duty to his nation.

At last, the phone calls from journalists stopped. Enough of the questions: "Mr. Roller, are you doing this because you want revenge?" You were released from having to restate your wish for justice repeatedly.

After the verdict, there was no elation. No popping of champagne corks or celebrations. And no word from you about how you felt.

Chapter 25

The Shadows

We heaved a couple suitcases into the tiny elevator and left the rest of the luggage for a second run. Max and I squeezed in, his head butting up against my armpit. He pressed the cream Bakelite button marked with a *4*. Aged ten, he still enjoyed playing at lobby boy whenever we came to visit Zagreb. The elevator shuddered, then inched its way slowly upward, coming to a halt about a foot below floor level.

The front door to the apartment was already open. Mama stood in the frame. Max charged out of the elevator and hurled himself at his grandma's midriff. She steadied herself against the wall, then put her arms around him. I joined them in the bear hug. Inside the apartment, across the corridor, I could see you sitting at the head of the dining table, facing the entrance. You made a Y shape with your arms, beckoning us to come in. The corners of your mouth arched upward. We rushed over and showered you with kisses.

In the melee of unpacking, you remained sitting in your chair. In the winter months prior to our visit, you'd experienced some difficulties walking. You'd lost some feeling in your right foot. Doctors seemed unable to help you.

"They look at his foot and ignore the rest of his body," Mama complained. She updated me on your condition as we got dinner ready in the kitchen. She hadn't been well herself, her porous spine delivering crushing spasms of pain that made her wince periodically.

"There are days when he cannot get out of bed," Mama continued. "Today he made a special effort because you were arriving from London."

At dinner, you barely touched your food and hardly said a word. The rest of us chattered, pretending nothing had changed. Meal over, Mama pushed you out of the dining room with you still seated in your office chair. The castors left long scratch marks on the parquet floor. She managed well enough until she reached the raised door trim between the room and the corridor. She pushed and shoved, her face getting red with the effort. She tried to cajole you into standing up for a few seconds so she could lift the chair over the threshold. You sat impassively, looking at the floor. Marek and I jumped up, offered help.

"No, no! There's no need for all of you to get up!" Mama insisted.

Ignoring her protestations, we heaved you around the hall and into the bedroom. I detected a musty smell coming off your head. I wondered when your hair was last washed. Before I got a chance to ask, Mama said, "I can manage from here. Go and tend to your family."

Later that evening, I raised the issue of a wheelchair with Mama. I offered to go out and choose one with her while we were in Zagreb.

"He's not always like this," Mama said defensively. "He has good days and bad days. He can walk on some days. And in any case, I'd struggle with the doorsteps even if he was in a wheelchair."

"Maybe it's time to think about some live-in help or a day nurse to assist with dressing and bath time?" I suggested. Mama dismissed the idea outright.

"I don't want some nosy parker snooping around my home," she snorted.

The next morning, I went into your bedroom with the gifts we'd brought from London. You were sitting in bed, propped up on a mound of over-sized pillows. Your knobby knees were outlined by the thin, yellow blanket faded from multiple rounds in the washing machine. There was a strange muddy-brown stain on the edge of the blanket.

"Look, Tata. I've got something for you," I said in a cheery voice and retrieved a large box of After Eight mints from a shopping bag. "I know these are your favorites." I placed the carton on your lap, but there was no reaction. You sat and stared at your hands folded in front of you.

"Talk to him for a while. He'll like that," Mama said as she disappeared to the bathroom for her ablutions.

I sat on the bed next to you and told you all about my new job. I was convinced that would perk you up. You always wanted to know about my latest achievements at work. When you were well, you questioned me about new projects and papers published. Every time I was promoted at work, you bragged to your friends, like a proud peacock. But this time, you didn't even look at me. You stared over my shoulder at the wall behind me. I wasn't sure you'd taken in any of what I'd said. A half-hour later, you were still silent. You reminded me of the Picasso sketch of a cockerel, beak crooked and claws broken, lying limp on a kitchen table, waiting for the darkness. The glint in your eye that kept you alive in Jasenovac had gone.

Despondent, I placed the mints on the bedside table and went in search of Max. Perhaps he could cheer up his grandad with his childish prattle. But he'd gone out with his father to the open-air market to buy flowers for our Easter Sunday celebrations.

When Mama finished her bath, we returned to the bedroom together. You sat, bolt upright, on the edge of the bed, feet on the floor, box of mints open on your lap. You pulled the thin wafers of chocolate out of their slippery, black envelopes one by one and stuffed them greedily into your mouth. Startled by our arrival, you looked up at us like a naughty boy caught raiding the biscuit tin. For a fleeting moment, I saw the old twinkle in your eye.

"You piggy," Mama exclaimed and ran over to you with a box of tissues to clean up your chin and fingers. "Doing the dying-swan routine all morning," she laughed, patting your cheek in a pretend slap. "And now look what you've done!"

"Can we have some?" I said. You nodded. We sat next to you, Mama and I on either side of you, and tucked into the chocolates. But the twinkle never came back.

A fortnight later, you were gone.

Chapter 26

The Visit

It was June 2018, fifteen years after you passed away. I was on my annual pilgrimage to Zagreb, but this time, my visit was different.

I figured I owed it to you. It was not enough to read about places, look at photographs, and study maps. A personal visit was essential to get a real feel for a location. On this trip, I was visiting Jasenovac to get a sense of what it was like for you to be there.

The early-morning train out of Zagreb snaked its way through the Pannonian Flatlands of Slavonia toward Novska, where I would meet Ivo Pejaković, director of the Jasenovac Memorial site. He had kindly offered to drive us around for the day.

Young wheat shoots colored the countryside a pale green. Swathes of crimson poppies lined the banks of the railroad track, like a red carpet rolled out for a special guest. The train stopped every few minutes to take on new passengers or disgorge the few already on the train.

My stop was next. I felt apprehensive. Would Ivo be there to meet me as we agreed? Would the visit upset me? Perhaps I would feel nothing. I knew roughly what to expect. I'd seen photographs and videos of the memorial site. I'd pored over maps and scores of images of the central monument, a giant concrete water lily set at the center of a landscaped park. I was not expecting to see kilns or brickworks. No torture chambers remained. Bombed by the Allies and mined by the Ustaša, the remnants of the camp were picked over by local villagers and used to repair their housing stock after World War II ended.

Ivo was there as planned. He was tall, with a prominent, square jaw. His dark hair, streaked through with grays, blended with the dark colors of his leather jacket and open-necked shirt. His handshake was warm and welcoming, but his demeanor was formal, as behooves the chief custodian of a war memorial. A local lad, Ivo studied history at the university in Zagreb and became director of the Jasenovac site after working there as a curator for several years.

Ivo drove us to the memorial park, a triangular expanse of green wedged between the road and the River Sava. As we approached, the monolithic water lily emerged from the flat plain around it. The rigid petals, like gray fingers, reached for the sky above.

We arrived in the parking lot. There was no gate, no fencing around the site.

"That's right," said Ivo when I queried the lack of security. "It's intentional. Anyone can visit, 24/7. We've had only one incident of vandalism since the museum reopened in 1997." I was reminded Jasenovac was at the heart of some of the fiercest fighting in the 1990s war. The site was ransacked by Serb forces, and the museum contents, removed. After mediation by the US Holocaust Memorial Museum, the collection was returned in 2001, but half the artifacts were missing.

We walked toward the main building on-site, a single-story pallid edifice with a flat roof and hard-edged walls of cold concrete. Clipped leylandii bushes and lawns softened the otherwise austere look of the complex. The building had two wings joined together by a covered walkway, its roof supported by slim columns through which I glimpsed the monumental water lily again, its dark shape sharply silhouetted against the blue sky.

We entered the smaller of the two wings and sat in a bland meeting room to talk and share documents and photos. I gave Ivo copies of your photos from the 1966 opening of the site. He gave me copies of four documents with your signature on them. They were short statements about some of your comrades incarcerated in the camp. There was nothing in them implicating any of the individuals of any wrongdoing. I was puzzled about their purpose.

"They didn't trust each other, even after the war was over," Ivo explained. "The party wanted survivors to vouch for their comrades' loyalty." The years of conspiracy and secrecy necessitated by the illegal status of the Communist Party prior to the war sowed the seeds of mutual distrust in peacetime. Like a chill-damaged pear, the internal rot was not at first obvious but slowly worked its way from the inside out.

We turned to the subject of Dinko Šakić and his behavior during his trial.

"Your father was not the only person Šakić laughed at during the trial," said Ivo. "With some witnesses, he didn't bother listening at all. When Šime Klaić testified, Šakić read a magazine on the table in front of him."

We left the office wing of the building and headed for a grassy riverbank where one of Ivo's colleagues was waiting with a group of visitors. She was about to take us on a guided tour of the site. She led us up an embankment from which there was a wide-angle view of the meandering river, the manicured lawns, and a freight train on a siding. Neat footpaths made of railway sleepers wound past a couple of small lakes, replete with flowering water lilies. Their delicate softness was in stark contrast to the brutalist 1960s architecture of the monument at the heart of the park.

"The camp opened in 1941 on the site of a brickworks originally owned by the family Bačić," our guide began. "It was originally a labor camp, but its real purpose did not become apparent until the following year. There were six camps across an area of fifty square kilometers. This camp, known as *Ciglana*, or Brickworks, eventually had a three-meter wall on three sides and a double row of barbed wire on the south side."

As our guide talked, I looked around at the other visitors in our group. There was a handful of people huddled together, men and women, whispering to each other. I couldn't make out their accents. Ivo caught my eye and told me they were from Prijedor. My skin bristled at the name. The town was in Bosnia, forty kilometers south of Jasenovac across the River Sava and Kozara Mountain. The region was a hotbed of ethnic cleansing in the 1990s and home to Omarska concentration camp, where Bosnian Serb paramilitaries starved, tortured, raped, and murdered their Muslim and Croat victims, many of whom had been their former neighbors, schoolmates, and teachers. The ethnicities of the persecutors and the persecuted were different in Jasenovac in 1942 and in Omarska fifty years later, but the outcome was the same. Images of cadaverous men, their sunken eyes peering through a barbed-wire fence, flashed across TV screens all around the world. History had repeated itself. I wondered which side the visitors were on in 1992.

There was another group of visitors, dressed in shorts and sneakers. They were American, possibly Texan, judging from their accents, in their teens and twenties. I wondered if they were descendants of immigrants from these parts. They were respectful, keeping their voices down.

Three cyclists, a grandma, mom, and child, joined us a few minutes after the guide had started her talk. They remained silent throughout. I was trying to focus on what our guide was saying, but the incessant buzz of horseflies was distracting. I waved my hand in front of my face to swat them away.

"The prisoners were brought in by train, of which you can see a reconstruction ahead of you," the guide pointed at the siding. I felt a slight sense of disappointment. Perhaps foolishly, I imagined the cattle cars and locomotive would be originals from the 1940s. But the reconstruction was convincing enough. The cracked paintwork and rusty barbed wire crisscrossing the narrow air vents gave the train a patina of age. I was reminded of the 1998 news clip in which you stood in front of this train with the BBC correspondent Jon Silverman. The crew was reporting on the Šakić trial and had taken you to Jasenovac for an interview.

"I prefer not to remember all the killings I saw. And I saw plenty of them," you'd said to Silverman in English.

"The cattle cars were built and donated as a gift to the memorial park by Slovenia," our guide continued.

A mare brayed in the distance.

"Many of the prisoners selected for liquidation were taken across the River Sava to the village of Gradina. There are many mass graves there, now in a different country. There is a separate museum there."

Her voice waxed and waned in my head.

"The camp was at its worst in 1942 during the Kozara offensive . . . "

I heard the faint cry of a cockerel.

Did she mention the children of Kozara Mountain? I was not sure if she did. She invited us to walk with her toward the central monument.

"Of the two lakes you see in the park, the bigger one didn't exist in the 1940s. It was a hole that prisoners extracted clay from. The smaller lake is original. It provided water for the camp, but it was contaminated."

A farm dog howled across the river.

"The original design for the park envisioned a monumental central water lily with several smaller ones scattered in the fields around it. However, concrete was expensive in the 1960s, so the smaller ones were never erected," our guide continued as she led us to a bronze bas-relief showing a three-dimensional map of the camp. Railway sleepers lining the paths creaked gently beneath our feet.

"The mounds and depressions in the ground in front of you represent the main buildings of the camp." We continued toward the colossal flower, its petals offering themselves up to the sky like an outstretched hand. An opening at the base of the stalk let us through into the heart of the monument.

"The original plan was to have a crypt, but there was a danger the entire structure would sink into the soft clay of the floodplain beneath it, so the design was adjusted," said the guide.

The concrete was as stark on the inside as on the outside, softened only slightly by a wall of railway sleepers at the far end of the interior. A bronze plaque engraved with a verse from the epic poem *The Pit* by Ivan Kovačić and a single wreath of flowers were the only adornments within.[1]

Our guide completed the formal tour and invited us to walk around the parkland on our own. Ivo returned to his office. We would meet again after I'd visited the museum.

Heart-shaped leaves floated on the two lakes. Between them, tiny spherical buds in cadmium yellow thrust themselves upward on thick, sap-green stalks. Rushes whispered in the wind. I was beguiled by the tranquil beauty of this place. I kept having to remind myself that it was once a killing ground.

I headed toward the museum building. At the entrance, visitors were invited to look inside a book listing all the known victims of the camp. The size of the book was shocking. It was thousands of pages long. The title *Jasenovac: Žrtva je Pojedinac, Every Victim Is an Individual*, hinted at the focus of the exhibition inside. It was devoted to the memory of the people murdered in the camp. Here, they were not just numbers. Their full names were listed with brief biographical details and a source reference where more information could be found. I leafed through the alphabetical list, searching for more information about Schwartz, the blind comrade you dedicated your longest poem to. There were hundreds of them on the list with different spellings, Schwartz and Švarc. Without a first name, I had no chance of finding out more about your comrade or his family.

I stepped inside the museum. The walls of the windowless rooms were painted black. Glass panels hung vertically from the ceiling, each engraved with the names of the victims in alphabetical order. I craned my neck upward. There were so many that it was impossible to read them all. At eye level, several screens showed rolling footage of testimonies by survivors of the camp. An aluminum food ration in a display case reminded me of the one you mentioned in your unfinished manuscript. Further down, almost at ankle level, I spotted a mallet and a knife, the preferred instruments of death in Jasenovac. By comparison with Nazi extermination camps, where gas-chamber operators killed behind walls and out of sight, here death was up close and personal, each victim the focus of a single sadistic individual.

The exhibition in its present form opened three years after you passed away. I wondered what you would have made of it.

I returned to Ivo's office, and he drove us to Stara Gradiška, twenty miles away along the bank of the River Sava. On the way there, we passed through Jasenovac village. I asked Ivo to stop at the train station. I was astonished to find two stations. One was a derelict double-story brick building, its windows knocked out of their frames and the roof missing. Black soot around the top of the crumbling walls hinted at what must have been a raging fire. The top branches of a tree growing inside the station peeped over the parapet. Long fingers of ivy trailed up the left wall of the building. A casualty of the 1990s war. Next to it was the new station—a single-story prefab made of aluminum panels and glass. It was locked. In front of the buildings, on the same level, three railway lines with overhead power cables stretched into the distance, a mass of poppies growing between the sleepers. Their exuberant red heads swayed in the warm breeze.

We arrived in Stara Gradiška. Ivo parked on the green median next to a derelict factory, its elongated, rectangular form covered with a sloping roof of rusting corrugated iron. In stark contrast, the modernistic round church across the road had whitewashed walls and a separate, chimneylike bell tower.

"Which way, Ivo?" I asked. He pointed toward the thicket of trees along the road. I caught sight of a crumbling archway that may once have housed a gate within it. On closer inspection, I noticed there was a wall extending from the arch to the left, but it was almost entirely submerged under a jumble of ivy and bindweed.

"This was the outer wall of the prison," Ivo explained.

We left the road and took a shortcut through a pine copse, needles crunching underfoot.

"We're nearly there," said Ivo, pointing ahead. I was expecting to see a fortress with prison wings extending on either side of the dreaded tower in which you endured your bout of typhus. Instead, I faced an abandoned ruin rising out of a sea of waist-high nettles. There was a hint of a once-imposing brick building, about three floors high, with dark archways punched into its side at ground level. On the first floor, some of the windows still retained their iron bars. I wondered if these were the bars that cooled your fevered forehead when you were ill. A thick green canopy of trees hovered where the roof would have been.

Perhaps sensing my disappointment, Ivo walked over to the makeshift wire-mesh fencing surrounding the site and lifted a section of it up. Ignoring the signs warning passersby of falling masonry, we dipped under the fence, fought our way through the brambles, and entered the building through one of the arches. Ivo strode ahead confidently. I followed him in.

We were in a long, wide corridor stretching on either side of our point of entry. Some light penetrated through the arches, but the atmosphere was gloomy, a sudden change from the bright sunshine outside. Skeins of dried paintwork hung loosely off the arched ceilings. The walls were pared back to the bare brick, the plaster crumbling in the rising damp. The floor was uneven. I tapped my way ahead, trailing behind Ivo. The greenish-ocher hues reminded me of an equally dimly lit watercolor by Vincent van Gogh of the asylum in Saint-Rémy. Unlike you, the artist admitted himself voluntarily. Like you, he was in a place of anguish, enclosed by stone walls and isolated from the rest of the world. He drew solace from the fields he could see through the barred window of his cell. They inspired him to paint the blazing sun and the sheafs of wheat undulating in his characteristic sweeps of sulfur yellow and purple. Even the more somber colors of his wintry paintings projected calmness and peace. They lacked the desolation you expressed in your poem of the snow-covered fields you saw outside the tower.

"Is this all that's left?" I asked Ivo.

"Yes. We would like to restore the building and turn it into a museum, but the works would be expensive. We intend to apply for EU funding . . . "

We walked back to the car, and Ivo drove me to the train station in Novska. I thanked him for his time and hospitality.

So that was Jasenovac. A tripoint of three fallen empires: Austrian, Ottoman, and French. Did I get a sense of what it was like for you? No. On a sunny day in late spring, it took a leap of faith to imagine the cold and the hunger you'd experienced. A glimpse of the weapons used to murder prisoners and the dank corridors of Stara Gradiška merely hinted at some of the horrors. I learned a lot, picked up new documents from Ivo, and bought a stack of books in the museum shop. The memorial site was a welcome place of contemplation, an oasis of calm. But it had none of the impact of your video-recorded story about the mother with the four children from Kozara Mountain.

The next day, I would go to another place of contemplation, the Mirogoj Cemetery in Zagreb.

* * *

The walk from the family home to the main square took less than fifteen minutes at a leisurely pace. Along the way, an old man with an accordion played a passable version of your favorite Russian romance song, "Ochi Charnye." You used to hum it while playing solitaire. I stopped in front of a shop window, pretending to be interested in the Croatian checkerboard football shirts on display, and waited for him to finish the song. I fumbled in my purse, extracted a couple of coins, and dropped them into the busker's hat.

I rounded the corner and entered the main square. Art deco buildings rubbed shoulders with neoclassical and baroque facades restored to their pastel-colored originals after decades of neglect. Gone were the gray cloaks of soot and rendering eaten away to the bare brick by smog. Hues of peach, primrose yellow, and pale fawn replaced the drabness that used to give the center an air of shabby chic long before the term became fashionable. The only contemporary structure on the square, a ten-story cuboid building ambitiously referred to by the locals as *neboder*, or skyscraper, had been reclad in shiny, mirrored panels in a nod to modernism.

I made my way from the square up the steep incline toward the cathedral. The twin towers stood erect in their neogothic glory, piercing the clear blue sky above. The tarpaulin on the scaffolding around the southerly tower flapped gently in the warm breeze. It had taken years to restore the north tower. A few more years, and the south tower would be in pristine condition, too.

I boarded the bendy blue bus 106 heading for Mirogoj Cemetery. The vehicle moved swiftly up the winding roads, its spine bending deftly like a giant caterpillar. Apartment blocks gave way to detached houses with gardens, leaving panoramic views of the city behind us. Still climbing, we passed a string of stonemasons' workshops, their courtyards littered with marble and granite slabs ready for engraving. We drove past the arcades, their copper domes shimmering into the distance as far as the eye could see. Solid brick on the outside but open and colonnaded on the inside of the cemetery, the arcades had taken the nineteenth-century town planners many years to build. Their vaulted walkways housed the graves of writers, academics, politicians, nobility, and heroes. I disembarked at the main entrance and crossed the road to the wooden roundhouse with its flower and candle stalls.

Loaded up with floral offerings, I headed back toward the cemetery. The Church of Christ the King towered over the main gate, its verdigris cupola dominating the string of smaller ones topping the arcades. A cascade of green Virginia creeper tumbled down the crescent of columns joining the church with the arcades. In fall, the leaves would turn a vivid crimson.

I headed into the parkland, laid out in a geometric checkerboard pattern, the walkways lined with pines pedantically clipped into cones. Neatly cropped lawns and rose bushes gave way to rows of mature birch, oak, and horse chestnut trees. Elaborate tombstones, chapels, and statues alternated with plain marble or granite memorials dedicated to the dead of all faiths. It didn't matter if they were Catholics, Orthodox, Protestants, Jews, Muslims, Latter-Day Saints, or nonbelievers. In the land of the dead, they were all the same. If only they could get on so well in the realm of the living.

I was at the family grave, a simple dais cloaked in a thick blanket of ivy. A couple of lofty pine trees hovered over the central headstone, a spartan slab of polished black granite engraved with gilded letters. There was Grandad Krešimir and Grandma Hana, the generation born at the tail end of the nineteenth century. Then there was you and Mama, buried eighteen months apart, and Uncle Kegla and Auntie Dina, gone within six months of each other. Arguably, your generation endured the worst of twentieth-century excesses. The country you were born in changed borders three times in your lifetime. As a child, you lived in the Kingdom of Yugoslavia. Then it was the fascist Independent State of Croatia, which was anything but independent. The country was reunited under communist rule for forty-five years, only to disintegrate again into splinters in the 1990s wars.

Of all the family, you and Mama traveled the most, but you always returned to Zagreb, the city you called home. I remembered Sister Marie-Berthe and our afternoons in the pineapple garden at the convent in Entebbe. You'd engaged her to nurture my French, the language you considered most noble of all, the language of literature, poetry, and the human condition. She'd returned to her native Paris in 1973, after Idi Amin made life difficult in Uganda. In her last letter to me, she compared you to Ulysses, a man who traveled widely but eventually found happiness by returning to the land of his forebears. She finished off with, *"La Patrie est toujours le plus beau pays du monde,"* "Your homeland is always the most beautiful country in the world."

I positioned the flowers in the center of the ivy and lit the candles. I stepped back a little to view the grave. How peaceful it all seemed. I imagined what it would be like to tell you about my writing.

"I've written a book, you know," I started, my voice shaky.

"Have you?" your face beamed. "What sort of book? Some exciting new science, perhaps."

"No. It's about you. A quest to get to know you. A search for my hidden dad."

"About me?" A look of bemused incomprehension swept over your face.

"I've uncovered your secret. I found your unfinished manuscript. And your poems. And the Shoah Foundation tape you never told me about. And what you did after leaving the party," I blurted it all out at once, a spitting torrent of words.

You sat fidgeting.

"My book has your writing in it, too."

Your face was impassive. I couldn't tell what you were thinking.

"You know," I blustered on, "my PhD adviser used to say, 'If it isn't written down, it doesn't exist. You might as well not have bothered doing the experiment.' Well, he was right. It's as true with history as it is in science. If events and experiences aren't written down or recorded on tape, future generations may wonder if they ever happened."

Long pause.

"I understand why you hid these things. You tried to protect me, to protect your family, to protect yourself. Maybe, like Viktor Frankl in his memoir *Man's Search for Meaning*, you suspected that people who'd never experienced a concentration camp wouldn't understand. I certainly would not have understood in my twenties or even in middle age. Maybe now, in the fall of my life, I can begin to understand."

"Have you double-checked your facts?" you asked.

Was that a sheepish grin I detected on your face?

"I have. Double-checked and triple-checked. That's not to say I haven't made any mistakes. Facts and figures. We love them, don't we? Numbers have no feelings, no emotions. They are the perfect antidote to feeling upset, not having to think about how we feel."

"Nothing wrong with facts and figures. On the contrary, a bit of number crunching does you good," you said.

"I agree. I like doing it myself."

Another pause.

"I had many questions for you when I was writing the book. Art Spiegelman interviewed his father, a Holocaust survivor, for his graphic memoir *Maus*. I couldn't interview you. All I had was inert evidence. I had to chase shadows of a life left behind. You are still a bit of mystery to me."

"Oh no, you haven't gone all soft and sentimental on me, have you?"

"I have told my own story about you. Others who have known you may see things differently. Someone said once, 'We all see what we want to believe. We are all unreliable narrators.' It's not just about you. It's about me and Mama and our life together as a family. Our recollections tangled together like the intricate pattern on the Qum rug you bought in Baghdad, telling stories of a lifetime, of a family. It's about belonging, too."

"So where do you belong?"

"I belong in London. It's been forty years, you know . . . "

You nodded but said nothing. My mind wandered. London, the city that welcomed me with open arms when I was a student. The city that gave me my first break in science, loyal friends, and a family of my own to nurture. Yugoslavia, our Jugoslavija, was a place where I once belonged, but I had come to realize and accept that this precious homeland, if it ever existed other than in my childish imagination, vanished a long time ago. It was not somewhere I could physically visit by hopping on an airplane. Fortunately, I could still reach it through memory and by writing down those memories.

"So be it," you said. "And don't worry about us. You know, it's not so bad here. You can eat, drink, and smoke as much as you like without consequences."

The mist around you cleared to reveal a cherrywood table, like the one we used to sit around on our summer holidays at the seaside. There was Mama in a floral dress, tapping her cigarette in the ashtray in front of her. Auntie Dina and Uncle Kegla and Grandma and Grandpa were all there, in short sleeves and tanned, smiling and waving at me. You all had glasses in your hands, whiskey for you and Mama, wine for everyone else. You raised your glasses and drank.

I smiled and waved back. You gradually disappeared back into the mist.

I turned around and walked back slowly, through the rose garden toward the cemetery gate and the bus stop.

In the distance, I heard a rooster sing.

Suggested Reading

In the six years it has taken me to translate my father's writing and pen my own story about him, I have read many primary and secondary sources of information on Jasenovac concentration camp. Foremost among these, in terms of scope and depth, have been the publications of prolific writer and eminent Croatian historian Professor Ivo Goldstein, culminating in his 950-page magnum opus *Jasenovac* (Zagreb: Fraktura, 2018). However, this scholarly book, like many other camp-specific publications, is in Croatian and has not to date been translated into English.

For Anglophone readers, the selection of camp-specific readings is rather more limited, but the following may be of interest:

Goldstein, Ivo. "Resistance to Centralism." In *Yugoslavia from a Historical Perspective*, ed. Sonja Biserko, 126–62. Belgrade: Helsinki Committee for Human Rights in Serbia, 2017. https://www.helsinki.org.rs/doc/yugoslavia%20from%20a%20historical%20perspective.pdf.

Mojzes, Paul. *Balkan Genocides: Holocaust and Ethnic Cleansing in the Twentieth Century*. Lanham, MD: Rowman & Littlefield, 2015.

Pejaković, Ivo. "Jasenovac Memorial Site and Difficult Heritage." *Témoigner—Entre Histoire et Mémoire* 114 (December 2012): 48–58.

In addition, useful websites include the Jasenovac Memorial Site, available in English and Croatian at https://jusp-jasenovac.hr, the US Holocaust Memorial Museum at https://ushmm.org, and the Shoah Foundation at https://sfi.usc.edu.

Author's Note

This is a book of memory. Inevitably, others will remember events and conversations differently, but I have done my best to tell a truthful story.

My memoir is a tribute to the courage of my father and all those like him who have survived wartime trauma that is unimaginable to those of us who have been fortunate enough to live in peace throughout our lives. I wrote this book to honor their memory and their lives.

I have been asked by some readers if I knew what happened to Dragan's prewar and wartime friends, mentioned in his unfinished manuscript. Vladislav (Vlado) Psotka and Milan Špalj died in the death cell referred to in my father's manuscript as building K in Stara Gradiška. Milan Špalj had been a prominent leader of the Communist Youth League. He was arrested in 1941, tortured by the police in Zagreb, and deported to Jasenovac, where he arrived on February 18, 1942, with the same transport as my father. He was awarded the Yugoslav Order of the People's Hero (*Narodni Heroj*) posthumously in 1953.

According to Đorđe Mihovilović [*Ćelija Smrti* (*Death Cell*), Jasenovac: Jasenovac Memorial Site, 2013, 159 pp.), Biserka Bronzin and her brothers Suncoslav and Ognjeslav were all active members of the Communist Youth League of Yugoslavia. Suncoslav was deported to Stara Gradiška in December 1941. He tried to escape but was caught and killed in July 1942. Ognjeslav also perished in the war, but there is some uncertainty about whether he was killed in Stara Gradiška or in Zagreb. Biserka was released after her arrest and reportedly survived the war, but I have not been able to trace any more information about her.

Acknowledgments

There are many people and organizations without whose help and encouragement I would never have started, persevered with, or finished this book.

First and foremost, I would like to thank my creative writing teachers: Julia Blackburn for getting me started on life writing; Dr. Stephen Carver for believing in my project when all I had were a few scribbled anecdotes; Paul Kingsnorth for getting me over the finishing line; and Dan Smith for helping me shape a long, rambling manuscript into a more compact and digestible tome.

I am grateful to all my beta readers for their constructive feedback, especially Zeenath, Miranda, Roy, and Emma; Teresa and Marek and their Streatham Book Club; Dr. Alice Little; and fellow writers and tutors at the Oxford Centre for Life Writing.

Many thanks to Ivo Pejaković, director of the Jasenovac Memorial Site, Croatia, for our helpful discussions, exchange of materials, and my unforgettable day in Jasenovac and Stara Gradiška in 2018.

Special thanks are due to the USC Shoah Foundation for recording my father's testimony in 1998, thereby preserving his story for posterity. A big thank-you to Crispin Brooks, Sandra Aguilar, and Ita Gordon for teaching me the skills of indexing and Dr. Badema Pitic for advice on citing from oral testimonies.

Finally, I thank Ashley Dodge, Laney Ackley, and the team at Rowman & Littlefield for publishing this book and turning a dream into reality.

Notes

CHAPTER 3

1. Miroslav Krleža (1893–1981) was a Croatian writer, poet, and polemicist. He was critical of conformism in all three guises of his homeland: Austria-Hungary, the Kingdom of Yugoslavia, and communist Yugoslavia. Émile Zola (1840–1902) was a contrarian French writer. He is buried with Victor Hugo and Alexandre Dumas in the Panthéon in Paris. Ivan Turgenev (1818–1883), a contemporary of Fyodor Dostoevsky and Leo Tolstoy, was a Russian writer highly critical of nineteenth-century Russian society.

2. The Molotov Ribbentrop Pact was a nonaggression agreement between the Soviet Union and Nazi Germany, named after the Soviet and German foreign ministers who signed it in August 1939.

3. France Prešeren (1800–1849) was a Slovenian poet of romantic and patriotic works. He is regarded as Slovenia's national poet.

CHAPTER 4

1. Ernst Toller (1893–1939) was a German writer and left-wing politician. He served as president of the short-lived and unrecognized Bavarian Soviet Republic in 1919. Zygmunt Nowakowski (1891–1963) was a Polish writer and actor. Ilya Ilf (1897–1937) and Yevgeny Petrov (1902–1942) were popular Soviet writers between the two world wars. They cowrote several satirical novels, plays, and short stories lampooning both the Soviet and American systems.

2. St. Nicholas Day is the Christian feast day of St. Nicholas, the bringer of gifts. It is celebrated on December 6 in continental Europe. The American Santa Claus and the British Father Christmas were both derived from St. Nicholas.

3. Mikhail Sholokhov (1905–1984) was a Russian writer who was awarded the Nobel Prize in literature in 1965.

4. The Tripartite Pact was a military alliance between Germany, Italy, and Japan signed in September 1940. Hungary, Romania, Slovakia, and Bulgaria joined the pact in the following six months. The Kingdom of Yugoslavia joined on March 25, 1941,

precipitating a coup two days later. The fascist Independent State of Croatia joined in June 1941.

CHAPTER 5

1. Ante Pavelić (1889–1959) founded and led the Croatian ultranationalist Ustaša organization (see note 2).
2. The Ustaša were ultranationalist Croatian paramilitaries that aligned themselves with the Nazis and formed the fascist Independent State of Croatia from 1941 to 1945.
3. The love song "Lili Marleen" was popular throughout Europe during World War II.

CHAPTER 6

1. "The Erika" was a German Army marching song popular during World War II.
2. The Serbian King Alexander of Yugoslavia (1888–1934) reigned from 1921 to 1934, when he was assassinated in Marseille during a state visit to France. The shooter was Bulgarian, but the assassination was orchestrated by the Ustaša leader Ante Pavelić, who lived in Italy at the time.

CHAPTER 9

1. Primo Levi, *If This Is a Man* and *The Truce*, combined volume (London: Abacus, 1987). Also *The Drowned and the Saved* (London: Abacus, 2013).

CHAPTER 12

1. The Non-Aligned Movement started during the Cold War as an antidote to the polarizing influence of the pro-Soviet Warsaw Pact and pro-Western capitalist countries, many of which belonged to NATO. The movement was formally established in 1961 in Belgrade, Yugoslavia, through the initiative of Yugoslav President Josip Broz Tito, Indian Prime Minister Jawaharlal Nehru, Egyptian President Gamal Abdel Nasser, Ghanaian President Kwame Nkrumah, and Indonesian President Sukarno.

CHAPTER 15

1. George Orwell, *Animal Farm* (New York: New American Library, 1974), 52–53.

CHAPTER 17

1. Joseph Conrad, *Heart of Darkness* (London: Penguin, 1999); V. S. Naipaul, *In a Free State* (London: Picador, 1971).

CHAPTER 18

1. Fidel Castro (1926–2016) was a Cuban revolutionary who served as leader of communist Cuba from 1959 to 2008.

CHAPTER 20

1. Karl May (1842–1912) was a German author who sold millions of books in his native German, as well as in translation. Published in the 1890s, his book series Winnetou, set in the American West, was hugely popular with young people throughout the twentieth century in central and eastern Europe, including Yugoslavia.

CHAPTER 24

1. Dragan Roller, interview 48670 by Jasminka Domaš, *Visual History Archive*, USC Shoah Foundation, October 12, 1998, https://vha.usc.edu/testimony/48670.

CHAPTER 26

1. Ivan Goran Kovačić (1913–1943) was a Croatian poet and writer. His poem *Jama, The Pit*, is a condemnation of the atrocities perpetrated by the Ustaša in World War II.

Index

About the Author

Sibel Roller is a writer of twentieth-century nonfiction and fiction focused on hitherto unheard voices and unusual perspectives. She grew up in eight countries on four continents but now lives in London. Educated at Hunter College in New York, Johns Hopkins University in Baltimore, and Queen Elizabeth College (University of London), her early career was in science research and teaching. She is professor emerita at London South Bank University.

https://sibelrollerauthor.com